Packet Guide to Routing and Switching

Bruce Hartpence

Beijing · Boston · Farnham · Sebastopol · Tokyo

Packet Guide to Routing and Switching

By Bruce Hartpence

Printed in the United States of America.

Published by O'Reilly Media, Inc., 1005 Gravenstein Highway North, Sebastopol, CA 95472.

O'Reilly books may be purchased for educational, business, or sales promotional use. Online editions are also available for most titles (*http://safaribooksonline.com*). For more information, contact our corporate/institutional sales department: 800-998-9938 or *corporate@oreilly.com*.

Editors: Shawn Wallace and Mike Hendrickson
Production Editor: Jasmine Perez
Proofreader: O'Reilly Production Services

Interior Designer: David Futato
Cover Designer: Karen Montgomery
Illustrator: Robert Romano

August 2011:   First Edition

Revision History for the First Edition
2011-08-15:   First release
2012-09-28:   Second release
2016-11-11:   Third release

See *http://oreilly.com/catalog/errata.csp?isbn=9781449306557* for release details.

978-1-449-49306-7

[LSI]

To Christina, Brooke, Nick, and Sydney—eternal gratitude for the love and the laughs that keep coming.

Table of Contents

Preface

For a long time, I was very happy building Ethernet networks, working with switches and then moving to 802.11. It took awhile, but eventually I realized that the world of interconnected networks cannot be reached with Layer 2 alone. In addition, as you spread your wings from the Layer 2 broadcast domains, you encounter the wonders of virtual local area networks and trunks. I became an "all over" networking sort of guy. Like my own progression, this book moves up to the next layers and ideas.

If you read the *Packet Guide to Core Network Protocols* (O'Reilly), you have a handle on the type of communication seen on every single network (ARP, ICMP, IP, Ethernet), regardless of operating system or networking equipment vendor. This book now moves to the advanced link and internetwork layer protocols that will enable the reader to expand to internetworks and larger topologies.

Like the first book, each chapter will tear apart a particular protocol or set of ideas, explaining the structure and operation. The discussion will be supported by ample packet captures. There is nothing theoretical about the stuff between these covers: the topologies depicted in each chapter were built in a lab as the chapters took form.

And like the first book, what you see here will be part of every network that you encounter. So, the practices, ideas and protocols seen here will continue to help you on your way for many years to come. I'll also continue to refer to and work with networking tables including routing (host and router), source address, and ARP tables.

Recently, many in the networking profession experienced, or at least paid attention to, IPv6 day. But the results were largely unimpressive. Several challenges—such as properly operating 6to4 tunnels, filters blocking some IPv6 messaging, and a seeming lack of support for security features—indicate that IPv4 will be with us for some time to come. That said, many of the chapters touch on IPv6, including some basic configurations and a comparison to IPv4 operation.

Each chapter contains a collection of review questions to remind the reader about key ideas. A series of lab experiences ranging from basic to advanced are also included.

These experiences are designed such that the reader can perform them with the help of the chapter, welding the ideas into place.

I hope you enjoy this book and that it helps you on your way to networking greatness.

Audience

As this book contains both ground-up explanations and advanced ideas, it is appropriate for those just beginning as well as the pros out there, who might need a refresher. Whether you are working with small networks or interconnecting larger ones, the principles contained remain true.

This book is meant to be a companion to *The Packet Guide to Core Network Protocols*. Both books stand on their own, but this book assumes that you understand the concepts and protocols explained previously, including ARP, ICMP, IP, equipment, Ethernet, and masking. Occasionally I'll throw in a little review, but these sections will be few and far between.

Contents of This Book

Chapter 1, Routing and Switching Strategies
> This chapter ties the book together, covering the integrated nature of the forwarding decisions made on the network and introduces many of the concepts that form the basis of later chapters. The chapter addresses key ideas, including classification of protocols, static versus dynamic topologies, and the reasons for installing a particular route.

Chapter 2, Host Routing
> This chapter picks up where the discussion of masks in Chapter 1 leaves off. Hosts are like routers in many ways, and possessing a routing table is just one of them. Reading this chapter will show you how to process a host routing table and how traffic starts out across a network. Conversations crossing routers will also be examined, with special attention paid to addressing and frame construction.

Chapter 3, Spanning Tree and Rapid Spanning Tree
> Loops are problematic for Ethernet networks. The Spanning Tree Protocol is an integral part of every network containing switches and works to protect the topology against them. It can also affect the performance of your network and consume bandwidth. This chapter covers Spanning Tree and the faster Rapid Spanning Tree protocol.

Chapter 4, VLANs and Trunking
> As good as switches have been for modern communication topologies, once the Layer 2 network grows beyond a certain size, bottlenecks and security concerns start to assert themselves. VLANs are a valuable tool used to address these prob-

lems. This chapter covers the design and operation of VLANs and includes sections for trunking protocols that allow VLANs to spread out over many switches.

Chapter 5, Routing Information Protocol

One of the first distance vector protocols, RIP is often used as a basis for understanding dynamic routing. However, RIP also has a place in small, modern communication networks. This chapter addresses the operation and structure of RIP. Also discussed are improvements to simple dynamic routing, including split horizon, poisoning, count to infinity, and triggered updates.

Chapter 6, Open Shortest Path First

OSPF is a link state protocol, and as such, is generally considered superior to protocols like RIP. This chapter will explain the operation of link state protocols and why convergence times are improved over distance vector. The protocol structure, addressing, and operation will be covered with support from packet captures.

Chapter 7, Network Address Translation

One of the reasons for the delay in full IPv6 deployment is the success of network address translation (NAT). NAT converts internal private (RFC 1918) addresses to globally unique IP addresses used on the Internet. Most home and many small office networks use this highly effective networking technology. This chapter will explain NAT operation and run through several examples depicting the translation tables and the traffic resulting from its deployment.

Chapter 8, Multicast

Multicast messaging is used when transmissions must reach a collection of nodes without using broadcast addressing. By default, routers do not forward multicast traffic. In order for nodes to reach multicast streams across a network, the Interior Group Management Protocol (IGMP) and protocol independent multicast (PIM) are configured on network devices. This chapter will explain the structure of these protocols, their operation, and multicast addressing for both IPv4 and IPv6.

Conventions Used in This Book

The following typographical conventions are used in this book:

Plain text

Indicates menu titles, menu options, menu buttons, and keyboard accelerators (such as Alt and Ctrl).

Italic

Indicates new terms, URLs, email addresses, filenames, file extensions, pathnames, directories, and Unix utilities.

`Constant width`

Indicates commands, options, switches, variables, attributes, keys, functions, types, classes, namespaces, methods, modules, properties, parameters, values, objects, events, event handlers, XML tags, HTML tags, macros, the contents of files, or the output from commands.

`Constant width bold`

Shows commands or other text that should be typed literally by the user.

`Constant width italic`

Shows text that should be replaced with user-supplied values.

 This icon signifies a tip, suggestion, or general note.

 This icon indicates a warning or caution.

Using Code Examples

This book is here to help you get your job done. In general, you may use the code in this book in your programs and documentation. You do not need to contact us for permission unless you're reproducing a significant portion of the code. For example, writing a program that uses several chunks of code from this book does not require permission. Selling or distributing a CD-ROM of examples from O'Reilly books does require permission. Answering a question by citing this book and quoting example code does not require permission. Incorporating a significant amount of example code from this book into your product's documentation does require permission.

We appreciate, but do not require, attribution. An attribution usually includes the title, author, publisher, and ISBN. For example: "*Packet Guide to Routing and Switching* by Bruce Hartpence (O'Reilly). Copyright 2011 Bruce Hartpence, 978-1-449-30655-7."

If you feel your use of code examples falls outside fair use or the permission given above, feel free to contact us at *permissions@oreilly.com*.

Safari® Books Online

 Safari Books Online (*www.safaribooksonline.com*) is an on-demand digital library that delivers expert content in both book and video form from the world's leading authors in technology and business.

Technology professionals, software developers, web designers, and business and creative professionals use Safari Books Online as their primary resource for research, problem solving, learning, and certification training.

Safari Books Online offers a range of plans and pricing for enterprise, government, and education, and individuals.

Members have access to thousands of books, training videos, and prepublication manuscripts in one fully searchable database from publishers like O'Reilly Media, Prentice Hall Professional, Addison-Wesley Professional, Microsoft Press, Sams, Que, Peachpit Press, Focal Press, Cisco Press, John Wiley & Sons, Syngress, Morgan Kaufmann, IBM Redbooks, Packt, Adobe Press, FT Press, Apress, Manning, New Riders, McGraw-Hill, Jones & Bartlett, Course Technology, and hundreds more. For more information about Safari Books Online, please visit us online.

How to Contact Us

Please address comments and questions concerning this book to the publisher:

O'Reilly Media, Inc.
1005 Gravenstein Highway North
Sebastopol, CA 95472
(800) 998-9938 (in the United States or Canada)
(707) 829-0515 (international or local)
(707) 829-0104 (fax)

We have a web page for this book, where we list errata, examples, and any additional information. You can access this page at:

http://www.oreilly.com/catalog/9781449306557

To comment or ask technical questions about this book, send email to:

bookquestions@oreilly.com

For more information about our books, courses, conferences, and news, see our website at *http://www.oreilly.com*.

Find us on Facebook: *http://facebook.com/oreilly*

Follow us on Twitter: *http://twitter.com/oreillymedia*

Watch us on YouTube: *http://www.youtube.com/oreillymedia*

Content Updates

September 28, 2012

- Swapped Switch 2 and Switch 3 in Figure 3-1.
- Swapped Switch 2 and Switch 3 in Figure 3-5.
- Changed the direction of the arrow between Switch 2 and Switch 3 in Figure 3-14.
- Fixed a minor issue from change lowest bridge ID to highest bridge ID.
- Fixed a typo in Question 10 of Chapter 3 from teo to two.
- Made some minor changes to Questions 5, 6, and 7 of Chapter 5.

Acknowledgments

This book follows closely on the heels of the first one. So, members of my family and many of the folks in my department have been putting up with my writing activities for several months now. Cables everywhere, signs hanging on equipment, demands for coffee, and general grumpiness were par for the course. Thanks to all of you for putting up with my shenanigans.

I'd like to thank the folks at O'Reilly for making both of these writing experiences the best they could be, and especially for helping a new writer get his legs.

Special thanks to my writing conscience: Jim Leone, who helps keep me on track and away from excessive pronouns. I also had loads of help from Jonathan Weissman, who not only shares a love of all things networking, but also helped me keep the fields in the correct order and the redundant phrases at bay.

CHAPTER 1

Routing and Switching Strategies

The previous book in this series, *The Packet Guide to Core Network Protocols*, covered the IPv4 protocols, masking, and devices that are part of every network. Now it's time to take on the routing and switching for the network. There are an astonishing number of table-based decisions that have to be made in order to get a single packet across a network, let alone across a series of networks. Not limited to routers, switches, and access points, these decisions are made at each and every device, including hosts. As networks are constructed and devices configured to forward packets and frames, network administrators must make critical decisions affecting performance, security, and optimization.

When moving to advanced ideas, the net admin should know how and why networking tables are constructed, and in what cases manual changes will be beneficial. This chapter provides details about the routing and switching operations, as well as design elements. This chapter assumes that the reader understands the basic operation of routers and switches, as well as the standard suite of protocols including Ethernet, Internet Protocol (IP), Address Resolution Protocol (ARP), and the Internet Control Message Protocol (ICMP).

Switching: Forwarding and Filtering Traffic

Most protocols are foregone conclusions, so when building networks, many of the choices are not choices at all. It is highly probable that a network will be a mixture of Ethernet and 802.11 nodes. These nodes will run the Internet Protocol at Layer 3 of the Transmission Control Protocol/Internet Protocol (TCP/IP) networking model (see Figure 1-1). The applications will be designed for TCP or the User Datagram Protocol (UDP).

There are many types of switching: packet, circuit, multilayer, virtual circuit, wide area network (WAN), local area network (LAN). Circuiting and virtual circuit switching almost always refer to WAN or telephone technologies, and as such, will not be part of our discussion. Packet switching usually concerns a router or perhaps a WAN switch. Multilayer switching is a technique for improving the processing of IP packets, but most vendors have different ideas as to the best approach. Often, LAN switches are deployed without any thought to how multilayer switching might improve performance. In fact, other than routing between VLANs, administrators are rarely interested in how advanced features might be used on the network. Since this book is about IP-based networking, switching will almost always refer to Ethernet frames and the routing will be that of IP packets.

Application	FTP, telnet, email, games, printing, HTTP
Transport	Transmission control Protocol (TCP), User Datagram Protocol (UDP)
Internet (Internetwork)	Internet Protocol (IP), ICMP, IGMP
Link layer (Network)	Ethernet, 802.11
Physical	Ethernet, 802.11

Figure 1-1. TCP/IP model

Switches operate at Layer 2 of the TCP/IP (and OSI) model and are the workhorses of most networks. The operation of switches and bridges is defined in the IEEE 802.1D standard. The standard also describes the behavior of other Layer 2 protocols, such as the Spanning Tree Protocol, which will be covered in Chapter 3.

In network design, we often talk about the "access" layer or how host devices are connected to the network. Switches and access points (we'll ignore the use of hubs and collision domains) cover all of the bases. In addition to forwarding Ethernet frames based on Media Access Control (MAC) addresses and processing the Cyclical Redundancy Check (CRC), switches provide a couple of very important services:

- Filter out traffic that should not be forwarded, such as local unicast frames
- Prevent the forwarding of collisions
- Prevent the forwarding of frames with errors

Switches also provide a collection of features that are part of most medium and large networks:

- Virtual local area networks (VLANs)
- Simple network management protocol (SNMP)
- Remote management
- Statistics collection
- Port mirroring
- Security such as 802.1X port-based authentication

Any device connected to a network, regardless of its specialization, still has to follow the rules of that network. Thus, switches still obey the rules for Ethernet access and collision detection. They also go through the same auto-negotiation operations that Ethernet hosts complete. There are several different link types used when installing switches. They can be connected directly together in point-to-point configurations, connected to shared media or to hosts. Depending on the location in the network, the requirements for performance and security can be significantly different. Core or backbone switches and routers may have the requirement of extremely high through-put, while switches connected to critical elements may be configured for stricter security. Many switches have absolutely no configuration changes, and are simply pulled out of the box and run with default factory settings.

Forwarding Based on MAC Addresses

To forward or filter Ethernet frames, the switch consults a source address table (SAT) before transmitting a frame to the destination. The SAT is also called a MAC address table or content addressable memory (CAM). Only the destination indicated in the table receives the transmission. In general, a switch receives a frame, reads the MAC addresses, performs the Cyclical Redundancy Check (CRC) for error control, and finally forwards the frame to the correct port. Broadcast and multicast frames are typically forwarded everywhere except the original source port. Figure 1-2 depicts a typical topology with a switch at the center.

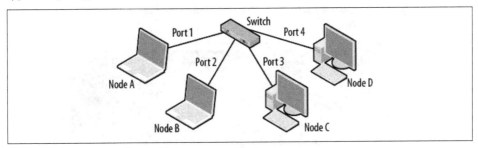

Figure 1-2. Basic switch topology

Network nodes have unique MAC addresses and Ethernet frames indentify the source and destination by these MAC addresses. A MAC address is a 6-byte value, such as 00:12:34:56:78:99, which is assigned to the host. The SAT is a mapping between the MAC addresses and the switch ports. This table also keeps track of the virtual local area networks, or VLANs, configured on the switch. On most switches, all ports are in VLAN 1 by default. The source address table for the network shown in Figure 1-2 might look like Table 1-1.

Table 1-1. Switch source address table

MAC Address	VLAN	Port
Node A MAC	1	1
Node B MAC	1	2
Node C MAC	1	3
Node D MAC	1	4

If the address is known, the frame is forwarded to the correct port. If the address is unknown, the frame is sent to every port except the source port. This is called flooding. If the destination MAC address is a broadcast address (in the form ff:ff:ff:ff:ff:ff), the frame is again sent everywhere except the original source port. In many cases, this is also the behavior for multicast frames. Recall that multicast frames commonly begin with a hexadecimal 01 in the first byte. The range of a multicast frame can be affected by using the Interior Group Management Protocol (IGMP). Switches can perform IGMP snooping in order to determine which ports should receive the multicast traffic. IGMP is also defined in the IEEE 802.1D standard. VLANs can reduce the effect of flooding or broadcasting because they can be used to break the switch into smaller logical segments. We'll talk about VLANs in Chapter 4.

Figure 1-3 displays the source address table from an operating Cisco switch. This output was obtained using the show mac-address-table command for the Cisco switch. The term *"dynamic"* means that the switch learned the address by examining frames sent by the attached nodes.

```
Non-static Address Table:
Destination Address   Address Type   VLAN   Destination Port
--------------------   ------------   ----   ----------------
0004.9b4b.5701        Dynamic          1     FastEthernet0/1
0004.9b4b.5701        Dynamic          2     FastEthernet0/1
0004.9b4b.5701        Dynamic          3     FastEthernet0/1
000e.0c76.5ad4        Dynamic          2     FastEthernet0/7
000e.0c77.20e4        Dynamic          2     FastEthernet0/1
000e.0c77.2322        Dynamic          3     FastEthernet0/1
0011.212c.15e0        Dynamic          3     FastEthernet0/23
0011.212c.15e1        Dynamic          2     FastEthernet0/13
```

Figure 1-3. Cisco switch SAT

Note that there are three VLANs and port 1 (FastEthernet0/1) has several associated MAC addresses. This is because another switch was connected at that point. An example of this type of topology in shown in Figure 1-4. Two switches are interconnected via Port 3 on Switch 1 and Port 3 on Switch 2. As normal traffic flows, the switches will learn where all of the MAC destinations are by recording the source MACs from the Ethernet transmissions.

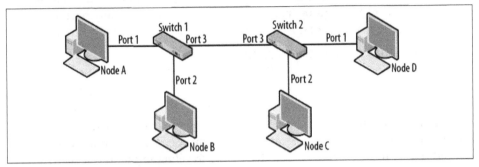

Figure 1-4. Two switch topology

In topologies such as this, it is impossible for a switch to connect directly to each destination. For example, the only piece of information Switch 2 will possess is the source MAC from its perspective. So, from the perspective of Switch 2, all frames appear to have come from the single port (3) connected to Switch 1. The reverse is also true. Building on what is known of source address tables and the learning process, the SATs for the two switches would look like Table 1-2.

Table 1-2. SAT for two switch topology

Switch 1			Switch 2		
MAC address	VLAN	Port	MAC address	VLAN	Port
Node A	1	1	Node A	1	3
Node B	1	2	Node B	1	3
Node C	1	3	Node C	1	2
Node D	1	3	Node D	1	1

When Node A sends traffic to Node D, Switch 1 forwards the traffic out Port 3. Switch 2 receives the frame and forwards the frame to Port 1.

Figure 1-3 also depicts several VLANs. What isn't clear from these SATs or topology diagrams is how traffic moves from one VLAN to another. Interconnected switches configured with VLANs are typically connected together via *trunk lines*. In addition, Layer 2 switches need a router or routing functionality to forward traffic between VLANs. With the advent of multiplayer switches, the boundary between routers and switches is getting a bit blurry. VLANs and trunks will be covered in-depth in Chapter 4.

One other very nice feature of a switch is port mirroring. Mirroring copies the traffic from one port and sends it to another. This is important because over the last several years, hubs have been almost entirely removed from the network. But without hubs, it can be a challenge to "see" the traffic that is flowing on the network. With mirroring, a management host can be installed and collect traffic from any port or VLAN. The following are examples of the commands that might be issued on a Cisco switch:

```
monitor session 1 source interface Fa0/24
monitor session 1 destination interface Fa0/9 encapsulation dot1q
```

The first command describes the source of the traffic to be monitored. The second command not only specifies the destination, but the type of frame encapsulation as well. In this case, the traffic monitored is actually flowing over a trunk line. Trunks are part of Chapter 4. Mirroring commands can also specify the direction of the desired traffic. It is possible to select the traffic traveling to or from a specific host. Typically, both directions are the default.

Figure 1-5 depicts an example in which Nodes A and B are communicating and the network admin would like to see what they are up to. So, the traffic coming to and from Node B is mirrored to the management node. Since the conversation is between Node A and B, a port connected to either one of them will suffice.

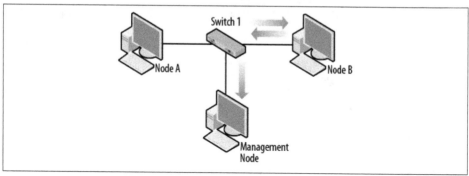

Figure 1-5. Port mirroring

Routing: Finding Paths

When building networks, we typically divide routing into two components: host and router. Routers handle traffic flowing between networks but hosts make many decisions long before the packets hit the network. Most routing protocols used to find pathways to destinations are router based, however.

Hosts are typically configured one of two ways: statically with an IP address, default gateway, and domain name server, or with values learned via the Dynamic Host Configuration Protocol (DHCP). Hosts send all traffic going off the local network to the default gateway, with the hope that the gateway can route the packets to the destination. One of my favorite questions to ask is "What is the first thing that a host does before sending a packet?" Before doing anything else, a host must process its routing table. Chapter 2 of this book is devoted to host-based routing. Historically, there have been some network technologies in which the hosts were more active. For example, IBM's Token Ring utilized discovery frames to find destination nodes on different network segments or rings. However, this is primarily a Layer 2 function, and is not part of contemporary Ethernet- and IP-based networks. Recent years have seen a return to utilizing the host of handling the routing function in the area of ad hoc networking.

Ad hoc routing typically does not run on the traditional network infrastructure. Applications include sensor networks, battlefield communications, and disaster scenarios in which the infrastructure is gone. In these situations, nodes will handle forwarding of traffic to other nodes. Related ideas are the ad hoc applications and 802.11 ad hoc networks. It is important to realize that with the 802.11 standard, nodes can connect in an ad hoc network but do not forward traffic for other nodes. If a wireless node is not within range of the source host, it will miss the transmission.

Ad hoc routing protocols are designed to solve this particular problem by empowering the nodes to handle the routing/forwarding function. Interesting problems crop up when the "router" may not be wired into the network: things such as movement of the wireless nodes, power saving, processing capability, and memory may be affected. In addition, the application is important. Are the nodes actually sensors which have very little in the way of resources? Are they moving quickly? These challenges have resulted in several ad hoc routing protocols being developed, such as Ad hoc On Demand Distance Vector (AODV), Fisheye State Routing (FSR), and Optimized Link State Routing (OLSR).

But these ideas are all a little beyond the scope of this book. The point being made here is that hosts and the host routing table are very active in the processing of packets. Historically, nodes on some networks were even more involved, and if ad hoc routing protocols are any indication, those days are not gone for good.

Routing Devices

Routers operate at the internetwork layer of the TCP/IP model and process IP addresses based on their routing table. A router's main function is to forward traffic to destination networks via the destination address in an IP packet. Routers also resolve MAC addresses (particularly their own) by using the Address Resolution Protocol (ARP). It is important to remember that Layer 2 (link layer) frames and MAC addresses do not live beyond the router. This means that an Ethernet frame is destroyed when it hits a router. When operating in a network, a router can act as the default gateway for hosts, as in most home networks. A router may be installed as an intermediate hop between other routers without any direct connectivity to hosts. In addition to routing, routers can be asked to perform a number of other tasks, such as network address translation, managing access control lists, terminating virtual private network or quality of service.

Basic router functionality is comprised of three major components:

- Routing process
- Routing protocols
- Routing table

The routing process is the actual movement of IP packets from one port to another and the routing table holds the information used by the routing process. Routing protocols such as the Routing Information Protocol (RIP) or Open Shortest Path First (OSPF) are used to communicate with other routers and may end up "installing" routes in the routing table for use by the routing process. When a router is configured, the routing table is constructed by bringing interfaces up and providing the interfaces with IP addresses. A simple Cisco routing table is shown in Figure 1-6.

```
Gateway of last resort is not set

C    192.168.15.0/24 is directly connected, FastEthernet0/1
C    192.168.20.0/24 is directly connected, FastEthernet0/0
```

Figure 1-6. Router routing table

When processing packets, routers "traverse" the routing table looking for the best possible pathway match. The routing table shown in Figure 1-6 indicates that the router knows of two networks: `192.168.15.0` and `192.168.20.0`. Note that this router does not have a default gateway or "gateway of last resort." This means that if the destination IP address is anywhere beyond the two networks listed, the router has no idea how to get there. If you said to yourself, "Ahh, ICMP destination unreachable message," give yourself a gold star.

Routing tables can be comprised of several different route types: directly connected, static, and dynamic. Two directly connected routes are seen in Figure 1-6. These are the networks on which the router has an interface and are accompanied by the letter "C" and the particular interface, such as `FastEthernet0/1`. Directly connected routes have preference over and above any other route.

> The 0/1 from the interface is a designator for the blade and port in the router chassis.

Static Routes

Static entries are those that are manually installed on a router by the network administrator. For specific destinations, and in small or stable network environments, manually configured static routes can be used very successfully. By using static routes, the *network administrator* has determined the pathway to be used to a particular destination network. The static route will supersede any pathway learned via a routing protocol because of the administrative distance, discussed later in this chapter.

Another important idea that is central to routing is the *next hop*. The next hop is a router that is one step closer to the destination from the perspective of a particular router. The next hop is the router to send packets to next. In many networks, a series of next hops are used. A medium-sized routed topology is shown in Figure 1-7. So, from the perspective of R1, R2 would be the next hop used to get to both the 192.168.3.0 and 192.168.4.0 networks.

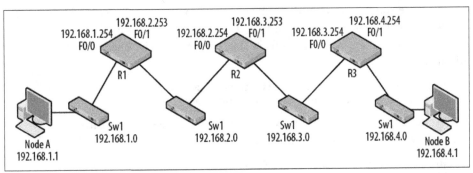

Figure 1-7. Small routed topology

This topology has three routers, which are cabled to each other via the switches shown. There are several ways to emulate a topology such as this, but this configuration was chosen for clarity. Initially, nothing has been configured except that the interfaces have been "brought up" and given IP addresses. To bring up an interface, it has to have been given the no shutdown command and have a link pulse. The routing tables of the routers will only contain the directly connected routes. Each router is only aware of the two networks for which is has interfaces. Table 1-3 depicts the routing tables at this point.

Table 1-3. Starting routing tables

R1	R2	R3
C 192.168.1.0 F0/0	C 192.168.2.0 F0/0	C 192.168.3.0 F0/0
C 192.168.2.0 F0/1	C 192.168.3.0 F0/1	C 192.168.4.0 F0/1

What is clear from these tables is that the routers do not have a complete picture of the whole network. For example, Node A is connected to Switch 1 and is trying to contact Node B on Switch 4. After processing its host routing table (see Chapter 2), it will forward the traffic to its default gateway (192.168.1.254) on R1. R1 will now consult its routing table and discover that it only has entries for networks on the left side of the topology. Without knowledge of the destination network, R1 will issue the ICMP destination unreachable message.

 Just for fun: The 192.168.1.0 and 192.168.4.0 networks are called stub networks because they have only one pathway in or out.

How is this problem solved? In small networks such as this, the network administrator can issue routing commands to the routers providing them with additional forwarding information. These would be the static routes. For Cisco routers, the command ip route is used. It has three fields that have to be filled in by the network administrator:

```
ip route destination-network destination-network-mask
next-hop-IP-address (forwarding router interface)
```

For example, R1 could be told how to get to the 192.168.3.0 and the 192.168.4.0 networks with the following commands:

```
ip route 192.168.3.0 255.255.255.0 192.168.2.254
ip route 192.168.4.0 255.255.255.0 192.168.2.254
```

The commands are almost identical except for the destination network. A couple important points: the last field specifying the forwarding router interface (192.168.2.254) is a neighboring router that can be reached by R1. With these two commands, the behavior is that from R1 the traffic is destined for the two networks specified should be sent to R2. The mask is also the mask of the destination network and not the mask used locally. It is possible that these masks are different. This correct form is called a recursive route.

After issuing the commands on R1, the routing tables would be updated as listed in Table 1-4:

Table 1-4. Updated R1 routing table

R1	R2	R3
C 192.168.1.0 F0/0	C 192.168.2.0 F0/0	C 192.168.3.0 F0/0
C 192.168.2.0 F0/1	C 192.168.3.0 F0/1	C 192.168.4.0 F0/1
S 192.168.3.0 via 192.168.2.254		
S 192.168.4.0 via 192.168.2.254		

While this is an improvement, it only solves part of the problem. Now R1 understands that traffic bound for these networks has to go to R2, but what does R2 do next? In the case of the `192.168.3.0` network, everything is fine since this is directly connected to R2. R2 can ARP for hosts since they will be on the same network. But since traffic is going to `192.168.4.0`, R2 requires some assistance from the administrator in the form of the following command:

```
ip route 192.168.4.0 255.255.255.0 192.168.3.254
```

The routing table is updated accordingly and we can breathe a sigh of relief as the packets finally made it to the `192.168.4.0` network.

Table 1-5. Updated R2 routing table

R1	R2	R3
C 192.168.1.0 F0/0	C 192.168.2.0 F0/0	C 192.168.3.0 F0/0
C 192.168.2.0 F0/1	C 192.168.3.0 F0/1	C 192.168.4.0 F0/1
S 192.168.3.0 via 192.168.2.254	S 192.168.4.0 via 192.168.3.254	
S 192.168.4.0 via 192.168.2.254		

Getting to the destination network is only half the battle—packets still have to get back. Examining the routing table on R3, it can be seen that the router does not understand where the `192.168.1.0` network can be found. The packet from Node A would have gotten there, but when Node B tries to respond, it will receive an ICMP destination unreachable message from R3. From the perspective of Node A, it will appear as though the transmission was never answered. To be complete, `ip route` commands for all of the unknown networks would have to be issued on each router and the routing tables updated. After all of the `ip route` commands have been issued, the routing table would look like the entries seen in Table 1-6.

Table 1-6. Completed routing tables

R1	R2	R3
C 192.168.1.0 F0/0	C 192.168.2.0 F0/0	C 192.168.3.0 F0/0
C 192.168.2.0 F0/1	C 192.168.3.0 F0/1	C 192.168.4.0 F0/1
S 192.168.3.0 via 192.168.2.254	S 192.168.1.0 via 192.168.2.253	S 192.168.1.0 via 192.168.3.253
S 192.168.4.0 via 192.168.2.254	S 192.168.4.0 via 192.168.3.254	S 192.168.2.0 via 192.168.3.253

The actual routing table for R2 and the `ip route` commands issued on R2 are both shown in Figure 1-8.

```
Router(config)#
Router(config)#ip route 192.168.1.0 255.255.255.0 192.168.2.253
Router(config)#ip route 192.168.4.0 255.255.255.0 192.168.3.254
Router(config)#

Gateway of last resort is not set

S    192.168.4.0/24 [1/0] via 192.168.3.254
S    192.168.1.0/24 [1/0] via 192.168.2.253
C    192.168.2.0/24 is directly connected, FastEthernet0/0
C    192.168.3.0/24 is directly connected, FastEthernet0/1
Router#
```

Figure 1-8. R2 routing table with static route commands

In the last few routing tables, all of the destination networks can be reached either because they are directly connected or have a static route which points to a neighbor router that might be able to help. I have used the term "might" because when using static routes, there is actually an assumption that the forwarding router chosen knows something about the pathway to the destination. This is not always the case, as was described before the routing tables were fully populated.

 There are several options regarding the arguments for the `ip route` command and there are times when the usage seen in this chapter should be modified. Serial links provide an example in which the last field should be an interface rather than a next hop ip address.

Digging a Little Deeper—Common Mistakes

Reviewing the changes outlined in Figure 1-8, there are two common mistakes made when trying to configure static routing. These will be reviewed from the perspective of R2. The following is a mistake:

```
ip route 192.168.1.0 255.255.255.0 192.168.2.254
```

This command asks the router to forward traffic to itself. In effect this says, "R2 doesn't know where the `192.168.1.0` network is, so let's send it to R2." This also makes little sense to the router and so it usually responds with the message shown in Figure 1-9. The network administrator and the router stare at each other for a bit, and then the admin is likely to try the second common mistake. This also occurs when addresses are entered incorrectly. The proper form is shown in Figure 1-8.

```
Router(config)#
Router(config)#ip route 192.168.1.0 255.255.255.0 192.168.2.254
%Invalid next hop address (it's this router)
Router(config)#
```

Figure 1-9. Error message for circular routing

The second mistake does not actually specify a forwarding router IP address, but rather a physical interface. This results in higher processing load on the router, and is usually reserved for use with interior routing protocols. The command and the resulting routing table are shown in Figure 1-10. Though they are static routes, the routing table indicates that the `192.168.1.0` and `192.168.4.0` networks are directly connected. The topology shows that this is clearly not the case.

```
ip classless
ip route 192.168.1.0 255.255.255.0 FastEthernet0/0
ip route 192.168.4.0 255.255.255.0 FastEthernet0/1
ip http server

Gateway of last resort is not set

S    192.168.4.0/24 is directly connected, FastEthernet0/1
S    192.168.1.0/24 is directly connected, FastEthernet0/0
C    192.168.2.0/24 is directly connected, FastEthernet0/0
C    192.168.3.0/24 is directly connected, FastEthernet0/1
Router#
```

Figure 1-10. Mistake 2

The reason for the higher processing is that the command is not specific enough and the router actually has no idea where to send the traffic. It is similar to a person who, wishing to mail a letter, addresses the letter but then simply opens the front door and throws the letter outside, hoping that it will get to the destination. What is really interesting is the effect on network traffic. The Address Resolution Protocol (ARP) traffic is limited to the local area network or subnet. This means that ARP messages are not generally forwarded by routers and hosts do not ARP for nodes not on their own network. An exception can be found in Proxy ARP, but it is rarely used. Lastly, MAC addresses typically do not have any meaning beyond their own network. But look what happens when the commands shown in Figure 1-10 are used. Figure 1-11 shows that R3 (`192.168.3.254`) is sending an ARP request for `192.168.1.1`, a node on a distant network. This breaks all of the basic behaviors and is just plain wrong. It makes me uncomfortable just looking at it.

```
⊞ Ethernet II, Src: Cisco_2c:0c:80 (00:11:21:2c:0c:80), Dst: Broadcast (ff:ff:ff:ff:ff:ff)
⊟ Address Resolution Protocol (request)
    Hardware type: Ethernet (0x0001)
    Protocol type: IP (0x0800)
    Hardware size: 6
    Protocol size: 4
    Opcode: request (0x0001)
    [Is gratuitous: False]
    Sender MAC address: Cisco_2c:0c:80 (00:11:21:2c:0c:80)
    Sender IP address: 192.168.3.254 (192.168.3.254)
    Target MAC address: 00:00:00_00:00:00 (00:00:00:00:00:00)
    Target IP address: 192.168.1.1 (192.168.1.1)
```

Figure 1-11. Nonlocal ARP traffic

Default Routes

It is often the case that several destinations can be reached via the same pathway. In cases like this, the routing table can continue to grow even though many of the routes share common fields. This was true in the routing tables for both R1 and R3. Routing table entries sharing the same pathway can be replaced with a smaller set of routes. The best examples are default routes and aggregation. Aggregation or route summarization is a technique for reducing the number of entries in a routing table by shortening the prefix length. The effect is to collect a series of destinations into a single entry.

The default route is a special case of a static route. Normally we think of default gateways or routers for hosts. Routers can also have default gateways. Like a host, when the routing table is exhausted and no matches are found for the destination, the default route is used. In Cisco-speak, this is called the gateway of last resort. Again, just like static routes, the network administrator is assuming that the next hop router knows something that the current router does not: how to get to either the destination or the next hop. Figure 1-12 shows the topology with the candidate default routes based on the information from Table 1-6.

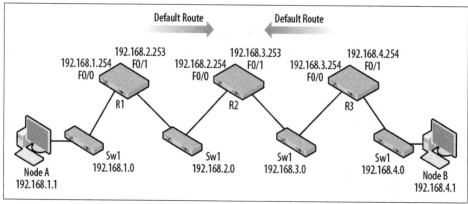

Figure 1-12. Default routes

For R1, all destinations not directly connected must be reached by forwarding traffic to 192.168.2.254. For R3, all destinations not directly connected must be reached by forwarding traffic to 192.168.3.253. Therefore, some of the routing table entries could be replaced with a default route. For a router, a default route or gateway of last resort is installed with a special set of arguments in the ip route command. Instead of specifying the destination network and the destination network mask, default routes use all 0's. You may recall that in processing a routing table with masks, AND-ing any IP address with a mask of 0.0.0.0 results in 0.0.0.0. This means that any destination will result in all zeroes (0.0.0.0) and the ANDing process for this ip route line will also be all zeroes, matching every destination:

```
ip route 0.0.0.0 0.0.0.0 forwarding router interface
```

For R1:

```
ip route 0.0.0.0 0.0.0.0 192.168.2.254
```

and for R4:

```
ip route 0.0.0.0 0.0.0.0 192.168.3.253
```

The routing tables would be updated as in Table 1-7.

Table 1-7. Updated routing tables with default routes

R1	R2	R3
C 192.168.1.0 F0/0	C 192.168.2.0 F0/0	C 192.168.3.0 F0/0
C 192.168.2.0 F0/1	C 192.168.3.0 F0/1	C 192.168.4.0 F0/1
S 0.0.0.0/0 via 192.168.2.254	S 192.168.1.0 via 192.168.2.253	S 0.0.0.0/0 via 192.168.3.253
	S 192.168.4.0 via 192.168.3.254	

Again, there are a couple of important points to note. While the routing tables for R1 and R3 have been improved, R2 still has the same number of routes. In this case, a default route pointing to R1 or R3 would not help much because R2 would still need another route for the network in the opposite direction. Additionally, we would be risking a routing loop. Lastly, going from four routes down to three may not seem like much of an improvement for R1 and R3, but this is a small network. Production networks can be much larger and have hundreds of routes.

Dynamic Routes

Dynamic routes are those learned via routing protocols, such as Routing Information Protocol (RIP) or Open Shortest Path First (OSPF). When building a network, the approach used to handle routing is an important decision. Static routes require less processing, but changes to network topology cannot be addressed quickly. If the pathway to a destination changes, or if a router is offline, pathways or routes will be lost. Static routes also offer no protection from operator error. Typically, static routes are used when the topology is stable and the network architecture is fairly straightforward. In other words, when the network conditions are well understood. We often assume that if the network admin installs the route, if must be correct. Dynamic routing protocols can protect us from these topology changes and errors between the keyboard and the chair. Most routing protocols also provide protection from routing loops and old, incorrect information. Many also handle load balancing and multiple pathways to destinations.

Routing Protocols

Before we discuss individual routing protocols in the later chapters, it is necessary to discuss types or characteristics of protocols. The idea is to pick the right protocol for the job and to do this we have to examine the algorithm and operational details. There are several ways to look at or define different protocols.

Single versus multipath

Routing protocols use an algorithm to determine the best path to the destination. If there is only one path, the decision is quite simple. In the event that several pathways exist, the routing protocol has a choice: it may take only the best possible path, leaving others to languish until needed, or it could install multiple pathways to the destination. The former is called a *single path* protocol. It may be that two pathways are equal in all respects and the router cannot make a choice as to which is better. The protocol can choose to send some portion of the data via each pathway. In this case, the protocol may be performing some form of load balancing to improve network throughput, in which case it would be considered *multipath*. Lastly, some consideration must be given to backup paths and the protocols' ability to failover should the preferred path be unavailable.

Interior versus exterior

Most routing protocols have established limitations. A clear example is the Routing Information Protocol (RIP), which cannot handle networks with more than 15 hops. Protocols are also designed to include in their calculations certain network parameters, such as cost or utilization. Thus, it may be that a particular protocol is completely inappropriate for a given network topology. Those designed for a group of networks under single administrative control (an autonomous system) are called *interior* routing protocols. We will see in later chapters that some interior routing protocols should stick to small groups of networks. Those designed for much larger scale topologies such as WAN connectivity and those deployed by ISPs are called *exterior*. Exterior protocols tend to link autonomous systems together. The Border Gateway Protocol (BGP) is an exterior routing protocol.

Flat versus hierarchical

When implementing a routing protocol, routers have a specific set of tasks to perform, such as advertising routing information, handling topology changes, and determining best path. If all of the routers are performing the same set of tasks, the protocol is said to be *flat*. This is the case with RIP. However, if there are other functions assigned to a subset of the routers, the protocol may be operating in a *hierarchical* manner. For example, some protocols define backbone and nonbackbone sections of the network. Traffic tends to flow from nonbackbone to backbone sections. Protocols often create boundaries around these sections called domains or areas. Peer routers communicate within a domain and backbone routers communicate between domains. OSPF is considered to be hierarchical because of its area-based organization. All OSPF routers understand forwarding within an area. Some of the routers understand inter-area forwarding and have additional knowledge of the overall topology.

Link state versus distance vector

These two terms refer to the algorithm used by the protocol to determine routes to use. Distance vector protocols are also called Bellman-Ford (for the original designers). You may recall from physics class that a vector is an object that describes magnitude and direction. An example might be that a runner was traveling 6 MPH and heading north. *Distance vector* routing protocols use the same idea in that they describe distance to the destination, commonly in terms of hop count (number of routers), and a direction in the form of the next hop IP address or interface to use. So, the destination network is X number of hops away and sends packets to a particular router. Neighboring routers send a portion of their routing table to each other and then send periodic updates. But there isn't much information other than hop count and direction. It is therefore difficult to make a decision based on the quality of the path. RIP is a distance vector protocol. Distance vector protocols are generally slow to "converge the topology" when compared to link state protocols. Convergence refers to the process of establishing a steady state topology after changes have occurred.

Link state protocols utilize greater detail about the links or connections between routers in order to make more informed decisions. For example, while two pathways might cover the same distance in order to get to the destination, if one path is based on 1Gbps Ethernet and the other is based on slower Frame Relay, the former path is chosen—even if the hop count is the same. This routing information is also flooded to the entire topology to speed up convergence. After the information has been flooded, routers keep in regular contact with each other via "hello" messages indicating that nothing has changed. For these reasons, link state protocols tend to converge more quickly. The protocols are based on Dijkstra's algorithm for finding the best path between points on a graph. OSPF is an example of a link state routing protocol.

A protocol like RIP can now be characterized as dynamic, router based, single path, interior, flat, and distance vector. Why RIP has these characteristics will be covered in Chapter 5. OSPF would be dynamic, router based, multipath, interior, hierarchical, and link state. We'll take an in-depth look at OSPF in Chapter 6.

Choosing or Installing a Route

As the routing table is built via dynamically learned routes, the router has to decide whether a route should be installed in the table. With static routes, the router doesn't have much choice. Additionally, as packets are received by the router, it must decide which route is the best for the given destination. For both of these decisions, three values are compared: prefix length, administrative distance, and metric values, in order of importance. These three are typically discussed in the context of Cisco routers. However, other vendors use similar processes and values in their routing table construction and decisions.

Prefix length

Prefix length is based on the number of bits in the mask because the mask determines the network address. The greater the number of 1's in the mask, the longer the prefix length. For example, an IP address of 192.168.1.5 with a mask of 255.255.255.0 has a network address of 192.168.1.0. Thus, the prefix length is 24. The same IP address with a mask of 255.255.0.0 has a prefix length of 16 and a network address of 192.168.0.0. When building a routing table or forwarding packets, longer prefixes are preferred because they get a packet closer to the destination. For example, if you were trying to mail a letter to someone living in the east, but all you knew was that they lived in Boston, the mail plane would drop the letter over the city in hopes that it would reach the destination. Providing the street gets the letter a little closer, and adding the house number finally gets it to the destination. So the address got longer and longer.

Similarly, to send a packet to me here at RIT (no denial-of-service attacks, please), routing table entries using a network address of 129.21.0.0 get it to this general area, but RIT is a big place. Routers eventually list the correct subnet by using a longer prefix, and get the packet much closer. Prefix length is the number one consideration in this process.

Administrative distance

The second consideration is the *administrative distance*. There are times when a router will receive information from different protocols. If the prefix lengths are the same, how does the router determine which information is the best? You might hear about two new restaurants from different friends. Experience tells you which of your friends has the better advice regarding food. Similarly, some routing protocols are better than others. Administrative distance is a number that can describe the value of information learned via a routing protocol or of the routing table entries already installed.

Every routing protocol has an administrative distance, and this is included in the routing table entries. Lower values are preferred and so, given two routes with an equal prefix length, the lower administrative distance will be chosen. Some common examples include those shown in Table 1-8.

Table 1-8. Protocol administrative distances

Route type	Administrative distance
Static	1
EIGRP	90
OSPF	110
RIP	120

Based on these values, OSPF information is considered superior to that of RIP. Given the same prefix length, you would take the OSPF information over that of RIP. However, if RIP advertises a route with a prefix length of 24 compared to an OSPF prefix length of 22, the RIP information will be installed or used. In a routing table, bracketed numbers include the administrative distance:

> *RIP - 192.168.1.0 255.255.255.0 [120]*
> *OSPF - 192.168.1.0 255.255.252.0 [110]*

Note that based on the administrative distance, static routes are considered superior to any learned route and directly connected routes are superior to static.

Metric

Metric is the last comparison value for route information. Metric is used to compare routes that are learned via the same routing protocol when they have the same prefix length. The metric values are dependent upon the routing protocol—RIP uses hop count while OSPF uses a formula to derive its dimensionless metric. It is inappropriate to use the metric to directly compare information from different protocols. For example, two pathways to the same destination are received by a router via RIP packets and so have the same administrative distance. Assuming the masks used have the same prefix length, the deciding factor will be the metric. One path utilizes 4 hops to get to the destination while the other only requires 3. Clearly one path is shorter and so will be installed in the routing table. The routing table would include entries such as:

192.168.1.0 255.255.255.0 [120/3] via 192.168.1.254

Inside the bracket, the hop count is appended to the administrative distance.

Routing Loops

There are several topologies that create problems for both Ethernet and IP. A looped architecture is one of the most challenging. Layer 2 protocols like Ethernet do not have a mechanism to handle loops, so Radia Perlman rode to the rescue with the Spanning Tree Protocol. At Layer 3, we are afforded some measure of protection because IP includes a time to live field. As packets continue around a looped topology, each router will decrement this field by one until it reaches zero. At this point, the IP packet is no longer sent along. A simple looped topology is shown in Figure 1-13.

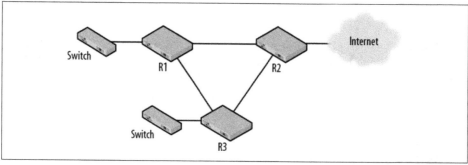

Figure 1-13. Routing loop

In this topology, nodes connected to the switches would use R1 and R2 as their default gateways. R1 and R2 would in turn use R3 as their gateway of last resort in order to get to external destinations. Routing between R1 and R2 might be handled via static or dynamic routes. As we discussed previously, the problem with static routes is that they do not respond to changing network conditions or handle loops. Any mistakes in configuration or with certain kinds of failure and packets could continuously circulate or be lost.

But routing loops are not always bad. For example, if connectivity for the nodes attached to the switches is considered critical, a routing loop might be installed to ensure that the network is very reliable. The links between R1/R3 and R2/R3 might span long distances, such as the connections to a service provider. Routing/failover protocols might be used to maintain this set of redundant links, especially if the topology is more complex than the one in Figure 1-13. Routing loops can also be installed in order to provide load balancing between links. Protocols like Hot Standby Routing Protocol (HSRP), Virtual Router Redundancy Protocol (VRRP), and the

Gateway Load Balancing Protocol (GLBP) are all designed to help prevent single point of failure instances and potentially balance traffic over the links.

Figure 1-13 is a very straightforward sort of loop, but it is by no means the only way to wind up with a looped topology. Misconfiguration or lost connectivity can easily result in a loop, even where physical loops are not present. Networks actually have two topologies, physical and logical. The physical topology can be traced by following cables, or at least a good set of labels. The logical topology can only be understood by examining configurations and the flow of traffic. An example in which the physical and logical topologies do not match can be seen in Figure 1-14.

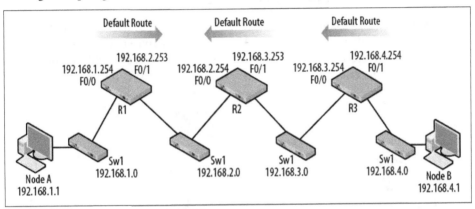

Figure 1-14. Physically linear, logical loop

When discussing static and default routes earlier in this chapter, the routing tables were simplified through the use of the default route on R1 and R3. But providing a default on R2 doesn't simplify the routing table. We will now see why placing a default route on R2 might not be a very good idea for a completely different reason. Assume that the routing tables are built and the default routes have been assigned as depicted in Figure 1-14. R2 is now using R1 for a default route.

Table 1-9. Default routing into routing loop

R1	R2	R3
C 192.168.1.0 F0/0	C 192.168.2.0 F0/0	C 192.168.3.0 F0/0
C 192.168.2.0 F0/1	C 192.168.3.0 F0/1	C 192.168.4.0 F0/1
S 0.0.0.0/0 via 192.168.2.254	S 0.0.0.0/0 via 192.168.2.253	S 0.0.0.0/0 via 192.168.3.253

What happens if Node A pings a device not on this particular set of networks, such as 192.168.5.1? The ICMP echo request would be sent to the default gateway of Node A (192.168.1.254) and R1 would discover that it did not know where the destination was. R1 would send the packet to its gateway of last resort: 192.168.2.254. R2 would process its routing table and discover that it did not know where the destination

(192.168.5.1) was either. R2 also has a gateway of last resort but the problem is that it is R1. Thus, the packet is sent right back to R1. Presto—logical loop. R1 receives the packets, processes its routing table, and the whole thing starts over again until the time to live field in the packet expires. Whether the configuration was done on purpose or by mistake, the results are the same. Figure 1-15 depicts an Internet Control Message Protocol (ICMP) packet that results from a time to live (TTL) field being reduced to 0, though for a different conversation. ICMP has the responsibility of informing network hosts when problems such as this occur. Within the ICMP packet, the time to live field is set to 255. But this is not true of all IP packets. Each router decrements this field as the packet is forwarded.

The topology seen in Figure 1-14 is an isolated topology, and in practice would be connected to the outside world or to another series of routers that eventually sent traffic offsite. So, the default gateway and the routing tables would be configured accordingly. But never underestimate our ability to set things up improperly.

```
Ethernet II, Src: Cisco_28:1b:e0 (00:05:5e:28:1b:e0), Dst: Standard_08:e0:27 (00:e0:29:08:e0:27)
Internet Protocol, Src: 192.168.3.253 (192.168.3.253), Dst: 192.168.3.1 (192.168.3.1)
    Version: 4
    Header length: 20 bytes
    Differentiated Services Field: 0xc0 (DSCP 0x30: Class Selector 6; ECN: 0x00)
    Total Length: 56
    Identification: 0x02db (731)
    Flags: 0x00
    Fragment offset: 0
    Time to live: 255
    Protocol: ICMP (0x01)
    Header checksum: 0x2fdb [correct]
    Source: 192.168.3.253 (192.168.3.253)
    Destination: 192.168.3.1 (192.168.3.1)
Internet Control Message Protocol
    Type: 11 (Time-to-live exceeded)
    Code: 0 (Time to live exceeded in transit)
    Checksum: 0x9fa3 [correct]
    Internet Protocol, Src: 192.168.3.1 (192.168.3.1), Dst: 192.168.1.254 (192.168.1.254)
    Internet Control Message Protocol
```

Figure 1-15. ICMP Time Exceeded

There are times when link failures can create loops. For example, if in Figure 1-14, the R3 interface connected to the 192.168.4.0 were to be shutdown, the route would be removed from the routing table of R3. However, the other routers in the topology would still believe that the 192.168.4.0 network is still available via R3. The question is: What does R3 do when traffic for the 192.168.4.0 network arrives?

Table 1-10. Correct routing tables—again

R1	R2	R3
C 192.168.1.0 F0/0	C 192.168.2.0 F0/0	C 192.168.3.0 F0/0
C 192.168.2.0 F0/1	C 192.168.3.0 F0/1	C 192.168.4.0 F0/1
S 0.0.0.0/0 via 192.168.2.254	S 192.168.1.0 via 192.168.2.253	S 0.0.0.0/0 via 192.168.3.253
	S 192.168.4.0 via 192.168.3.254	

As we can see, R3 receives the packet and, not knowing where the destination is, would sends it to the gateway of last resort (R2). This is because when the interface is shutdown, R3 removes the 192.168.4.0 network from its routing table, resulting in another routing loop. For these reasons, whenever there is a doubt about the stability of the network or when complexity starts to grow, rely on dynamic routing.

Discard or Null Routing

Sometimes the best designs simply do not fit the topology at hand. When this happens, attempts to simplify or optimize the network can create real headaches. For example, aggregation is often used to shrink or simplify routing tables. To aggregate a series of routes, the number of downstream routes to be aggregated should be based on powers of 2. When network masks used to aggregate routes are modified, the changes are based on powers of 2. Now let's consider an example: imagine that the network administrator wishes to clean up the routing tables of the small, aggregated topology shown in Figure 1-16.

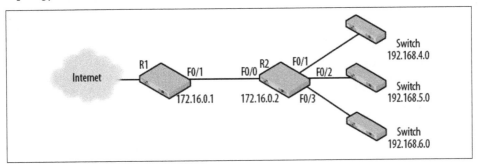

Figure 1-16. Aggregated topology

The routing tables for R1 and R2 are shown in Table 1-11. In this example, we are not concerned with the outside connectivity for R1.

Table 1-11. Routing tables, aggregated topology

R1	R2
C 172.16.0.0/16 F0/1	C 172.16.0.0/16 F0/0
S 192.168.4.0/24 via 172.16.0.2	C 192.168.4.0/24 F0/1
S 192.168.5.0/24 via 172.16.0.2	C 192.168.5.0/24 F0/2
S 192.168.6.0/24 via 172.16.0.2	C 192.168.6.0/24 F0/3
	S 0.0.0.0/0 via 172.16.0.1

The routing tables show that R2 is using R1 as a default gateway and that R1 is accessing several networks via R2. The network administrator looks at these and decides to aggregate them together in order to make the routing table of R1 simpler. This is accomplished by manipulating the mask associated with the downstream routes on R1.

Table 1-12. Routing tables, aggregated topology with network administrator "fix"

R1	R2
C 172.16.0.0/16 F0/1	C 172.16.0.0/16 F0/0
S 192.168.4.0/22 via 172.16.0.2	C 192.168.4.0/24 F0/1
	C 192.168.5.0/24 F0/2
	C 192.168.6.0/24 F0/3
	S 0.0.0.0/0 via 172.16.0.1

The resulting entry in R1 now encompasses the following addresses: `192.168.4.0`–`192.168.7.255`. But what happens when an address such as `192.168.7.1` is pinged from outside of R1? The traffic would be forwarded to R2, but since the route is not part of the table on R2, it would use its default route to send the traffic right back to R1. And again we have a routing loop. One solution for this problem would be to install null routes on R2 in order to prevent it from sending traffic back to R1. This can be for the aggregated address or the smaller address space, so variations of this command can be used on either router.

```
ip route 192.168.4.0 255.255.252.0 null0
```

In order to prevent this route from stopping all traffic, a higher administrative distance can be assigned to the route.

IPv6

Though IPv6 is not the focus of this book, it doesn't hurt to take a peek. The hard part about IPv6 is learning all of the addressing and terms. After that, you have to prepare your mind for values that look quite a bit different. But, from a routing perspective, many of the techniques are the same. Figure 1-17 depicts the same topology used earlier, but it is now an IPv6 topology. The /64 is the CIDR notation for the masks used.

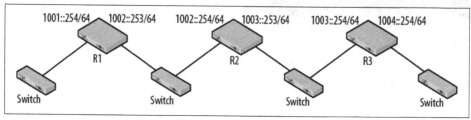

Figure 1-17. IPv6 topology

In order to build a topology, there are a couple of necessary changes to the configuration of each router. As can be seen, each router interface has an IPv6 address. For R1, the IPv4 and IPv6 commands are quite similar:

```
ip address 192.168.1.254 255.255.255.0    ipv6 address    1001::254/64
```

Again, the major difference is in the structure of the address. The colons in the IPv6 address suppress long strings of zeroes. The /64 is a classless interdomain routing (CIDR) shortcut for the mask. Routing is set up with two commands: `ipv6 unicast-routing` and `ipv6 route`. The second command is for the static routes. For R1, routes for the 1003::/64 and 1004::/64 networks are required.

```
ipv6 route 1003::/64 1002::254
ipv6 route 1004::/64 1002::254
```

The routing table for IPv6-based routers can be a little confusing at first, but after breaking it down, the similarities begin to emerge. Figure 1-18 displays the routing table for R1. Note the use of directly connected and static routes. One addition is the local (L) or link local entry. This refers to the interface of the router. The mask for these entries is /128 or all ones. This is the same as the IPv4 host entry. FF00 is the multicast entry. The brackets associated with each entry still show the administrative distance and metric.

```
IPv6 Routing Table - Default - 7 entries
Codes: C - Connected, L - Local, S - Static, U - Per-user Static route
       B - BGP, M - MIPv6, R - RIP, I1 - ISIS L1
       I2 - ISIS L2, IA - ISIS interarea, IS - ISIS summary, D - EIGRP
       EX - EIGRP external
       O - OSPF Intra, OI - OSPF Inter, OE1 - OSPF ext 1, OE2 - OSPF ext 2
       ON1 - OSPF NSSA ext 1, ON2 - OSPF NSSA ext 2
C   1001::/64 [0/0]
       via FastEthernet0/0, directly connected
L   1001::254/128 [0/0]
       via FastEthernet0/0, receive
C   1002::/64 [0/0]
       via FastEthernet0/1, directly connected
L   1002::253/128 [0/0]
       via FastEthernet0/1, receive
S   1003::/64 [1/0]
       via 1002::254
S   1004::/64 [1/0]
       via 1002::254
L   FF00::/8 [0/0]
       via Null0, receive
```

Figure 1-18. R1 IPv6 routing table

Reading

The ideas discussed in this chapter are outlined in a collection of RFC and standards, or touched on when reading about a particular protocol. For example, the RFCs for

RIP and OSPF refer to several routing issues and so are listed here. When configuring network equipment, I have always found it useful to have two documents at hand: command references and configuration guides. The command references are a must, since they contain the actual commands and the arguments used with the commands. However, these are not very useful when trying to understand "best practices." This is where configuration guides come in. These documents, along with vendor whitepapers, provide an explanation of where it is appropriate to use a particular command or how to begin building your network. In the end, trial and error will guide you as you try to get things working and gain experience.

> IEEE 802.1D: Standard for Local and Metropolitan Area Networks: Media Access Control (MAC) Bridges
> RFC 1102: Policy Routing in Internet Protocols
> RFC 2328: OSPF version 2
> RFC 2453: RIP version 2
> RFC 3768: Virtual Router Redundancy Protocol

Summary

In this chapter, we discussed some of the larger issues associated with routing and switching. When building networks, it is important to understand general concepts such as static, default, and dynamic routing. As networks grow in size and complexity, skills that become important include the ability to develop sound topology decisions and evaluate routing protocols. VLANs, trunks, installation of routes, and looped architectures were also covered. The best network administrators not only understand the commands to use, but the reasons for the commands and how network decisions are made.

Review Questions

1. When connected together and running VLANs, trunk lines are often used.

    a. TRUE

    b. FALSE

2. Static routes are manually installed and have a lower administrative distance than dynamic routes.

    a. TRUE

    b. FALSE

3. Dynamic routes are used whenever the network topology changes.

    a. TRUE

b. FALSE

4. Which of the following is the proper order of importance for route selection?

   a. Admin distance, prefix length, metric

   b. Prefix length, admin distance, metric

   c. Metric, prefix length, admin distance

5. The next hop router should be an interface on a router connected to your network.

   a. TRUE

   b. FALSE

6. Directly connected routes will be installed as soon as an interface is "up".

   a. TRUE

   b. FALSE

7. Match the following terms to their definitions.

   a. Metric   1. Number of bits in the mask

   b. Admin Distance   2. Value comparing information from the same
                             routing protocol
   c. Prefix Length
                          3. Quality comparison between routing protocols

8. RIP and OSPF are both what type of routing protocol?

   a. Distance vector

   b. Host based

   c. Hierarchical

   d. Interior

9. What addresses are encompassed by the following routing table entry: `172.31.32.0/19`?

10. Routing loops only occur on physically looped networks.

    a. TRUE

    b. FALSE

Review Answers

1. TRUE

2. TRUE

3. FALSE

4. B

5. TRUE

6. TRUE

7. a) 2 b) 3 c) 1

8. D

9. 172.31.32.0–172.31.63.255

10. FALSE

Lab Activities

Activity 1—Interconnected Switches and SATs

Materials: Two switches, two computers

1. Connect two switches via a crossover cable or uplink.

2. Connect the two computers, one on each switch.

3. Explore the SAT on each switch. Pay attention to the VLAN, port and MAC address listings. Handy Cisco command: `show mac-address-table`.

4. Experiment with either moving the computers or adding more nodes.

5. Before reviewing the table after each experiment, predict what the SAT content will be and why.

Activity 2—Static Routing Topology

Materials: Three routers, two computers

1. Wire the topology shown in Figure 1-7. Note: The topology can be reduced to two routers with the same requirements, though not as many.

2. Give each of the router interfaces and the computers IP addresses.

3. Examine the routing tables of each of the routers once the interfaces are up. Handy Cisco command: `show ip route`.

4. Experiment using PING. Which destinations are reachable and which are not?

5. Working from left to right, begin adding static routes in order to solve connectivity problems. Handy Cisco command: `ip route destination network destination mask forwarding router interface`.

6. Once all destinations can be PINGed from all interfaces, you are done.

Activity 3—Convert to Default Routes

Materials: Three routers, two computers, Wireshark

1. Using the topology from the previous activity, convert the static routes on R1 and R3 to default routes. Note: This activity can be confusing if only two routers are used, since there will not be a clear reason to choose the default route.

2. Examine the routing tables from each router. Select a couple destinations and process the routing tables manually, checking to see if the process can be followed step by step.

3. Now experiment with the captures themselves. Starting from a computer or interface, and assuming that the ARP tables are clear, try to explain every packet that will be generated as a result of a PING to an IP address at least one hop away.

4. Complete the PING and examine the captures in order to determine the correct answer. Were you correct? If not, why not?

Activity 4—Routing Loop

Materials: Three routers, two computers, Wireshark

1. Using the same topology, convert the routing table on R2 to default routes.

2. What addresses can be PINGed and what addresses cannot?

3. What happens in the command shell when you PING an address not on the topology?

4. Start up Wireshark and examine the traffic on the network as a result of your PING offsite.

5. What happens to the IP TTL field?

6. Where was the loop and what caused it?

7. What was the ICMP traffic generated as a result?

Activity 5—Null Route

Materials: Three routers, two computers, Wireshark

1. In the topology above, install null routes to fix the routing loop. Recall the null argument to the ip route command.

2. Does this solve the connectivity problem or simply hide the difficulty?

CHAPTER 2

Host Routing

"Seems like an awful lot just to get a packet from one side of the room to the other."
—An anonymous networking student

Chapter 1 discussed several of the issues associated with forwarding traffic across a network. Communication flows from one host to another (usually a server of some kind) and then back again. Switch source address and router routing tables are critical to this process. But, no matter what the purpose of the transmission, several operations must take place before packets can enter the network, beginning with the host routing table. Integrated ideas include masking, address resolution, and default gateways.

The Decision Process

From the moment a source host generates a chunk of data for transmission, work begins that will eventually result in an Ethernet frame being transmitted. From the application layer on down, the data is encapsulated in a series of headers until it reaches the bottom of the protocol stack. For example, accessing a web page uses the hypertext transfer protocol (HTTP) to move information between the web server and the host. HTTP uses the transmission control protocol (TCP) at Layer 4 followed by IP and then Ethernet or 802.11. If we assume Ethernet, the encapsulated data would look like that seen in Figure 2-1.

```
Ethernet II, Src: WesternD_89:ba:fa (00:00:c0:89:ba:fa), Dst: Cisco_2c:0c:80 (00:11:21:2c:0c:80)
Internet Protocol, Src: 192.168.1.1 (192.168.1.1), Dst: 192.168.1.254 (192.168.1.254)
Transmission Control Protocol, Src Port: cma (1050), Dst Port: http (80), Seq: 1, Ack: 1, Len: 405
Hypertext Transfer Protocol
```

Figure 2-1. Encapsulation

As the encapsulation nears completion, the source and destination MAC addresses have to be filled in. The same is true for addressing at other layers but the IP addresses and port numbers are straightforward, as the host is communicating with an IP-based server and using well known ports. Actually, the source MAC is also straightforward, since the host is generating the frame. So, the question becomes: What address should be placed in the destination MAC address field of the Ethernet frame?

If the host can figure out the correct destination IP address, the address resolution protocol (ARP) will provide the answer. Stated another way, we have to ask for the right MAC address. The answer depends on whether the destination is on the same network as the source host. The following pages provide a couple of examples. The topology in Figure 2-2 contains two networks (192.168.15.0 and 192.168.20.0) separated by a router. Nodes A and B are on the same network and Node C is on a different network.

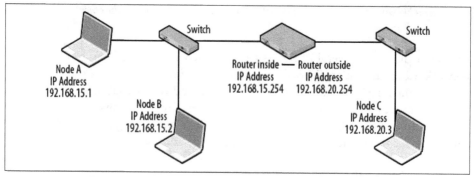

Figure 2-2. Small Topology

Sending traffic to nodes on the same network is very straightforward. The transmissions simply go from the source IP and MAC address to the destination node's IP and MAC address. In fact, since we use ARP to figure out the destination MAC and switches use the MAC address table (a.k.a., the source address table) to forward Ethernet frames, we often say that for nodes on the same network, the forwarding decisions are all at Layer 2.

What can make this process a little tricky is that traffic for the opposite network has to somehow get to the router. ARP is not used to resolve MAC addresses on other networks. It turns out that if sending traffic off the network, hosts place the *MAC address of the router* into the Ethernet frame. This choice is made when the host processes its own local routing table. This is also known as the host routing table. The routing table for Node A is shown in Figure 2-3. This output was obtained by issuing the route print command in the command shell of a Windows-based computer.

```
C:\>route print
=================================================================
Interface List
0x1 ...................... MS TCP Loopback interface
0x30004 ...00 e0 29 44 12 65 ...... SMC EtherPower II 10/100 Ethernet Adapter
=================================================================
Active Routes:
Network Destination        Netmask          Gateway       Interface  Metric
        0.0.0.0          0.0.0.0     192.168.15.254   192.168.15.1     20
      127.0.0.0        255.0.0.0         127.0.0.1       127.0.0.1      1
   192.168.15.0    255.255.255.0      192.168.15.1    192.168.15.1     20
   192.168.15.1  255.255.255.255         127.0.0.1       127.0.0.1     20
 192.168.15.255  255.255.255.255      192.168.15.1    192.168.15.1     20
      224.0.0.0        240.0.0.0      192.168.15.1    192.168.15.1     20
255.255.255.255  255.255.255.255      192.168.15.1    192.168.15.1      1
Default Gateway:       192.168.15.254
=================================================================
Persistent Routes:
  None
```

Figure 2-3. Node A routing table

Most operating systems provide similar information. There are five columns and when processing this table, start with the bottom entry. Work begins with columns 1 and 2. The very first thing that a node must do is determine whether or not the destination is on the same network. The result markedly changes the subsequent steps taken and the Ethernet header. The mechanism used to determine the network is called ANDing. The companion book to this one, *The Packet Guide to Core Network Protocols*, has an entire chapter devoted to masking, but the following is a little masking review.

The network mask is used to determine the network ID of the IP address in question via the logical AND operation. With a logical AND, a binary value "ANDed" with a 0 results in a 0 for output. ANDing with a 1 leaves the original value. For example, converting the IP address 172.16.49.67 and mask of 255.255.224 to binary results in the following:

10101100 . 00010000 . 00110001 . 01000011
<u>11111111 . 11111111 . 11100000 . 00000000</u>

Performing a bitwise AND:

10101100 . 00010000 . 00100000 . 00000000

Converting to base 10 numbers reveals that this IP address is on the 172.16.32.0 network. The important thing to remember is that the host is trying to determine both the source and destination networks. The first operation pulls the destination seen in column 1. The second is the ANDing operation which takes the destination address for the transmission and the column 2 mask. The basic question: Are the resulting values the same? If not, try again.

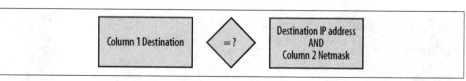

Figure 2-4. The basic question

In the following examples, Node A is attempting to communicate first with Node B on the same network, and then Node C on a different network. The flowchart shown in Figure 2-5 outlines the decision tree a host uses when trying to contact another node, regardless of the destination network. There are several integrated processes needed to explain how this works. Regardless of the destination, begin by parsing the host routing table. Steps 1 and 2 from Figure 2-5 work through each line of the table until either a match has been discovered or the table is out of entries.

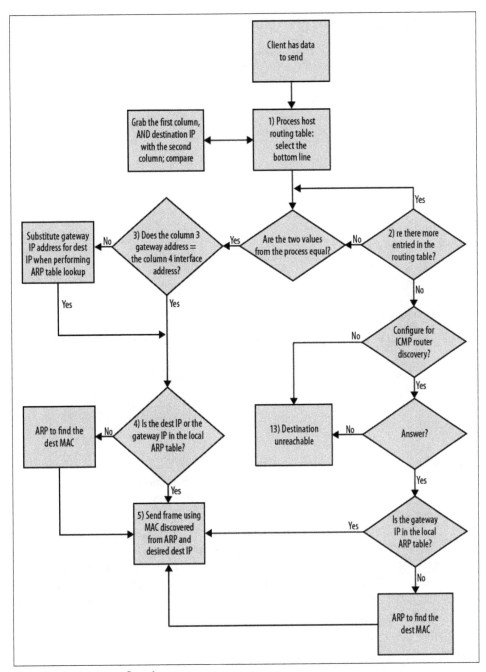

Figure 2-5. Decision flowchart

Case 1: Destination Is on the Same Network as the Source

For this example, it is assumed that Node A is trying to PING Node B. Using the table from Figure 2-3, the first decision would be:

```
                              192.168.15.2
255.255.255.255  Compare to   AND
                              255.255.255.255
                              192.168.15.2
```

Since these are not equal, the second line would be processed

```
                        192.168.15.2
224.0.0.0  Compare to   AND
                        240.0.0.0
                        192.0.0.0
```

These are also not the same.

For this case, the procedure continues until the fifth line up from the bottom.

```
                            192.168.15.2
192.168.15.0  Compare to    AND
                            255.255.255.0
                            192.168.15.0
```

Now that the values are a match, it is time to move to the left side of the flow chart and step 3. At this point, the interface to use the gateway must be determined. Step 3 asks if the column 3 and column 4 IP addresses are the same. The interfaces shown in column 4 are simply the IP addresses assigned to the network interface cards of the host. The gateways shown in column 3 will either be the same network interfaces or routers attached to the network. From Figure 2-3, the interface IP address is either 192.168.15.1 or loopback. Line 5 of the routing table indicates that for this destination, the interface IP address and the gateway IP address are both 192.168.15.1. This means that *the interface is the gateway*. In other words, there is no need to send this to a default gateway because the destination is on the same network and can be contacted directly.

Having established that the destination is on the same network, the host begins building the Ethernet frame but the destination MAC address is needed. Step 4 moves to ARP. The purpose of ARP is to determine the MAC address of the destination host. This information is stored locally in the host ARP table. First the ARP table is checked in order to see if the host already knows the correct MAC address. If an entry for the destination IP is not found, then an ARP request must be sent. Once the address is learned, the Ethernet frame can be constructed and transmitted to the destination.

Case 2: Destination Is on a Different Network than the Source

Case 2 begins with the same step as Case 1 (i.e., with processing the host routing table). The only difference is the destination IP address. A different line in the host routing table will provide the answer. This time the destination IP address is Node C: 192.168.20.1. The first ANDing decision would look like this:

	255.255.255.255		192.168.20.1
	AND	Compare to	AND
	255.255.255.255		255.255.255.255
Results	255.255.255.255		192.168.20.1

For this destination, the process would continue until the very last line of the routing table, if reached. This line is special because it happens to be the default gateway as indicated by 0.0.0.0 being used on both the destination network and netmask columns. This is called the "match all" line because of the ANDing process results.

	0.0.0.0		192.168.20.1
	AND	Compare to	AND
	0.0.0.0		0.0.0.0
Results	0.0.0.0		0.0.0.0

No matter the destination, the ANDing process results will be the same. As in Case 1, it is now time for step 3. This time, the values seen in columns 3 and 4 turn out to be different. When the two values are not the same, the source host realizes that the destination is on a different network and so must send the traffic to its default gateway in order to reach the destination. The default gateway line and change in gateway are circled in Figure 2-6.

Back at the flow chart and step 3, when the gateway is different than the interface, the node must ARP for the gateway address. This is because the frame must be sent off of the network. The only way to do this is to take the IP packet destined for Node C and wrap it in an Ethernet frame that is sent to the router. By checking the ARP table or ARPing for 192.168.15.254, the MAC address of the default gateway can be learned and the frame can be built.

```
C:\>route print
=======================================================================
Interface List
0x1 ......................... MS TCP Loopback interface
0x30004 ...00 e0 29 44 12 65 ...... SMC EtherPower II 10/100 Ethernet Adapter
=======================================================================
Active Routes:
Network Destination        Netmask          Gateway          Interface  Metric
        0.0.0.0            0.0.0.0      192.168.15.254    192.168.15.1       20
      127.0.0.0          255.0.0.0          127.0.0.1         127.0.0.1        1
   192.168.15.0      255.255.255.0      192.168.15.1      192.168.15.1       20
   192.168.15.1    255.255.255.255        127.0.0.1         127.0.0.1       20
 192.168.15.255    255.255.255.255     192.168.15.1      192.168.15.1       20
       224.0.0.0        240.0.0.0      192.168.15.1      192.168.15.1       20
 255.255.255.255   255.255.255.255     192.168.15.1      192.168.15.1        1
Default Gateway:       192.168.15.254
=======================================================================
Persistent Routes:
  None
```

Figure 2-6. Default gateway fields

Don't confuse the default gateway entry of 0.0.0.0 with the IP address of 0.0.0.0.

What If the Default Gateway Is Not Known?

Part of the Figure 2-5 flow chart deals with the sticky problem of not having a default gateway or having an incorrect entry. If a host is using DHCP, it is probable that a gateway address (along with IP address, mask, and DNS) has been provided, but it is not a guarantee. The same can be said of statically configured hosts. A default gateway is correct if the IP address is on the same network as the source host. In Figure 2-6, the addresses 192.168.15.1 and 192.168.15.254 are on the same network. If the gateway entry (192.168.15.254) is missing or incorrect, the output shown in Figure 2-7 will appear in the command shell.

```
C:\>ping 192.168.20.1

Pinging 192.168.20.1 with 32 bytes of data:

Destination host unreachable.
Destination host unreachable.
Destination host unreachable.
Destination host unreachable.

Ping statistics for 192.168.20.1:
    Packets: Sent = 4, Received = 0, Lost = 4 (100% loss),
```

Figure 2-7. Output as a result of a missing default gateway

A couple of things to remember regarding this output:

- No packets were generated as a result of this problem—this is a message generated by the local operating system on the source host.

- This is often confused with the ICMP destination unreachable message, but they are NOT the same thing. Though the same phrase is used, if the output is a result of an ICMP message, a source IP address will be included.

There are simple solutions to the missing default gateway problem, such as repairing the DHCP server configuration or repairing the statically configured settings. However, ICMP router solicitation and advertisement messages can also be used. This method is typically not running by default and must be configured on both the router and the host. While they are not common on wired LANs, applications like Mobile IP and some sections of the cellular infrastructure make use of these ICMP messages. A router solicitation is shown in Figure 2-8. Note that the solicitation is sent to the "all routers" multicast address of 224.0.0.2.

```
Ethernet II, Src: Standard_08:e0:27 (00:e0:29:08:e0:27), Dst: IPv4mcast_00:00:02 (01:00:5e:00:00:02)
Internet Protocol, Src: 192.168.3.1 (192.168.3.1), Dst: 224.0.0.2 (224.0.0.2)
Internet Control Message Protocol
  Type: 10 (Router solicitation)
  Code: 0 ()
  Checksum: 0xf5ff [correct]
```

Figure 2-8. ICMP router solicitation

Following the flowchart, in the absence of a default gateway, and without configuring the host for ICMP router solicitations (and the router for advertisements), the host will wind up at unlucky step 13—destination unreachable. A host routing table without a default gateway is shown in Figure 2-9.

```
C:\>route print
===========================================================================
Interface List
0x1 ........................... MS TCP Loopback interface
0x30004 ...00 e0 29 44 12 65 ...... SMC EtherPower II 10/100 Ethernet Adapter
===========================================================================
Active Routes:
Network Destination        Netmask          Gateway       Interface  Metric
      127.0.0.0        255.0.0.0       127.0.0.1       127.0.0.1       1
    192.168.15.0    255.255.255.0    192.168.15.1    192.168.15.1      20
    192.168.15.1  255.255.255.255      127.0.0.1       127.0.0.1      20
  192.168.15.255  255.255.255.255    192.168.15.1    192.168.15.1      20
      224.0.0.0        240.0.0.0    192.168.15.1    192.168.15.1      20
 255.255.255.255  255.255.255.255    192.168.15.1    192.168.15.1       1
===========================================================================
Persistent Routes:
  None
```

Figure 2-9. Routing table missing default gateway

Host Routing Tables

Back to the host routing table shown in Figure 2-9. As the routing table is processed, entries can be found that match the specialized addresses associated with IP. These address types, values, and the line from the Node A routing table are shown below. The line numbers are listed top to bottom, but remember that the host routing table is processed from the bottom up.

Table 2-1. Special Addresses

Purpose	Address	Line in routing table
Loopback	127.0.0.0	1
Network ID	192.168.15.0	2
Host IP address	192.168.15.1	3
Directed Broadcast	192.168.15.255	4
Multicast	224.0.0.0	5
Limited Broadcast	255.255.255.255	6

 One address that appears regularly on many networks, but is missing from Figure 2-9 is 169.254.0.0. This address is from the IETF Zero Configuration standard and usually appears when the host does not receive an address via DHCP or static configuration.

As mentioned previously, the information contained in a host routing table is similar regardless of the operating system, but there are some differences worth pointing out. Figure 2-10 depicts a routing table from a Windows 7 computer configured in the same way.

The biggest difference is in column 3. When the gateway and the interface IP addresses are the same, the destination is on the same network. Another way to look at this is that the destination can be reached via the link attached to the source host. This is considered to be "on link." IPv6 refers to this type of entry as "link-local." There is also a change to the fifth column, which describes the metric. For hosts, metric is typically tied to the speed of the link. Hosts prefer higher speed connections. Recalling the discussion from Chapter 1 regarding metrics, routers have a significantly different meaning for metrics.

The last point to make regarding host routing tables is that the examples used thus far have been for single-homed hosts. This is a host with a single network interface like Node A, B, and C in Figure 2-2. Dual or multihomed computers will have two or more interfaces. Multihomed hosts have a corresponding increase in the number of routing table entries. Each interface must have a set of entries, such as the six described earlier in this section. An example of a multihomed host would be when a laptop is docked but still has the wireless interface active.

```
IPv4 Route Table
===========================================================================
Active Routes:
Network Destination        Netmask          Gateway       Interface  Metric
          0.0.0.0          0.0.0.0   192.168.15.254   192.168.15.1    286
        127.0.0.0        255.0.0.0        On-link       127.0.0.1    306
        127.0.0.1  255.255.255.255        On-link       127.0.0.1    306
  127.255.255.255  255.255.255.255        On-link       127.0.0.1    306
     192.168.15.0    255.255.255.0        On-link    192.168.15.1    286
     192.168.15.1  255.255.255.255        On-link    192.168.15.1    286
   192.168.15.255  255.255.255.255        On-link    192.168.15.1    286
        224.0.0.0        240.0.0.0        On-link       127.0.0.1    306
        224.0.0.0        240.0.0.0        On-link    192.168.15.1    286
  255.255.255.255  255.255.255.255        On-link       127.0.0.1    306
  255.255.255.255  255.255.255.255        On-link    192.168.15.1    286
===========================================================================
Persistent Routes:
  Network Address          Netmask  Gateway Address  Metric
          0.0.0.0          0.0.0.0   192.168.15.254  Default
===========================================================================

IPv6 Route Table
===========================================================================
Active Routes:
 If Metric Network Destination        Gateway
  1    306 ::1/128                     On-link
  1    306 ff00::/8                    On-link
===========================================================================
Persistent Routes:
  None
```

Figure 2-10. Windows 7 routing table

For single homed hosts, the gateway addresses are fairly straightforward in that the host will either direct traffic to its own network or to the default gateway as discussed above. But, if Internet Connection Sharing (ICS) were to be used in order to have an interface on two networks, the routing table changes quite a bit. This topology is shown in Figure 2-11.

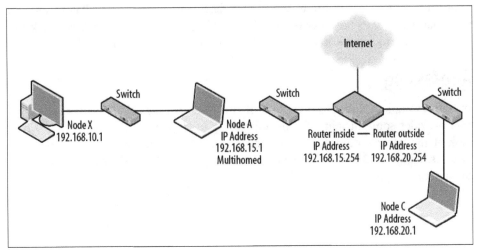

Figure 2-11. Node A is a multihomed host

Taking another look at the routing table for Node A, it can be seen that not only has the number of routing table entries doubled, but there are two default gateways. There are also two persistent routes indicating the networks to which the host has a direct connection.

```
IPv4 Route Table
===========================================================================
Active Routes:
Network Destination        Netmask          Gateway       Interface  Metric
          0.0.0.0          0.0.0.0   192.168.15.254   192.168.15.1     286
          0.0.0.0          0.0.0.0   192.168.10.254   192.168.10.1     281
        127.0.0.0        255.0.0.0         On-link        127.0.0.1     306
        127.0.0.1  255.255.255.255         On-link        127.0.0.1     306
  127.255.255.255  255.255.255.255         On-link        127.0.0.1     306
     192.168.10.0    255.255.255.0         On-link     192.168.10.1     281
     192.168.10.1  255.255.255.255         On-link     192.168.10.1     281
   192.168.10.255  255.255.255.255         On-link     192.168.10.1     281
     192.168.15.0    255.255.255.0         On-link     192.168.15.1     286
     192.168.15.1  255.255.255.255         On-link     192.168.15.1     286
   192.168.15.255  255.255.255.255         On-link     192.168.15.1     286
        224.0.0.0        240.0.0.0         On-link        127.0.0.1     306
        224.0.0.0        240.0.0.0         On-link     192.168.15.1     286
        224.0.0.0        240.0.0.0         On-link     192.168.10.1     281
  255.255.255.255  255.255.255.255         On-link        127.0.0.1     306
  255.255.255.255  255.255.255.255         On-link     192.168.15.1     286
  255.255.255.255  255.255.255.255         On-link     192.168.10.1     281
===========================================================================
Persistent Routes:
  Network Address          Netmask    Gateway Address    Metric
          0.0.0.0          0.0.0.0     192.168.15.254    Default
          0.0.0.0          0.0.0.0     192.168.10.254    Default
===========================================================================
```

Figure 2-12. Multihomed host routing table

Two gateways might seem like a good idea, but only one of the entries (typically the lower one) is used. In this case, the host would never send data to 192.168.15.254. It might be the case that the lower entry (192.168.10.254) is not preferred and in fact might not actually get traffic to the proper destination. Figure 2-11 has included a potential pathway to the Internet. Sending traffic to the 192.168.10.0 network is a dead end. Metrics can be used to affect the entry used, but this is unusual.

Addressing

In both examples (Node A pings Node B and Node A pings Node C), the ARP process provides some insight into the addressing used. This section will take a closer look at the packets flowing between the nodes and the addressing installed in the headers. Figure 2-13 depicts the original topology but includes the MAC addresses of the devices.

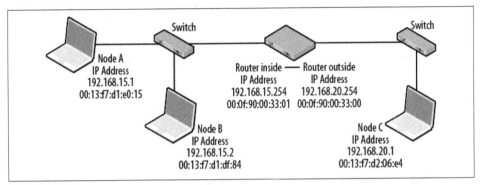

Figure 2-13. Topology with MAC Addresses

In Case 1, Node A pings (ICMP echo request) node Node B. This exchange does not require the router at all and the packets/frames involved are built solely with the IP and MAC addresses of the two nodes in question. The following packet has been expanded to show the first ICMP echo request sent between them. This particular packet was captured on Node A.

```
⊟ Ethernet II, Src: SmcNetwo_d1:e0:15 (00:13:f7:d1:e0:15), Dst: SmcNetwo_d1:df:84 (00:13:f7:d1:df:84)
  ⊞ Destination: SmcNetwo_d1:df:84 (00:13:f7:d1:df:84)
  ⊞ Source: SmcNetwo_d1:e0:15 (00:13:f7:d1:e0:15)
    Type: IP (0x0800)
⊟ Internet Protocol, Src: 192.168.15.1 (192.168.15.1), Dst: 192.168.15.2 (192.168.15.2)
    Version: 4
    Header length: 20 bytes
  ⊞ Differentiated Services Field: 0x00 (DSCP 0x00: Default; ECN: 0x00)
    Total Length: 60
    Identification: 0x2605 (9733)
  ⊞ Flags: 0x00
    Fragment offset: 0
    Time to live: 128
    Protocol: ICMP (0x01)
  ⊞ Header checksum: 0x7568 [correct]
    Source: 192.168.15.1 (192.168.15.1)
    Destination: 192.168.15.2 (192.168.15.2)
⊞ Internet Control Message Protocol
```

Figure 2-14. IP and MAC addresses used in Case 1

When communicating with a node off of the network (Node A pings Node C), an Ethernet frame is constructed and sent to the router rather than the destination node. The IP address information is still that of Nodes A and C. Under normal circumstances, routers do not rewrite the IP headers. One notable exception to this rule is network address translation (NAT). On the other hand, Layer 2 frames, such as Ethernet, are rewritten every time a router is traversed. The packet in Figure 2-15 has also been expanded after being caught on Node A, which shows the change in addressing at Layer 2.

```
Ethernet II, Src: SmcNetwo_d1:e0:15 (00:13:f7:d1:e0:15), Dst: Cisco_00:33:01 (00:0f:90:00:33:01)
  Destination: Cisco_00:33:01 (00:0f:90:00:33:01)
  Source: SmcNetwo_d1:e0:15 (00:13:f7:d1:e0:15)
  Type: IP (0x0800)
Internet Protocol, Src: 192.168.15.1 (192.168.15.1), Dst: 192.168.20.1 (192.168.20.1)
  Version: 4
  Header length: 20 bytes
  Differentiated Services Field: 0x00 (DSCP 0x00: Default; ECN: 0x00)
  Total Length: 60
  Identification: 0x25fa (9722)
  Flags: 0x00
  Fragment offset: 0
  Time to live: 128
  Protocol: ICMP (0x01)
  Header checksum: 0x7074 [correct]
  Source: 192.168.15.1 (192.168.15.1)
  Destination: 192.168.20.1 (192.168.20.1)
Internet Control Message Protocol
```

Figure 2-15. IP and MAC addresses used in Case 2

On the opposite side (192.168.20.0) of the router, the same type of substitution would occur. When the router forwards the ICMP echo request to Node C, the source MAC address would be that of the router, the destination would be that of Node C, but the IP addressing remains the same. Remember that in this topology, the router has two interfaces. The MAC addresses of the interfaces will be used and should be different. This is shown in Figure 2-16. For the return trip, the MAC addresses will be flipped with Node C sending to the router interface on its side. Back on the 192.168.15.0 network, the frame will come from the router interface on that side to Node A.

```
Ethernet II, Src: Cisco_00:33:00 (00:0f:90:00:33:00), Dst: SmcNetwo_d2:06:e4 (00:13:f7:d2:06:e4)
  Destination: SmcNetwo_d2:06:e4 (00:13:f7:d2:06:e4)
  Source: Cisco_00:33:00 (00:0f:90:00:33:00)
  Type: IP (0x0800)
Internet Protocol, Src: 192.168.15.1 (192.168.15.1), Dst: 192.168.20.1 (192.168.20.1)
  Version: 4
  Header length: 20 bytes
  Differentiated Services Field: 0x00 (DSCP 0x00: Default; ECN: 0x00)
  Total Length: 60
  Identification: 0x2635 (9781)
  Flags: 0x00
  Fragment offset: 0
  Time to live: 127
  Protocol: ICMP (0x01)
  Header checksum: 0x7139 [correct]
  Source: 192.168.15.1 (192.168.15.1)
  Destination: 192.168.20.1 (192.168.20.1)
Internet Control Message Protocol
```

Figure 2-16. Addressing used on the 192.168.20.0 network

Tracking the Packets

The addressing section above explains the packet forwarding mechanism and addresses used on both sides of the router. This section will provide an explanation of the complete set of packets involved and assumes empty ARP tables.

Case 1: Destination Is on the Same Network as the Source

Regardless of the destination, a node must first process the local host routing table to look for a match. Since Node A (192.168.15.1) and Node B (192.168.15.2) are on the same network, the match would be found before reaching the top (default gateway) table entry. The sending node would discover the interface and gateway addresses (columns 3 and 4) are the same, so the target/destination node can be contacted directly. Finding its ARP table empty, the sending node would participate in the following packet exchanges:

```
4 1.977590    SmcNetwo_d1:e0:15    Broadcast            ARP   who has 192.168.15.2? Tell 192.168.15.1
5 1.977780    SmcNetwo_d1:df:84    SmcNetwo_d1:e0:15    ARP   192.168.15.2 is at 00:13:f7:d1:df:84
6 1.977787    192.168.15.1         192.168.15.2         ICMP  Echo (ping) request
7 1.977992    192.168.15.2         192.168.15.1         ICMP  Echo (ping) reply
```

Figure 2-17. Conversation on the 192.168.15.0 network

Figure 2-17 shows the ARP request from 192.168.15.1 and the subsequent ARP reply packet. Node A has now learned the MAC address matching the destination IP and can build an Ethernet frame to encapsulate the ICMP echo request. Once the ICMP echo is sent, the reply comes back from 192.168.15.2.

Case 2: Destination Is on a Different Network than the Source

Case 2 is a bit more complicated than Case 1, but the same rules apply. Communication is initiated on one side of the router, but continues on the other side. Packets from both sides will be included. Again, Node A (192.168.15.1) must process its host routing table. This time, the matching entry is the default gateway table entry. Node A obtains the gateway address from column 3. Finding its ARP table empty, the sending node would participate in the following packet exchanges:

```
6 5.127439    SmcNetwo_d1:e0:15 Broadcast         ARP   who has 192.168.15.254? Tell 192.168.15.1
7 5.128503    Cisco_00:33:01    SmcNetwo_d1:e0:15 ARP   192.168.15.254 is at 00:0f:90:00:33:01
8 5.128510    192.168.15.1      192.168.20.1      ICMP  Echo (ping) request
```

Figure 2-18. Conversation crossing the networks, 192.168.15.0 network side

Node A sends the ARP request out looking for the MAC address of the router and, upon receiving the ARP reply, forwards the ICMP echo request to the router for processing. But this only gets the message to the router. On the opposite side, the router must now find Node C (192.168.20.1) and then forward the message on. This is shown in Figure 2-19.

```
4 1.005457    Cisco_00:33:00 Broadcast       ARP   who has 192.168.20.1? Tell 192.168.20.254
5 1.005463    SmcNetwo_d2:06 Cisco_00:33:00  ARP   192.168.20.1 is at 00:13:f7:d2:06:e4
6 1.697588    192.168.15.1   192.168.20.1    ICMP  Echo (ping) request
7 1.697612    192.168.20.1   192.168.15.1    ICMP  Echo (ping) reply
```

Figure 2-19. Conversation crossing the networks, 192.168.20.0 network side

The router is engaging in some of the same processes as the host. The router "ARPs" for Node C and, once it discovers the MAC address, forwards the original ICMP echo request by building the appropriate Ethernet frame. Node C receives the request and must generate an ICMP echo reply back to Node A. This whole process begins again but in the reverse direction. The only difference is that some of the ARP tables will already be populated.

Note: To be complete, the router has one additional step—it must also process its routing table. The table is included below.

```
Gateway of last resort is not set

C    192.168.15.0/24 is directly connected, FastEthernet0/1
C    192.168.20.0/24 is directly connected, FastEthernet0/0
```

Figure 2-20. Router routing table

Reading

This chapter is similar to Chapter 1 in that it is not protocol specific although there are a bunch of protocols represented. No matter what the destination, the first step is always to process the host routing table. After this has been completed and the correct entry found, the address resolution process is completed. Understanding the host routing table can be enhanced by the documentation for the operating system. One helpful resource is the Microsoft Developer Network or Technet (*http://technet.micro soft.com/en-us/*). For a little light reading, I've listed several of the protocol RFCs used in this process.

RFC 791: Internet Protocol DARPA Internet Program Protocol Specification
RFC 792: Internet Control Message Protocol
RFC 796: Address Mapping, J. Postel
RFC 826: Ethernet Address Resolution Protocol
RFC 894: A Standard for the Transmission of IP Datagrams over Ethernet Networks, C. Hornig
RFC 895: A Standard for the Transmission of IP Datagrams over Experimental Ethernet Networks, J. Postel
RFC 917: Internet Subnets
RFC 950: Internet Standard Subnetting Procedure
RFC 1256: ICMP Router Discovery Messages
RFC 1338: Supernetting: an Address Assignment and Aggregation Strategy
RFC 1519: CIDR: an Address Assignment and Aggregation Strategy

Summary

Understanding host-based routing involves a whole collection of integrated processes. Host routing tables, address resolution, masking, Ethernet headers, and the Internet protocol are all part of the story. The sequence of steps may depend on the location of the destination and this can affect the construction of the frame and the processing. Like all networking tables, the host routing table can be manipulated. Understanding these processes and their interrelated nature are central to good network administration to facilitate troubleshooting, optimization, and security.

Review Questions

1. What is the very first thing that a node must do before sending a packet?

2. What message is likely if the default gateway is missing?

3. What is the result of ANDing a binary 1 with a binary 0?

4. Hosts always ARP for destinations on their network.

5. Can a host ARP for a destination not on its network?

6. Routers will never modify the Ethernet frame, but they commonly modify IP headers.

   a. TRUE

   b. FALSE

7. In a host routing table, what will be an identifying characteristic of the gateway and interface columns for a host on the same network?

8. Do routers use the address resolution protocol?

9. Multihomed hosts are network nodes that have more than one active interface and they will have more host routing table entries.

   a. TRUE

   b. FALSE

10. In an ideal situation with ARP tables clear, how many one way packets will be generated if Node A issues the following command: ping -n 1 192.168.20.1? Why?

Review Answers

1. Process its host routing table.

2. Destination host unreachable

3. 0

4. False, if an ARP table entry exists, no ARP request is generated.

5. No

6. FALSE

7. The columns will have the same IP address.

8. Yes

9. TRUE

10. 8—Two ARP conversations and two sets of ICMP echo conversations.

Lab Activities

Activity 1—Build the Topology Depicted in Figure 2-2

Materials: Router and three hosts

1. Set up the IP addresses. Giving the router IP addresses will automatically popu-late the router routing table.

2. If you are using a Linksys or similar device, you will have to look at the options for disabling NAT. By default, home gateways use NAT and firewalls and will either mask or prevent the network traffic.

3. Once completed, test by PINGing all of the network devices.

Activity 2—Host Routing Table

Materials: Node A

1. Examine the host routing table of Node A using the route print command for MS Windows.

2. Pick two or three destinations. Determine via the ANDing process which of the entries in the routing table will match the destinations you've chosen.

3. Can you pick the gateway and interfaces to be used?

Activity 3—ARP Tables

Materials: Router, host command line, and ARP tables

1. Using the `arp -a` command, determine the contents of the ARP tables.

2. If present, record the MAC and IP addresses listed.

3. Clear the arp tables. This will vary depending on the device, but issuing the `arp` command without an argument will bring up the help page. Be sure to clear the ARP table of the router as well.

4. Why is this activity important? In order to see the full flow of packets and all of the processes, all of the tables must be cleared. You need not worry about switch SATs for this experiment.

Activity 4—Following the Traffic

Materials: Router, three hosts, and Wireshark

1. Begin a packet capture on all three nodes.

2. Ping between Node A and Nodes B and C.

3. Verify that you have captured ARP and ICMP traffic.

4. Using this chapter as a guide, see if you can follow the flow of traffic between the nodes. Be wary of the time stamps, as things happen quickly—especially when attempting to trace traffic across the router.

5. Is there any traffic present that did not pertain to the conversation you created? Why is it there? Common example will include Windows traffic, domain name service, and IPv6 multicast.

Activity 5—Addressing

Materials: Router, three hosts, and Wireshark

1. Once you have captured the traffic, open the packets and examine the addresses used.

2. Can you see the change in addressing from one side of the router to another?

3. Which addresses changed?

4. Do any of the addresses change in pinging between Node A and Node B?

CHAPTER 3

Spanning Tree and Rapid Spanning Tree

Ethernet structure and operation are well understood because the base protocol is consistent from one version to another and the standard behaves predictably in almost every topology. Since many of the decisions regarding Ethernet—such as the network interface, signaling, and equipment type—are pre-determined, one might say that Ethernet deployments are simple and straightforward. However, proper Ethernet network operation is also dependent on adherence to topology rules and other protocols, such as the address resolution protocol. So a simple network develops some interesting, and sometimes complex, characteristics.

This chapter is about the Spanning Tree Protocol and its faster version, the Rapid Spanning Tree Protocol. These protocols wage a continuing battle to prevent against loops in Ethernet networks. A loop in an Ethernet network is created when the topology is connected back to itself. This is a problem because unlike the Internet Protocol at Layer 3, Ethernet does not have any built in protection. Therefore, it cannot prevent frames from continuously circulating. When loops occur, user connectivity can be significantly degraded if not destroyed entirely.

The Spanning Tree Protocol is active by default, and is invisible to network administrators and users alike. But because it works and is "on" by default does not necessarily mean that we can ignore it. Sometimes spanning tree is very inefficient. "On by default" also means that the protocol is working behind the scenes. Spanning tree may have taken actions making the administrator oblivious to problems on the network. This chapter will cover spanning tree usage, operation, and security concerns. The spanning tree protocol is standardized in IEEE 802.1D. While the first version of the spanning tree protocol has been replaced by rapid spanning tree, the earlier version is often the default, so understanding the earlier standard is still important. Today, spanning tree runs on most bridges and switches with the exception of some wireless equipment.

Why Are Loops Bad?

The basic problem is that at Layer 2, Ethernet does not have any ability to remove continuously circulating frames or prevent loops. Unlike IP, which has a time to live (TTL) field, Ethernet devices such as hubs and switches will simply continue to forward frames even when a loop is present. At first glance, this may not seem like such a big deal, but when you consider that a single frame passing into a switch may cause several copies to be created, the impact becomes apparent. Let's look at a small topology. In Figure 3-1 three switches are connected in a loop.

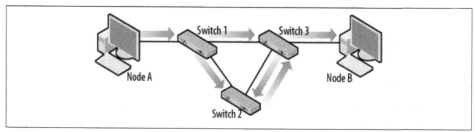

Figure 3-1. Switching loop

When Node A communicates with Node B, the first frame sent out is an ARP request which happens to be a broadcast. Basic switch behavior is to forward this frame out all ports except for the arrival port. In this case, Switch 1 sends the frame to both Switch 2 and Switch 3. Switch 2 and Switch 3 immediately forward this broadcast frame to each other. Right after that, they send it right back to Switch 1. Switch 1 now has two copies of the frame it originally sent and to make matters worse, it does not know that they are copies. So, Switch 1 forwards these copies right back around to Switch 2 and 3. And so on, and so on... To give you an idea of how bad it can get, switches normally transmitting dozens of frames per second can be forced to transmit hundreds or even thousands of frames per second. Backplane utilization can go from less than 10% to over 80% in less than a minute. Recalling the construction of an Ethernet frame and forwarding behavior of Layer 1 and 2 devices, there is nothing to address this problem. Enter the spanning tree protocol.

Radia Perlman is the woman responsible for the Spanning Tree algorithm. The story goes that while she was working at Digital Equipment Corp (DEC), she recognized the problem and went home to think about it. She solved it on Saturday and had time to write a poem about it on Sunday. We'll cover the protocol later but here is the poem.

    Algorhyme
    I think that I shall never see
    A graph more lovely than a tree.
    A tree whose crucial property
    Is loop-free connectivity.
    A tree which must be sure to span.

So packets can reach every LAN.
First the Root must be selected
By ID it is elected.
Least cost paths from Root are traced
In the tree these paths are placed.
A mesh is made by folks like me
Then bridges find a spanning tree.

The Structure of Spanning Tree BPDUs

Spanning tree requires that switches send out frames called bridge protocol data units (BPDUs) and the information contained within these BPDUs is received and processed by neighboring switches. The basic structure is shown in Figure 3-2.

There are three sections to the BPDU: protocol details, fields specific to the comparison algorithm, and the timer values. Each of these sections will be explained in greater detail later on, but to get us started, this frame is encapsulated in an 802.3 frame. Management frames such as Cisco Discovery Protocol often use 802.3 encapsulation while data frames use Ethernet Type II.

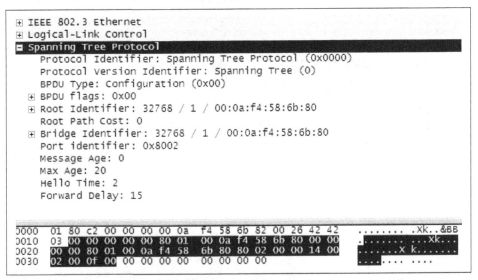

Figure 3-2. Bridge protocol data unit

The Comparison Algorithm

The whole point of spanning tree is to eliminate loops by automatically blocking ports on the network. It figures out which ports to block through the comparison algorithm. The comparison algorithm uses up to four fields to make the comparison: root identifier, root path cost, bridge identifier (transmitting bridge/switch), and the port identifier (transmitting port). From a spanning tree perspective, lower numbers are better. The order is important, with the root identifier being determined first. Figure 3-2 shows a decoded packet along with the hexadecimal version of the same packet. The spanning tree header is highlighted to show the associated hexadecimal values. Wireshark provides some clarification regarding the content of the BPDU, adding some information that is not present in the actual frame.

The information in these four fields is "compared" with information already known by the switch. The comparisons are used to make decisions regarding control of looped topologies. Spanning tree imposes a logical topology on the network by blocking ports from transmitting data frames. This means that the physical and logical topologies can differ.

Alliteration aside, the functions of the four fields follow:

Root identifier
> An eight-byte field that is a combination of the root bridge priority and the root bridge MAC address. A typical bridge priority value is 32768 (8000 in hex). The virtual local area network identifier (VLAN ID) can be added to this number. Since all of the ports on a Cisco switch start out in VLAN 1, the priority changes to 32768 + 1 (32769). The hexadecimal equivalent is 8001. In a converged or steady state topology, all BPDUs will have the same root ID. From Figure 3-2, the decoded view has a root ID of 32768/1/000af4586b80. Examining the hex section, the value 8001000af4586b80 starts after the first five bytes. This difference is the merging of the priority and VLAN id.

Root path cost
> A four-byte field describing the distance away from the root in terms of the number and speed of the links. In Figure 3-2, the path cost is 0, which means that we are looking a BPDU that came directly from the root bridge. The values for link speed are:

> | | |
> |---|---|
> | 10BaseT | 100 |
> | 100BaseT | 19 |
> | 1000Baset | 4 |

> BPDUs leaving the root bridge will have a path cost of 0 regardless of the link speed. All other BPDUs will have topology-based values. For example, in a 100BaseT network, BPDUs that are two switches downstream would have a root path cost of 38, as shown in Figure 3-3.

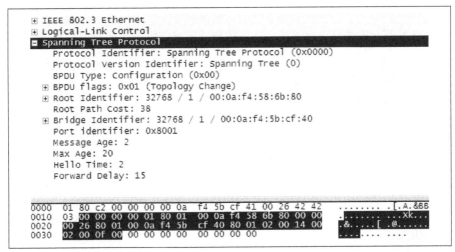

```
⊞ IEEE 802.3 Ethernet
⊞ Logical-Link Control
⊟ Spanning Tree Protocol
      Protocol Identifier: Spanning Tree Protocol (0x0000)
      Protocol Version Identifier: Spanning Tree (0)
      BPDU Type: Configuration (0x00)
  ⊞ BPDU flags: 0x01 (Topology Change)
  ⊞ Root Identifier: 32768 / 1 / 00:0a:f4:58:6b:80
      Root Path Cost: 38
  ⊞ Bridge Identifier: 32768 / 1 / 00:0a:f4:5b:cf:40
      Port identifier: 0x8001
      Message Age: 2
      Max Age: 20
      Hello Time: 2
      Forward Delay: 15


0000   01 80 c2 00 00 00 00 0a  f4 5b cf 41 00 26 42 42    ........ .[.A.&BB
0010   03 00 00 00 00 01 80 01  00 0a f4 58 6b 80 00 00    ........ ...xk...
0020   00 26 80 01 00 0a f4 5b  cf 40 80 01 02 00 14 00    .&.....[ .@......
0030   02 00 0f 00 00 00 00 00  00 00 00 00                .... ....
```

Figure 3-3. Increased path cost

Bridge identifier

An eight-byte field that is a combination of the transmitting bridge priority and the transmitting bridge MAC address. "Transmit" is the key here because it refers to the switch sending the BPDU. Again, the typical value for the bridge priority is 32768 (8000 in hex) with an addition for any VLANs. The switch sending the current BPDU fills in its own values here. Figure 3-3 is actually a BPDU caught on the same network as the BPDU seen in Figure 3-2, just farther from the root bridge. From Figure 3-3, not only has the path cost been incremented, but the bridge ID has changed. The root ID field stays the same since all of the switches in the topology agree on this value. The bridge ID is now 32768/1/000af45bcf40 (8001000af45bcf40 in hex) since a switch other than the root transmitted the frame. In Figure 3-2, the root ID and the bridge ID are the same, which is another indicator that the BPDU came from the root.

Port identifier

This is the last field in the comparison algorithm. These two bytes are a combination of the transmitting port priority and the port number. A common value for the port priority is 128 (80 in hex). From Figure 3-2 we can see that the value is 8002 so the BPDU came from port 2. Figure 3-3 shows a value of 8001, which means that while the two switches were using the same port priorities, the BPDUs were sent out on different ports and, based on the different bridge ID, separate switches.

The first task of the algorithm is to elect a root bridge. It is a straightforward procedure in which the bridge with the lowest priority and MAC address combination becomes the root bridge. If all switches start with the same priority (which is common) the switch with the lowest MAC address becomes the root bridge. It does not matter which switch starts the process because switches exchange BPDUs and the spanning tree topology can change based on the information received. After the election of a root bridge, the spanning tree algorithm elects designated bridges, sets port roles, and blocks ports to eliminate loops. The following sections will first cover the building blocks of the protocol and then go through the operational aspects tying all of them together.

Some Definitions

There are several terms used within the spanning tree protocol, and understanding these will help during the topology example:

Root bridge
> This is the switch with the lowest numerical value for its priority and MAC address.

Designated bridge
> As traffic leaving a segment of the network flows to the root switch, it may pass through (be forwarded by) another switch. This switch would be the designated bridge for that segment.

Root and designated ports
> Once the topology has stabilized, all switches downstream from the root switch will have ports that are closer to the root switch and those that are farther from the root. The ports that are closer are called root ports. Ports that are farther are called designated. Another way to look at this is to say that root ports point toward the root and that traffic on its way to the root switch flows out of these ports. There is only one root port per switch. Designated ports point away from the root switch and traffic on its way to the root switch flows into these. All ports on the root switch are considered designated. Root and designated labels are called the *port roles*.

Spanning Tree Addressing

Spanning tree uses a specific set of addresses. In Figure 3-4, the Ethernet and Logical Link Control (LLC) headers are expanded to show the specifics. This is another view of the frame shown in Figure 3-3.

Compare the Ethernet source address in Figure 3-4 (000af45bcf41) to the bridge ID (8001000af45bcf40) seen in Figure 3-3. Removing the bridge priority leaves 000af45bcf40. Note that the Ethernet source address has simply been incremented by 1. This particular BPDU came from port 1 on the switch because of the port ID of 8001 and now this is verified by the MAC addresses because the port number is simply added to the MAC address of the switch. If this BPDU would have come from port 10, then the port ID in the spanning tree data would have been 800a and the source MAC address seen in the Ethernet frame would have been 000af45bcf4a. So the switch and its individual ports have unique MAC addresses.

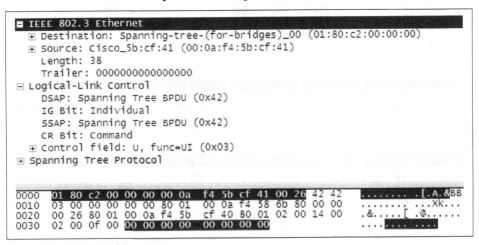

```
■ IEEE 802.3 Ethernet
    ⊞ Destination: Spanning-tree-(for-bridges)_00  (01:80:c2:00:00:00)
    ⊞ Source: Cisco_5b:cf:41 (00:0a:f4:5b:cf:41)
      Length: 38
      Trailer: 0000000000000000
  ⊟ Logical-Link Control
      DSAP: Spanning Tree BPDU (0x42)
      IG Bit: Individual
      SSAP: Spanning Tree BPDU (0x42)
      CR Bit: Command
    ⊞ Control field: U, func=UI (0x03)
  ⊞ Spanning Tree Protocol

0000   01 80 c2 00 00 00 00 0a  f4 5b cf 41 00 26 42 42   ........ .[.A.&BB
0010   03 00 00 00 00 00 80 01  00 0a f4 58 6b 80 00 00   ........ ...Xk...
0020   00 26 80 01 00 0a f4 5b  cf 40 80 01 02 00 14 00   .&.....[ .@......
0030   02 00 0f 00 00 00 00 00  00 00 00 00               ....▪... ....
```

Figure 3-4. BPDU addressing

 Occasionally you might have cause to convert a router to a bridge. In this case, the addressing does not follow this convention and the bridge ID will also vary.

The Ethernet destination MAC of 0180c2000000 is defined as the Bridge Group Address. All switches and bridges are supposed to understand and listen to this particular address. This is also why a Cisco switch can engage in spanning tree operations with a switch from another vendor. This address, along with the LLC Destination Service Access Point (DSAP) and the LLC Source Service Access Point (SSAP), are specified in IEEE 802.1D for use with the spanning tree protocol.

Port States

In an operating network, administrators are typically unaware of spanning tree port "states" because several are transitions. By the time one looks, ports that are sending/receiving traffic are already in a "forwarding" state. All ports start out in the "blocked" state. Movement between states is governed by a forwarding delay timer.

Blocked
> A port in this state can receive but not transmit BPDUs. It does not transmit or forward data frames. A port in this state may actually begin forwarding depending on the STP information received (or not received) from neighboring bridges.

Listening

This is the first transitional state and is entered when spanning tree detects that the port may have to participate in data frame forwarding. The port will receive and process BPDUs but does not forward data frames. In this state, ports begin sending BPDUs.

Learning

This state is similar to listening except that the port and switch now understand the topology and are preparing to forward data frames. The port will continue to receive and process BPDUs.

Forwarding

This is the final state. A port will now forward data frames even as it continues to process any new information from incoming BPDUs.

Shutdown/Disabled

A port that has been administratively shutdown is not participating in either forwarding of data frames or spanning tree (BPDU frames).

Spanning Tree Timers

Much of the operation of spanning tree is controlled via a series of timers. The values in use on a network can be seen in the ending BPDU data, such as in Figure 3-3 and Figure 3-7.

Hello

This timer controls the rate at which configuration BPDUs are issued from the root switch. A standard value is 2 seconds. When capturing packets this can actually get a bit annoying, as there are so many of them. The standard BPDU seen in Figure 3-4 is actually considered the "hello" message.

Max age

Switches keep track of how long they have had the current information. If the age of this information exceeds the max age timer value (20 seconds) the comparison algorithm may have to be rerun. The current age timer is reset every time new information is received via a BPDU. An example might be if the neighboring switch transmitting BPDUs was unplugged. The receiving switch would not receive anymore BPDUs and the age of the current information would start to climb. Eventually the receiver would have to find a new path to the root.

Forward delay

This timer monitors the time spent in each of the transitional port states. A 15 second limit is standard. This also provides insight into the delay between plugging in a computer and receiving a link light. The ports come up blocking, wait 15 seconds as they listen for BPDUs (listening), another 15 seconds before processing (learning) and forwarding. Therefore, a common delay for the link light is about 30 seconds.

The Operation of Spanning Tree

To better understand the operation of spanning tree, let's run through an example using a small topology. The MAC addresses and BPDU values will be the same as those seen in the previous packets. Figure 3-5 depicts this topology. Initially all three switches are powered off. The router simply indicates a pathway off of the network but is not involved in the spanning tree decisions. The bridge priorities are all set to 32768 + VLAN or 32769 (8001 in hex) assuming VLAN 1, and the port priorities are set to 128 (80 in hex). The process begins by powering Switch 1 and then adding switches, examining the process as we go.

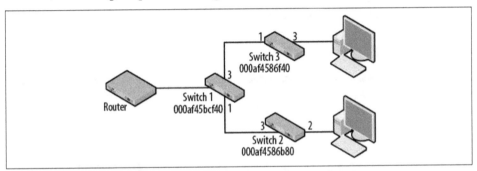

Figure 3-5. Small spanning tree topology

Step 1—Switch 1 Is Powered Up

When a Cisco switch is booting, all of the port link lights are amber, meaning that they are not currently forwarding traffic. In addition, when plugging a computer into a switch port, there is usually a delay before the link light goes green. This is because switch ports typically come up in the "blocking" state. The switch must first learn about the network topology before it starts forwarding traffic. This is to avoid creating an immediate loop.

Once Switch 1 has listened for and processed potential BPDU traffic, it is free to begin forwarding traffic. During this time, the ports have been transitioning between the various states. Using the debug spanning-tree events command on a Cisco switch yields the output in Figure 3-6.

```
Switch#
1d02h: %LINK-3-UPDOWN: Interface FastEthernet0/3, changed state to up
1d02h: set portid: VLAN0001 Fa0/3: new port id 8003
1d02h: STP: VLAN0001 Fa0/3 -> listening
1d02h: %LINEPROTO-5-UPDOWN: Line protocol on Interface FastEthernet0/3, changed state to up
1d02h: STP: VLAN0001 Fa0/3 -> learning
1d02h: STP: VLAN0001 Fa0/3 -> forwarding
Switch#
```

Figure 3-6. Port states

As port FastEthernet 0/3 (F0/3) comes up it transitions from blocking→listening→learning→forwarding, pausing for 15 seconds in listening and learning states.

Flowing out of ports 1 and 3 we would see the BPDUs in Figure 3-7. Note that the Ethernet source MAC addresses and the port IDs seen in the BPDU data correspond to the port transmitting the BPDU. Since Switch 1 is the only one running, it is the root switch and the transmitting switch as well. This is reflected in the BDPU root ID and bridge ID fields. The path cost for both BPDUs is 0.

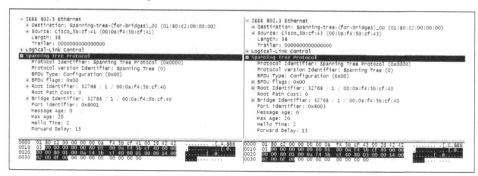

Figure 3-7. Step 1 BPDUs

The result of this step can also be seen with the show spanning-tree command.

From Figure 3-8, the root ID and the bridge ID are the same. The bridge priority is listed as 32769. Port F0/1 and F0/3 are forwarding with a cost of 19 (indicating 100Mbps) and a port priority of 128. The timer values are also listed.

```
Switch#
Switch#show spanning-tree

VLAN0001
  Spanning tree enabled protocol ieee
  Root ID     Priority    32769
              Address     000a.f45b.cf40
              This bridge is the root
              Hello Time   2 sec  Max Age 20 sec  Forward Delay 15 sec

  Bridge ID   Priority    32769  (priority 32768 sys-id-ext 1)
              Address     000a.f45b.cf40
              Hello Time   2 sec  Max Age 20 sec  Forward Delay 15 sec
              Aging Time 300

Interface         Role Sts Cost      Prio.Nbr Type
---------------- ---- --- --------- -------- --------------------------------
Fa0/1            Desg FWD 19        128.1    Shr
Fa0/3            Desg FWD 19        128.3    Shr

Switch#
```

Figure 3-8. Step 1 show spanning tree

Step 2—Switch 2 Is Powered Up

In steady state conditions, BPDUs flow away from the root bridge. This is simply because there is no need to inform upstream switches about network conditions since the upstream switches are the original source. This is true until something in the network changes. In this case, the MAC address of Switch 2 is lower than that of Switch 1. This means that if the bridge priorities are the same (they are), Switch 2 will become the new root. The ports on Switch 2 come up blocking but listen to the BPDUs coming from Switch 1. Switch 2 notices that the value contained in the root ID field is inferior to its own bridge ID and responds with a BPDU back to Switch 1 indicating that a coup d'etat is underway. Examining the debugging output on Switch 1, we can follow its reaction.

```
1d03h: STP: VLAN0001 heard root 32769-000a.f458.6b80 on Fa0/1
1d03h:       supersedes 32769-000a.f45b.cf40
1d03h: STP: VLAN0001 new root is 32769, 000a.f458.6b80 on port Fa0/1, cost 19
1d03h: STP: VLAN0001 sent Topology Change Notice on Fa0/1
```

Figure 3-9. Switch 1 debug output showing a new root switch

Capturing BPDUs between Switch 1 and Switch 2 shows that the BPDUs are now flowing from Switch 2 instead of Switch 1. The important details are that the root and bridge IDs have changed. Recall that since these are the same, this BPDU came from the root. This is supported by a root path cost of 0. Compare Figure 3-10 to Figure 3-7.

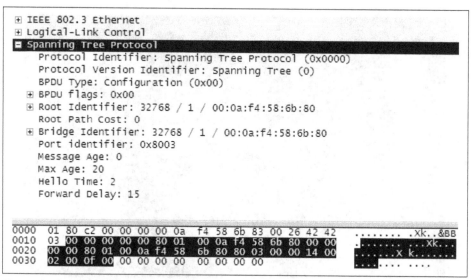

Figure 3-10. BPDU from the new root

The results can also be seen in the BPDUs transmitted from Switch 1 on the other side of the topology. In Figure 3-11 the BPDU was sent from the old root (bridge ID field) but Switch 2 is advertised as the new root in the root ID field (32768/1/000af4586b80).

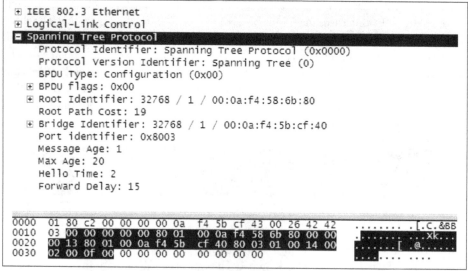

Figure 3-11. BPDU from old root advertising the new root

The path cost has also increased to 19 because traffic must now cross the 100Mbps Switch 1 in order to reach the root switch. Lastly, the summary on Switch 1 displays the changes to the topology in another form.

```
Switch#
Switch#sh spanning-tree

VLAN0001
  Spanning tree enabled protocol ieee
  Root ID    Priority    32769
             Address     000a.f458.6b80
             Cost        19
             Port        1 (FastEthernet0/1)
             Hello Time   2 sec  Max Age 20 sec  Forward Delay 15 sec

  Bridge ID  Priority    32769  (priority 32768 sys-id-ext 1)
             Address     000a.f45b.cf40
             Hello Time   2 sec  Max Age 20 sec  Forward Delay 15 sec
             Aging Time 300

Interface        Role Sts Cost      Prio.Nbr Type
---------------- ---- --- --------- -------- -------------------------
Fa0/1            Root FWD 19        128.1    Shr
Fa0/3            Desg FWD 19        128.3    Shr

Switch#
```

Figure 3-12. Switch1 show spanning tree with new root

Figure 3-9 contained the debugging results of Switch 1 receiving a BPDU from Switch 2. This event also changed the information output from the show spanning-tree command, as shown in Figure 3-12. Like most network processes, examining the packet captures and the output from the network devices provides a window into the operation of the protocol.

Step 3—Switch 3 Is Powered Up

With the addition of Switch 3, the topology is complete, though not yet converged. Based on MAC address and priority, all three switches will recognize Switch 2 as the root. BPDUs will flow away from Switch 2, advertising the topology information as they go. Adding Switch 3 does not change very much in the topology except to extend it. At the farthest point from Switch 2 (top computer in Figure 3-5), a capture would reveal that the path cost to the root is now 38 and that Switch 3 is the transmitting switch. This is shown in Figure 3-13.

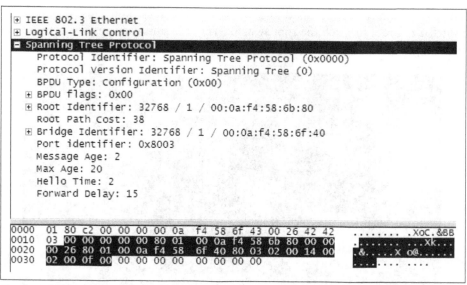

```
⊞ IEEE 802.3 Ethernet
⊞ Logical-Link Control
⊟ Spanning Tree Protocol
    Protocol Identifier: Spanning Tree Protocol (0x0000)
    Protocol Version Identifier: Spanning Tree (0)
    BPDU Type: Configuration (0x00)
  ⊞ BPDU flags: 0x00
  ⊞ Root Identifier: 32768 / 1 / 00:0a:f4:58:6b:80
    Root Path Cost: 38
  ⊞ Bridge Identifier: 32768 / 1 / 00:0a:f4:58:6f:40
    Port identifier: 0x8003
    Message Age: 2
    Max Age: 20
    Hello Time: 2
    Forward Delay: 15


0000  01 80 c2 00 00 00 00 0a  f4 58 6f 43 00 26 42 42   ........ .XoC.&BB
0010  03 00 00 00 00 00 80 01  00 0a f4 58 6b 80 00 00   ........ ...Xk...
0020  00 26 80 01 00 0a f4 58  6f 40 80 03 02 00 14 00   .&.....X o@......
0030  02 00 0f 00 00 00 00 00  00 00 00 00               ........ ....
```

Figure 3-13. BPDU transmitted by Switch 3

Note that the bridge ID has changed but the root ID has not. The path cost has increased to 38. The port ID is 8003.

After developing an understanding of the structure and basic operation of spanning tree, one might realize that given this small network, spanning tree is not necessary because the topology is not looped. But what if someone came along and connected Switch 2 to Switch 3 either by accident (happens all the time) or due to an interest in redundancy? That is where the fun begins. On to step 4.

Step 4—Creation of a Loop

When a physical loop is created by connecting Switches 2 and 3, spanning tree responds by blocking one of the ports in the topology. If more loops are created, more ports would be blocked until all of the loops were eliminated. Initially, the physical and logical topologies are the same. The decision as to which port is blocked is based entirely on the information used by the comparison algorithm. But we have another question to address first: How are loops detected? During normal operations, BPDUs flow away from the root. Stated another way, a switch should only receive information about the root switch from one direction. When a switch "hears" about the root via BPDUs on more than one port, a loop has occurred.

Regardless of the spanning tree version, switches react very quickly to eliminate the loop. As switches compare BPDU information, the switch with the highest values is the loser and must block a port. Figure 3-14 is a depiction of the new topology with the loop created. We know that based on the priorities and MAC addresses, Switch 2 became the root switch. Thus, all of the BPDUs seen in this network have the same value in the first field of the comparison algorithm.

Root ID – 32768/1/000af4586b80

The next field to consider is the path cost to the root. The root switch sends out a path cost of 0 from ports 2 and 3. Clearly these are the lowest path cost values and the root will not be asked to block a port. Switches 1 and 3 cannot improve upon either the root ID or the path cost. So, it is up to Switch 1 and 3 to decide which of the downstream ports will be blocked as they fire BPDUs at each other.

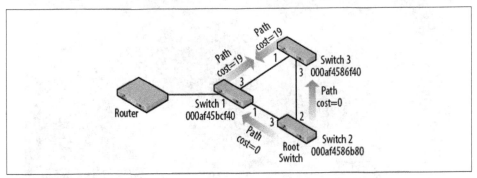

Figure 3-14. Looped topology

On the link between Switch 1 and Switch 3, BPDUs would be sent out with the same root ID and, as indicated in Figure 3-14, the same path cost. In this case, the decision as to which port to block comes down to the bridge ID. With the bridge priorities the same, the higher MAC address "loses" and Switch 1 must block a port. While the physical topology will continue as drawn in Figure 3-14, the logical topology will behave like the one seen in Figure 3-15 with port 3 on Switch 1 blocked and the loop is eliminated.

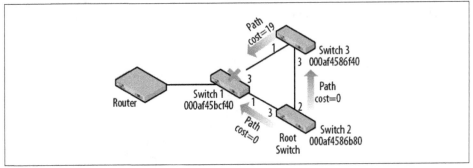

Figure 3-15. Resolved topology

The output of the show spanning tree command run on Switch 1 (Figure 3-16) depicts the topology changes made. Remember that the cable is still physically connected.

```
Switch#
2d02h: STP: VLAN0001 sent Topology Change Notice on Fa0/1
2d02h: STP: VLAN0001 Fa0/3 -> blocking
Switch#
Switch#sh span

VLAN0001
  Spanning tree enabled protocol ieee
  Root ID    Priority    32769
             Address     000a.f458.6b80
             Cost        19
             Port        1 (FastEthernet0/1)
             Hello Time   2 sec  Max Age 20 sec  Forward Delay 15 sec

  Bridge ID  Priority    32769  (priority 32768 sys-id-ext 1)
             Address     000a.f45b.cf40
             Hello Time   2 sec  Max Age 20 sec  Forward Delay 15 sec
             Aging Time 15

Interface        Role Sts Cost      Prio.Nbr Type
---------------- ---- --- --------- -------- -------------------------
Fa0/1            Root FWD 19        128.1    Shr
Fa0/3            Altn BLK 19        128.3    Shr

Switch#
```

Figure 3-16. Switch 1 show spanning tree with blocked port

At the top of Figure 3-16 the event is recorded and the final state is displayed at the bottom with the interface list. Root ports, designated ports, root bridges and designated bridges were defined in a previous section. Once the topology has stabilized we can now clearly see the roles of each network device and port. In Figure 3-17, the letters B, R, and D indicate blocked, root, and designated ports, respectively.

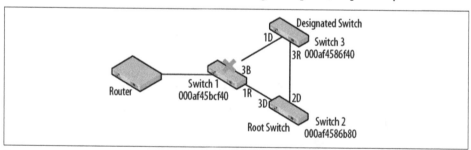

Figure 3-17. Switch and port roles

These roles can also be seen in the output from the show spanning tree command in Figure 3-12 and Figure 3-16.

Spanning Tree Messages

In order to arrive at this new stable configuration, the switches swapped quite a bit of information via BPDUs. The spanning tree protocol has a small collection of messages, including the steady state "hello" already seen. But with the introduction of a loop and the need to block a port, it is time to talk about the other message types. The 1-byte BPDU type is set based on the message used. The 1-byte BPDU flags field provides an indication of the operation underway. The steady state values are shown in Figure 3-18. This frame was captured immediately before the loop was introduced.

```
⊟ Spanning Tree Protocol
      Protocol Identifier: Spanning Tree Protocol (0x0000)
      Protocol Version Identifier: Spanning Tree (0)
      BPDU Type: Configuration (0x00)
   ⊟ BPDU flags: 0x00
         0... .... = Topology Change Acknowledgment: No
         .... ...0 = Topology Change: No
   ⊞ Root Identifier: 32768 / 1 / 00:0a:f4:58:6b:80
      Root Path Cost: 38
   ⊞ Bridge Identifier: 32768 / 1 / 00:0a:f4:58:6f:40
      Port Identifier: 0x8003
      Message Age: 2
      Max Age: 20
      Hello Time: 2
      Forward Delay: 15
```

Figure 3-18. BPDU type and flags

Configuration
    This is the standard message type. The BPDU type field is set to 00. The message contains all of the information discussed in this chapter. Figure 3-18 is an example of a configuration BPDU with the flags field set to 00.

Topology Change
    This BPDU is meant to indicate that a topology reconfiguration is underway. When the loop was created, Switches 1 and 3 exchanged BPDUs. Switch 3, understanding that there was a better path to the root, initiated a topology change or TC. There are a couple of events that will drive a topology change in a spanning tree topology: expiration of the max age timer, addition or removal of a switch, links going up/down, and receipt of new information via a BPDU. In the loop example, the trigger occurred when Switch 3 became aware of a second pathway to the root switch. The change to the flags field is shown in Figure 3-19.

```
⊟ Spanning Tree Protocol
     Protocol Identifier: Spanning Tree Protocol (0x0000)
     Protocol Version Identifier: Spanning Tree (0)
     BPDU Type: Configuration (0x00)
    ■ BPDU flags: 0x01 (Topology Change)
        0... .... = Topology Change Acknowledgment: No
        .... ...1 = Topology Change: Yes
    ⊞ Root Identifier: 32768 / 1 / 00:0a:f4:58:6b:80
```

Figure 3-19. Topology change flags

Topology Change Notification

Upon receipt of a BPDU from Switch 3, Switch 1 now realizes that the topology is changing; BPDUs will flow in the same direction but there is a loop. Switch 1 now sends a Topology Change Notification (TCN) back to the root as shown in Figure 3-20.

```
⊟ IEEE 802.3 Ethernet
   ⊞ Destination: Spanning-tree-(for-bridges)_00 (01:80:c2:00:00:00)
   ⊞ Source: Cisco_5b:cf:41 (00:0a:f4:5b:cf:41)
     Length: 7
     Trailer: 0000000000000000000000000000000000000000000000000000...
   ⊞ Logical-Link Control
   ⊟ Spanning Tree Protocol
        Protocol Identifier: Spanning Tree Protocol (0x0000)
        Protocol Version Identifier: Spanning Tree (0)
        BPDU Type: Topology Change Notification (0x80)

0000  01 80 c2 00 00 00 00 0a  f4 5b cf 41 00 07 42 42   ........ .[.A..BB
0010  03 00 00 00 80 00 00 00  00 00 00 00 00 00 00 00   ....■... ........
0020  00 00 00 00 00 00 00 00  00 00 00 00 00 00 00 00   ........ ........
0030  00 00 00 00 00 00 00 00  00 00 00 00               ........ ....
```

Figure 3-20. Topology change notification

The TCN BPDU does not contain any configuration information. A close look at the hex for the BPDU reveals that the trailer (padding of all 0's) is much larger to adhere to the Ethernet minimum frame size.

The topology change process continues long enough for all of the ports throughout the topology to transition to the proper state (forwarding or blocked). Per the standard, the forwarding delay timer cycles twice. So this amounts to about 30 seconds. You can actually count the number of configuration BPDUs during this time and usually come up with 15 or 16.

Topology Change Notification Acknowledgement

When a TCN is sent (in this case from 000af45bcf41 on Switch 1), the receiving switch returns an answer in the form of a TCN ACK message as seen in Figure 3-21. This message indicates its purpose via the flags field and provides the most up-to-date information regarding the topology.

```
⊞ IEEE 802.3 Ethernet
⊞ Logical-Link Control
⊟ Spanning Tree Protocol
    Protocol Identifier: Spanning Tree Protocol (0x0000)
    Protocol Version Identifier: Spanning Tree (0)
    BPDU Type: Configuration (0x00)
 ⊟ BPDU flags: 0x81 (Topology Change Acknowledgment, Topology Change)
        1... .... = Topology Change Acknowledgment: Yes
        .... ...1 = Topology Change: Yes
 ⊞ Root Identifier: 32768 / 1 / 00:0a:f4:58:6b:80
    Root Path Cost: 0
 ⊞ Bridge Identifier: 32768 / 1 / 00:0a:f4:58:6b:80
    Port Identifier: 0x8003
    Message Age: 0
    Max Age: 20
    Hello Time: 2
    Forward Delay: 15


0000   01 80 c2 00 00 00 00 0a  f4 58 6b 83 00 26 42 42   ........ .Xk..&BB
0010   03 00 00 00 00 00 81 80 01  00 0a f4 58 6b 80 00 00   .....▮.. ...Xk...
0020   00 00 80 01 00 0a f4 58  6b 80 80 03 00 00 14 00   ........X k......
0030   02 00 0f 00 00 00 00 00  00 00 00 00               ........ ....
```

Figure 3-21. TCN acknowledgement

The last note I'd like to make regarding the flags field is that it is 1 byte in length, yet only uses a couple message types. We'll store this little piece of information away for use later in the chapter.

Problems with Spanning Tree

Spanning tree is very good at eliminating loops. It took less than five seconds to solve the problem in our sample topology. However, when information is lost or when better pathways are created, spanning tree can be excruciatingly slow. For example, if the loop was removed from the topology by unplugging the cable between Switch 1 and 2 (reverting back to the one seen in Figure 3-5), spanning tree would not instantaneously "unblock" port 3 on Switch 1. Instead, we would have to wait for the information received by Switch 3 to age out. Switch 3 would no longer receive BPDUs from the root switch. Eventually the max age timer would expire and a topology change would begin. But how long would it take? The max age timer is 20 seconds, after which the TCN would be sent. The forwarding delay timer is 15 seconds for both the listening and learning states. So, port 3 on Switch 1 would remain blocked for 50 seconds even after the loop was gone. Any node connected to Switch 3 would be isolated for that entire time. As the network size or complexity increases, this length of time will also increase. This delay makes the original spanning tree inappropriate for a redundancy solution.

Another problem, and one of the reasons that it is good to understand the protocol, is that "automatic" spanning tree topologies can often be suboptimal in terms of forwarding. Assume that a host is connected to Switch 3 and attempts to open a web page. Based on the original blocking solution (port 3 on Switch 1), the traffic would have to flow around the entire topology as shown in Figure 3-22.

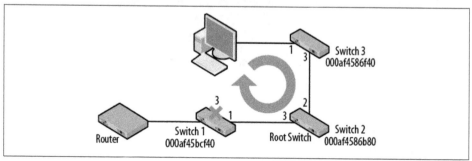

Figure 3-22. Suboptimal forwarding

In this case, the spanning tree eliminated the loop but created problems for traffic handling. In order to improve things for all nodes, the priority of Switch 1 could be changed such that it becomes the root. Recall that the bridge ID is a combination of bridge/switch priority followed by the MAC address. In Figure 3-23, the priority has been lowered to 4096 + 1 for the VLAN (1001 in hex) making Switch 1 the new root.

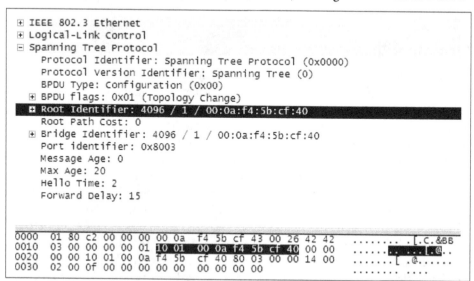

Figure 3-23. BPDU with priority change

The topology now resolves itself as shown in Figure 3-24. The pathway off the network for nodes connected to both Switch 2 and 3 is now straight through Switch 1. Port 3 on Switch 1 has been unblocked and port 3 on Switch 3 has been blocked.

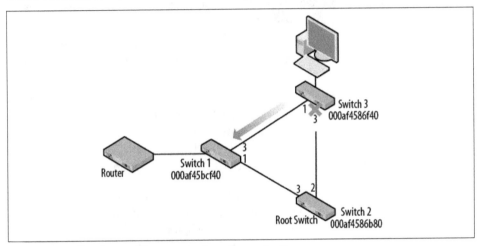

Figure 3-24. Topology with new root based on priority

Switch to Switch: A Special Case

Regardless of topology, the whole process begins with the election of a root switch based on priority and MAC address. From there, switches with the best path cost to the root become designated bridges for the traffic traveling off of a particular network segment. In the event of a path cost tie such as that seen earlier in this chapter, the nonroot switch having the highest bridge ID (priority and MAC address) loses and must block a port. But when does the port ID field get used?

In Figure 3-25, two switches are connected directly to each other in a loop. Again, spanning tree will step in and block one of the ports. In order to determine which one, the comparison algorithm must be used:

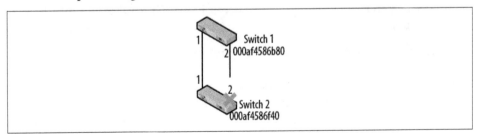

Figure 3-25. Special case

1. Elect a root Switch. Assuming that the priorities are the same (32768 + 1), the deciding factor is the MAC address. Switch 1 becomes the root.

2. Path Cost. BPDUs flow away from the root and since both BPDUs are also leaving the root, they will have a path cost of 0.

3. Compare bridge IDs. Bridge ID is the ID of the transmitting bridge. In this case, both BPDUs will have the same value of 8001:000af4586b80 since they both come from the root.

4. Compare port IDs. This is our last chance to stop the loop. All of the other fields have had the same values in each BPDU. However, when we compare the BPDU leaving ports 1 and 2, we finally see a difference. From port 1, the port ID is 8001 (priority of 128 and a port number of 1) while the BPDU leaving port 2 on Switch 1 has a port ID of 8002 (priority of 128 and a port number of 2).

Because of the information received from Switch 1, Switch 2 now decides to block its own port 2 which terminates the loop. It is important to realize that the information contained in the BPDUs had nothing to do with Switch 2.

Cisco Improvements

Rapid spanning tree protocol (RSTP) has been part of the standards literature for more than a decade. However, it has not always been supported by vendor equipment. Even if you had equipment supporting RSTP, it might not be compatible with older bridges and switches. Cisco deployed a series of improvement to STP in an effort to help speed up convergence and port forwarding.

Portfast

Spanning tree is for bridges and switches. Hosts do not care very much about the network topology. So, when a host is connected to the network, it is not really necessary to have them wait for the transitions between the port states. In fact, devices like voice over IP phones may actually suffer because of it. This is because the phone is attempting to complete a number of transactions early in the connection process.

The command `spanning-tree portfast` informs the port that it does not have to go through the listening and learning port states. It is very handy when working in a dynamic environment during troubleshooting or testing. However, this is only to be used with end nodes. Accidentally connecting an interface configured for portfast with another switch can create loops. The potential hazards are advertised by Cisco when you issue the command.

```
Switch(config-if)#spanning-tree portfast
%Warning: portfast should only be enabled on ports connected to a single
 host. Connecting hubs, concentrators, switches, bridges, etc... to this
 interface  when portfast is enabled, can cause temporary bridging loops.
 Use with CAUTION

%Portfast has been configured on FastEthernet0/11 but will only
 have effect when the interface is in a non-trunking mode.
Switch(config-if)#
```

Figure 3-26. Portfast warning

Uplinkfast

Uplinkfast is designed to help speed up convergence in cases where an alternate path to the root switch exists. One of the downfalls of spanning tree is that it can lead to lengthy convergence delays because of the timers, even though a failover pathway might exist. Even in the small topology discussed earlier, the convergence time was 50 seconds when the loop was removed.

Using the same topology, Switches 1 and 3 will be given the command spanning-tree uplinkfast and become members of an uplink group with their neighbors. There are a couple of changes to the BPDU; bridge priority and path cost are increased. This ensures that they will *not* become the root as they now have specified roles. Figure 3-27 depicts these BPDU changes.

Another look at the output from show spanning-tree reveals that the switch has a completely different view of the topology. The change noted in the BPDU is here but in addition, one will be listed as an alternate. To be complete, the blocked port was listed as alternates before (Figure 3-16) but they operated with the longer delays.

With uplinkfast configured, when the link to the root is lost, the switch immediately fails over to the secondary pathways through Switch 3. In addition, port 3 on Switch 1 starts forwarding. This takes about 1 second as opposed to nearly a minute.

```
⊞ IEEE 802.3 Ethernet
⊞ Logical-Link Control
⊟ Spanning Tree Protocol
    Protocol Identifier: Spanning Tree Protocol (0x0000)
    Protocol Version Identifier: Spanning Tree (0)
    BPDU Type: Configuration (0x00)
⊞ BPDU flags: 0x00
⊞ Root Identifier: 32768 / 1 / 00:0a:f4:58:6b:80
    Root Path Cost: 3019
⊞ Bridge Identifier: 49152 / 1 / 00:0a:f4:58:6f:40
    Port Identifier: 0x8001
    Message Age: 1
    Max Age: 20
    Hello Time: 2
    Forward Delay: 15
```

Figure 3-27. Uplinkfast BPDU

```
Switch#sh spanning-tree uplinkfast
UplinkFast is enabled

Station update rate set to 150 packets/sec.

UplinkFast statistics
-----------------------------
Number of transitions via uplinkFast (all VLANs)          : 0
Number of proxy multicast addresses transmitted (all VLANs) : 0

Name                     Interface List
------------------       ------------------------------------
VLAN0001                 Fa0/1(fwd), Fa0/3
Switch#
Switch#sh span

VLAN0001
  Spanning tree enabled protocol ieee
  Root ID    Priority    32769
             Address     000a.f458.6b80
             Cost        3019
             Port        1 (FastEthernet0/1)
             Hello Time   2 sec  Max Age 20 sec  Forward Delay 15 sec

  Bridge ID  Priority    49153  (priority 49152 sys-id-ext 1)
             Address     000a.f45b.cf40
             Hello Time   2 sec  Max Age 20 sec  Forward Delay 15 sec
             Aging Time 300
  Uplinkfast enabled

Interface          Role Sts Cost      Prio.Nbr Type
----------------   ---- --- --------- -------- --------------------
Fa0/1              Root FWD 3019       128.1    Shr
Fa0/3              Altn BLK 3019       128.3    Shr
```

Figure 3-28. Uplinkfast output

Backbonefast

The uplinkfast goal is to improve slow convergence time for a switch that has lost its connection to the root switch. But what about when a switch elsewhere in the topology loses the connection to the root? Normally it would be "every switch for itself" and max age timers would have to be exceeded before anything could be done. For example, in topology from Figure 3-17, Switch 2 is the root and Switch 1 is blocking port 3 to eliminate the loop. Uplinkfast helped with a loss of the connection between Switch 1 and 3. But if the link between Switch 2 (root) and Switch 3 were to be lost, is there anything Switch 1 can do to help?

With backbonefast, when Switch 3 loses its connection to the root, it responds by advertising itself as the root via a BPDU sent to Switch 1. However, Switch 1 is still connected to the original root and so recognizes the BPDU from Switch 3 as inferior. Switch 1 can use a special frame called a root link query (RLQ) to determine if the root is still present. If the root still lives, Switch 1 can transition blocked port 3 immediately to the listening state without waiting for the max age timer to expire. This saves about 20 seconds in convergence time over standard spanning tree.

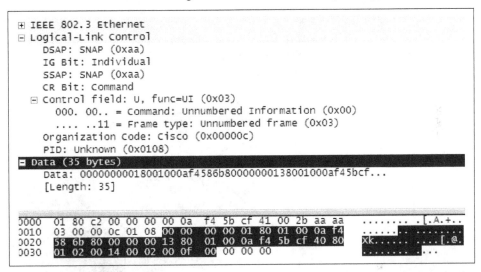

```
⊞ IEEE 802.3 Ethernet
⊟ Logical-Link Control
     DSAP: SNAP (0xaa)
     IG Bit: Individual
     SSAP: SNAP (0xaa)
     CR Bit: Command
  ⊟ Control field: U, func=UI (0x03)
       000. 00.. = Command: Unnumbered Information (0x00)
       .... ..11 = Frame type: Unnumbered frame (0x03)
     Organization Code: Cisco (0x00000c)
     PID: Unknown (0x0108)
⊟ Data (35 bytes)
     Data: 0000000018001000af4586b80000000138001000af45bcf...
     [Length: 35]

0000  01 80 c2 00 00 00 00 0a  f4 5b cf 41 00 2b aa aa   ........ .[.A.+..
0010  03 00 00 0c 01 08 00 00  00 00 01 80 01 00 0a f4   ........ ........
0020  58 6b 80 00 00 00 13 80  01 00 0a f4 5b cf 40 80   Xk...... ....[.@.
0030  01 02 00 14 00 02 00 0f  00 00 00 00               ........ .....
```

Figure 3-29. Root link query

Wireshark does not decode the entire root link query. Recall that this is highly proprietary and not commonly deployed. However, an examination of the data field shows us the MAC addresses of the switches involved. Even more telling is the conversation between the switches. This frame is generated from a nonroot switch upon receipt of the inferior BPDU. It is followed by an RLQ response from the root switch. Once the path to the root is established, the blocked port on Switch 1 immediately transitions to the listening state.

VLANs and Spanning Tree

Earlier in this chapter, there was an indicator that STP might be affected by VLANs. The bridge priority takes the VLAN ID into account by adding the value to 32768. From Chapter 4, VLANs are separate IP networks and exist as separate Layer 2 broadcast domains. It turns out that each VLAN can have its own instance of spanning tree running. This means that if needed, each VLAN could have a different logical topology than the other VLANs running on the same switches. In Cisco language, this is known as Per VLAN Spanning Tree, or PVST.

Consider the topology seen in Figure 3-30. On the surface, it is the exact same topology used earlier in this chapter, except that now there are VLANs running on the switches and the switches are interconnected with trunks. I've also added a set of servers for VLANs 4 and 5. By default, spanning tree would resolve the topology exactly as we have seen so far, even with the VLANs. This is because even with VLANs, spanning tree makes its decision the same way. While there are separate VLANs, the logical topologies will end up being the same, though they will be calculated independently.

The problem is that even on this small topology, we can see that VLAN 4 users on Switch 3 have to travel all the way around the network to access the servers. This is not true for the users on VLAN 5 since the servers are located in the center of the network. To make this more efficient, Switch 1 could be made the root for VLAN 4.

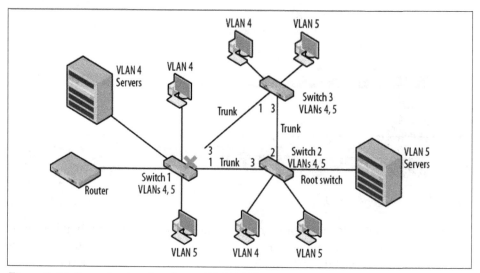

Figure 3-30. Spanning tree topology with VLANs

As before, we'll make a small change based on priorities. In Figure 3-24, the result of changing switch priorities is shown in the BPDU. What isn't obvious is that this priority change is actually for the VLAN. Specifically this was a change for VLAN 1 since in that case, all ports were in VLAN 1. The actual command used was `spanning tree vlan 1 priority 4096`. For this example, the command will be modified to `spanning tree vlan 4 priority 4096`. Note that VLAN 5 is not addressed because the root for VLAN 5 is right where it should be. The result is that the physical topology will not change but there will be *two* logical topologies as shown in Figure 3-31.

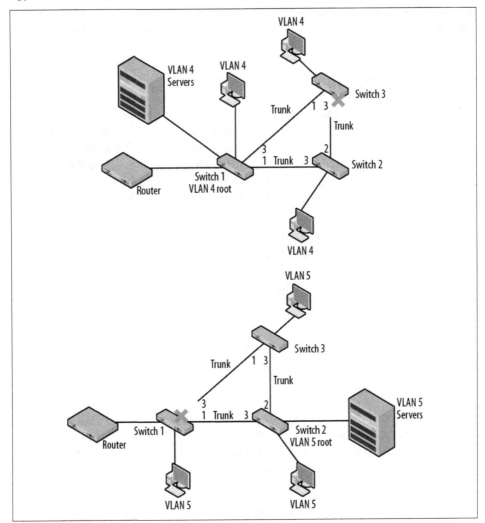

Figure 3-31. New spanning tree topologies based on VLAN

On the left, we can see that the topology has been modified to block port 3 on Switch 3. This modification brings the resources closer to the VLAN 4 users. The right side topology remains the same. Examining the `show spanning tree` output from earlier in the chapter (ex. Figure 3-16 and Figure 3-28), the VLAN ID is listed as part of the screen data. For the topologies shown in Figure 3-31, the output from the show spanning tree command would depict the two configurations by providing separate output for VLANs 4 and 5. It is important to realize that packet forwarding decisions are based not just on the MAC addresses but the VLAN IDs seen on the trunk lines as well. These details are covered in Chapter 4.

Another important benefit to creating multiple instances of spanning tree is that for a portion of the logical traffic, ports can now be brought into service that otherwise might have blocked traffic, improving throughput and performance.

The Rapid Spanning Tree Protocol

The Spanning Tree Protocol from IEEE 802.1D is highly effective at eliminating loops but very slow at converging in other situations such as recovering pathways. Most organizations do not depend on spanning tree or other Layer 2 solutions for redundancy, load balancing or failover. Routers often replace switches where these features are desired. Cisco added improvements such as portfast, uplinkfast and backbonefast address either slow convergence or port state transitions though not all of these are in regular use.

The Rapid Spanning Tree Protocol (RSTP), which is standardized in IEEE 802.1w, improves the performance of the original spanning tree and incorporates many of the functions seen in the Cisco enhancements. In addition, it is fast enough to become a dependable component of some robust, highly reliable networks.

A couple of the significant changes include:

- Switches quickly purge old information once new data is received
- Several new port roles are defined.
- Port states have also been modified.

In 802.1D spanning tree, once a port begins forwarding, there is no indication of the port role within the BPDU. From the BPDUs seen earlier in the chapter, we also know that while the BPDU type and flags field comprise 2 bytes of data, few values or types are used. RSTP makes use of these fields to convey additional information regarding the ports and therefore, the topology.

Rather than transitioning to forwarding and then simply becoming either a root or designated port, RSTP separates these two ideas and reduces the number of states.

Table 3-1. *Port state comparison*

802.1D	802.1w
Disabled	Discard
Blocked	Discard
Listening	Discard
Learning	Learning
Forwarding	Forwarding

Blocking becomes a port role and is divided into backup and alternate blocked ports. The roles of designated and root are now variables of the port and are sent along with the BPDU. Within the flags field, the port states (learning and forwarding) and the roles are sent along with the BPDU. This is in addition to a change to the protocol version and signaling. Recall that 802.1D messages are limited to configuration, topology change notification (TCN) and the TCN ACK. RSTP adds proposals and ACKs for the proposals. An example of these changes can be seen in Figure 3-32.

```
⊟ IEEE 802.3 Ethernet
  ⊞ Destination: Spanning-tree-(for-bridges)_00 (01:80:c2:00:00:00)
  ⊞ Source: Cisco_58:6b:82 (00:0a:f4:58:6b:82)
    Length: 39
    Trailer: 0000000000000
⊞ Logical-Link Control
⊟ Spanning Tree Protocol
    Protocol Identifier: Spanning Tree Protocol (0x0000)
    Protocol Version Identifier: Rapid Spanning Tree (2)
    BPDU Type: Rapid/Multiple Spanning Tree (0x02)
  ⊟ BPDU flags: 0x3c (Forwarding, Learning, Port Role: Designated)
        0... .... = Topology Change Acknowledgment: No
        .0.. .... = Agreement: No
        ..1. .... = Forwarding: Yes
        ...1 .... = Learning: Yes
        .... 11.. = Port Role: Designated (3)
        .... ..0. = Proposal: No
        .... ...0 = Topology Change: No
  ⊞ Root Identifier: 32768 / 1 / 00:0a:f4:58:6b:80
    Root Path Cost: 0
  ⊞ Bridge Identifier: 32768 / 1 / 00:0a:f4:58:6b:80
    Port Identifier: 0x8002
    Message Age: 0
    Max Age: 20

0000  01 80 c2 00 00 00 00 0a  f4 58 6b 82 00 27 42 42   ........ .Xk..'BB
0010  03 00 00 02 02 3c 80 01  00 0a f4 58 6b 80 00 00   .....<.. ...Xk..
0020  00 00 80 01 00 0a f4 58  6b 80 80 02 00 00 14 00   .......X k.......
0030  02 00 0f 00 00 00 00 00  00 00 00 00               ........ ....
```

Figure 3-32. *Rapid spanning tree fields*

Even with these changes, much of the protocol is the same. Root ports are still those receiving BPDUs and sending TCN BPDUs (point to the root switch) and designated ports still send BPDUs and receive TCN BPDUs (point away from the root switch). Switch and port priorities are also used in similar fashion.

The Operation of RSTP

Unlike 802.1D spanning tree, in which switches only send BPDUs if they have received one from upstream, RSTP switches send BPDUs every Hello time regardless. In addition, rather than wait for the max age timer of 20 seconds to expire, RSTP only waits for three Hello times (6 seconds) before aging out neighbor information. This means that there is faster failure detection and the Hello or configuration BPDU can be thought of as a "keep alive" message. RSTP also allows immediate acceptance of inferior BPDU information in the event that the path to the root switch is lost. This is similar to the behavior of backbonefast.

Ports are now identified according to their link type without the addition of vendor improvements. Edge ports are those that do not receive BPDUs and so transition to forwarding immediately without stopping in the other port states. This is similar to portfast. An edge port receiving a BPDU converts to a standard spanning tree port. Point-to-point links are those connecting switches directly together. These ports also transition quickly to the forwarding state because a loop is less likely. This is based on the port being full duplex. These link types can also be configured manually. Figure 3-33 depicts the output of the show spanning-tree command after RSTP has been enabled. Note the changes to the link types.

```
Switch#sh spa
3w0d: %SYS-5-CONFIG_I: Configured from console by console

VLAN0001
  Spanning tree enabled protocol rstp
  Root ID    Priority    32769
             Address     000a.f458.6b80
             Cost        19
             Port        3 (FastEthernet0/3)
             Hello Time  2 sec  Max Age 20 sec  Forward Delay 15 sec

  Bridge ID  Priority    32769  (priority 32768 sys-id-ext 1)
             Address     000a.f458.6f40
             Hello Time  2 sec  Max Age 20 sec  Forward Delay 15 sec
             Aging Time 300

Interface        Role Sts Cost      Prio.Nbr Type
---------------- ---- --- --------- -------- --------------------------
Fa0/1            Desg FWD 19        128.1    P2p
Fa0/3            Root FWD 19        128.3    Shr
Fa0/5            Desg FWD 19        128.5    Edge P2p
```

Figure 3-33. RSTP show spanning tree output

On point-to-point links, switches negotiate for permission to begin forwarding via proposal and agreement. Upon changes, ports go into "sync" by blocking/discarding or converting to edge ports. The negotiation elects root ports and transitions some ports directly to forwarding. For RSTP topology changes, switches start a topology change timer for all "nonedge" designated ports and the root port. Spanning tree MAC addresses are flushed for these ports. In this way, the new information is quickly reported to the other switches in the network. Convergence time is drastically reduced making RSTP part of redundancy and failover solutions.

Alternate and backup blocked ports

Alternate ports are blocked ports that still receive BPDUs from other bridges though better pathways exist. Building on the topology used earlier, I've added Switch 4 downstream of Switch 3. Upon loss of the "better" pathway to the root via Switch 3, the *alternate* port on Switch 1 will quickly transition to forwarding. This is similar to, but much faster than the idea of uplinkfast.

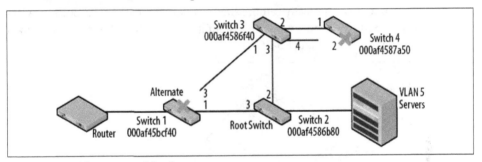

Figure 3-34. Alternate and backup ports

Backup ports receive BPDUs from their own switch but are the inferior port. In this case they are blocked but have no guarantee back to the root. This is also shown in Figure 3-34 on Switch 4. Looking closely at port 2 on Switch 4, we can understand why it was blocked. Comparing the BPDUs from Switch 3 to Switch 4, the BPDU leaving port 4 would be inferior. If port 2 on Switch 3 stopped sending BPDUs, port 4 on Switch 3 should take over. But Switch 4 is not guaranteed access to the root since the overall path did not change; it is still via Switch 3 and so is dependent upon connectivity elsewhere in the network. This is also one of the few cases where RSTP does not outperform 802.1D STP in terms of convergence.

Security

The security concerns with a protocol like spanning tree are not usually directed at loss of data or intrusion. Instead, administrators worry about network disruption or denial of service problems. Spanning tree topologies are relatively easy to disrupt by injecting traffic. Connecting to any port on a switch provides a vector for the injection. Programs like Yersinia allow attackers to craft the necessary packets. Attacks like this work because the switches and the protocol assume that the incoming packets have the correct information. For example, an attacker connecting to any one of the topologies discussed in this chapter might inject a "bad" BPDU. The attacking BPDU might have a root priority that is very low compared to the actual root. The "bad" BPDU causes a topology change with all pathways resolving toward the new root. Once the topology converges, the attacker can remove the BDPUs and force another topology change. Changes like this also cause a network traffic to flow toward the attacker, with the potential for exposing user data to the attacker. Defense against this sort of attack is left to commands such as `root guard` and `bpdu guard`, which limit the ability of attackers to inject bad BPDUs or supplant the valid root switch. Attacks like this can be home grown too. If a network administrator were to install a switch without considering the spanning tree topology, the very same scenario can occur.

Another concern for network administrators is in the wireless network. Many access points can be converted to wireless bridges. This is typically done to provide a network connection to geographically remote sites or nodes. Like an access point, a wireless bridge has both a wired and wireless interface. A little slip can result in a topology like that shown in Figure 3-35.

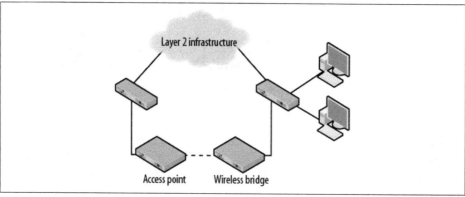

Figure 3-35. Wireless bridging loop

Depending on the type and vendor for the bridge, it may or may not participate in spanning tree. Imagine if the wireless bridge priority was lower than some of the wired switches. The topology would be forced to re-converge with the wireless bridge potentially becoming the root. Wireless bridges have nowhere near the capacity of wired switches. If the wireless bridge does not participate in spanning tree, it is possible that an unresolved loop may occur or that a port elsewhere in the topology would have to be blocked. This may limit connectivity for a section of the network.

Reading

IEEE 802.1D bridging standard, "IEEE Standard for Local and metropolitan area networks: Media Access Control (MAC) Bridges", (incorporates 802.1w), Jun. 2004.

IEEE 802.1Q VLAN standard, "IEEE Standards for Local and metropolitan area networks: Virtual Bridged Local Area Networks", (incorporates 802.1v and 802.1s), May 2006.

RFC 5556: Transparent Interconnection of Lots of Links (TRILL): Problem and Applicability Statement

Summary

Spanning tree is a protocol that is part of almost every single Layer 2 network. Because it runs by default, it is often misunderstood or ignored entirely. However, spanning tree, and the faster rapid spanning tree, may serve a critical role in the network in protecting the Ethernet network from Layer 2 loops. The scenarios and packets described in this chapter depict the operation and expected behavior of this ubiquitous process. Rapid and 802.1D spanning have many of the same behaviors, but because of improvements to convergence speed, rapid spanning tree is the better choice for redundancy in networks. Though the protocols have been around for awhile, and some of the functions have been supplanted by routers, work continues in the area of Layer 2 loop resolution. Projects like TRILL (Transparent Interconnection of Lots of Links) indicate that folks, especially Radia Perlman, are not done thinking about the problem.

Review Questions

1. Spanning tree is defined in what standard?
2. The main purpose of spanning tree is to eliminate logical loops.
   a. TRUE
   b. FALSE
3. What are the four fields used in the comparison algorithm?
4. What are the components of the root ID field?
5. What is the destination MAC address used on a BPDU?
6. Describe the difference between a root port and a designated port.
7. What are the values for the hello, max age and hello timers?
8. Name three Cisco improvements to spanning tree.

9. Rapid Spanning Tree is appropriate for maintaining high speed redundancy in networks.

    a. TRUE

    b. FALSE

10. Rapid spanning tree defined what two types of blocked ports?

Review Answers

1. 802.1D
2. TRUE
3. Root ID, path cost, bridge ID, port ID
4. Bridge priority and MAC address
5. 01:80:c2:00:00:00
6. Root ports point to the root switch and designated ports point away. Traffic flows into designated ports on its way to the root switch and out of root ports.
7. 15, 20 and 2 seconds
8. Portfast, uplinkfast and backbonefast
9. TRUE
10. Alternate and backup

Lab Activities

Activity 1—Capture of a BPDU

Materials: A computer with an active network connection to a switch and packet capture software (Wireshark)

1. If not already connected to the switch, connected the computer NIC to the switch.
2. Once the link light turns green, start the packet capture software.
3. Examine the packets captured and find a BPDU.
4. Open the BPDU and analyze the fields used by the comparison algorithm. What are the values?

Activity 2—BPDU Address Analysis

Materials: A computer with an active network connection to a switch and packet capture software (Wireshark)

1. Using the BPDU captured in Activity 1, examine the addressing used. Look for the following:

2. Source and destination MAC addresses

3. Root bridge MAC address

4. Transmit Bridge MAC address.

5. How are these related to each other? How are they used?

Activity 3—Looping the Switch Back to Itself

Materials: Managed Switch

1. Prior to starting this activity, determine what you are going to do and try to determine what will happen with this loop.

2. Using an Ethernet cable, loop one port on the switch to another.

3. What happens to the link lights?

4. In the management interface, what is the status of the ports? Are any blocked? If so, which one and why? Be very specific in your answer.

Activity 4—Looping Switches Together

Materials: Two or three managed switches, a computer capable of capturing packets

1. This activity assumes access to a collection of switches. Two will be sufficient for the experiments.

2. As in Activity 3, try to determine what will happen when the loop is created. Be very specific about what will happen and why.

3. Connect the 2 or 3 switches in a line. Which switch is the root? What will the BPDU look like at a point farthest from the root? Consider the four fields of the comparison algorithm.

4. Connect the switches in a loop. What port will be blocked? Why? What will the changes be to the BPDUs on each segment of the network?

Activity 5—Removing the Loop

Materials: Two or three managed switches, a computer capable of capturing packets

1. Using the topology from Activity 4, remove the physical loop you created.
2. How long does it take for the blocked port to move to the forwarding state?
3. What happens if you change the switch priorities on one of the nonroot switches? How long does it take for the effect to be reflected in the network topology and BPDUs?

CHAPTER 4

VLANs and Trunking

The move from hubs (shared networks) to switched networks was a big improvement. Control over collisions, increased throughput, and the additional features offered by switches all provide ample incentive to upgrade infrastructure. But Layer 2 switched topologies are not without their difficulties. Extensive flat topologies can create congested broadcast domains and can involve compromises with security, redundancy, and load balancing. These issues can be mitigated through the use of virtual local area networks, or VLANs. This chapter provides the structure and operation of VLANs as standardized in IEEE 802.1Q. This discussion will include trunking methods used for interconnecting devices on VLANs.

Problem: Big Broadcast Domains

With any single shared media LAN segment, transmissions propagate through the entire segment. As traffic activity increases, more collisions occur and transmitting nodes must back off and wait before attempting the transmission again. While the collision is cleared, other nodes must also wait, further increasing congestion on the LAN segment.

The left side of Figure 4-1 depicts a small network in which PC 2 and PC 4 attempt transmissions at the same time. The frames propagate away from the computers, eventually colliding with each other somewhere in between the two nodes as shown on the right. The increased voltage and power then propagate away from the scene of the collision. Note that the collision does not continue past the switches on either end. These are the boundaries of the *collision domain*. This is one of the primary reasons for switches replacing hubs. Hubs (and access points) simply do not scale well as network traffic increases.

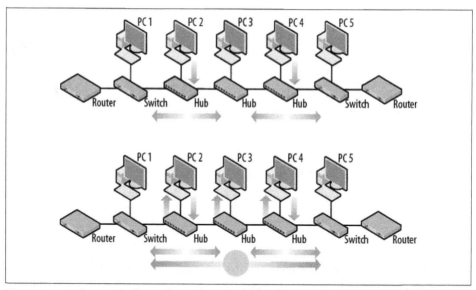

Figure 4-1. Before and after collision

The use of switches at Layer 2 eliminates much of the scaling problem because they filter out problems such as collisions. Instead, transmissions are now governed by the behavior of the switches and the broadcast domain. A *broadcast domain* defines the area over which a broadcast frame will propagate. For example, an ARP request issued by PC 3 results in a broadcast frame that propagates through the switches all the way to the routers as shown in Figure 4-2. A broadcast frame has the broadcast address (FF-FF-FF-FF-FF-FF) as the destination MAC.

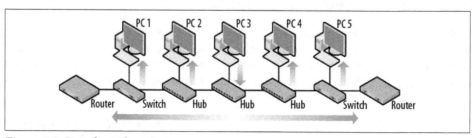

Figure 4-2. Broadcast domain

With the improved performance and filtering resulting from the use of switches, there is a temptation to create large Layer 2 topologies and add lots of nodes, but this creates a large broadcast domain. The problem is that all devices on a network (computers, printers, switching equipment, etc.) generate broadcast and multicast frames that traverse the entire broadcast domain, competing with data traffic for bandwidth. Much of this traffic is for management of the network and includes protocols for address resolution (ARP), dynamic host configuration (DHCP), spanning tree (STP), and an assortment of Windows tasks. Figure 4-3 illustrates the potential difficulty. Assume that PC1 has generated the following requests: ARP, Windows registration, and DHCP.

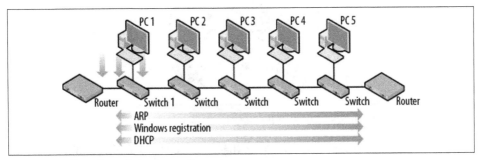

Figure 4-3. Broadcast frame growth

Because all of the requests use a broadcast frame, as they are received at Switch 1, the frames are forwarded in all directions. As the other switches in the topology follow suit, the frames traverse the entire network and are received at all other nodes and the routers.

As the number of network nodes increases, the amount of overhead also increases. Each switch might be connected to dozens of nodes, with each node generating the several broadcast frames. If enough traffic is created, even a switched network can have poor performance. Deploying VLANs can help solve this problem by breaking up the broadcast domain and separating the traffic.

What Is a VLAN?

A virtual local area network (VLAN) is a logical grouping of ports which is independent of location. A single VLAN (and the nodes connected in a single VLAN) will behave in the same way as if it was a separate Layer 3 network. VLAN membership need not be limited to sequential ports or even ports on the same switch. Figure 4-4 depicts a very common deployment in which nodes are connected to a switch and the switch is connected to a router. Looking at the left side, the automatic assumption would be that all of the nodes are on the same IP network since they all connect to the same router interface.

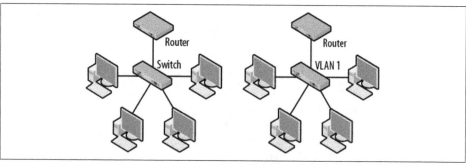

Figure 4-4. Basic switch and VLAN topology

What is not obvious from the topology on the left is that by default, all of these nodes are actually part of the same VLAN. So, another way to think about this topology is based on the VLAN as shown on the right. For example, with Cisco devices the default VLAN is VLAN 1. This is also called the management VLAN. Its initial configuration includes all ports as members and this reflected in the source address table or SAT. This table is often described as being used to forward frames to the proper Layer 2 port based on the destination MAC. With the introduction of VLANs, the source address table reflects the port to MAC address mapping on a per-VLAN basis resulting in more advanced forwarding decisions. Figure 4-5 displays the output from both the *show mac-address-table* and *show vlan* commands. All of the ports (Fa0/1 – Fa0/24) are in VLAN 1.

```
Switch#sh mac-address-table
          Mac Address Table
-------------------------------------------

Vlan    Mac Address       Type        Ports
----    -------------     --------    -----
 All    000c.85aa.ea40    STATIC      CPU
 All    0100.0ccc.cccc    STATIC      CPU
 All    0100.0ccc.cccd    STATIC      CPU
 All    0100.0cdd.dddd    STATIC      CPU
   1    000a.f458.6c58    DYNAMIC     Fa0/24
   1    0013.f7d1.de9b    DYNAMIC     Fa0/24
   1    0013.f7d1.e016    DYNAMIC     Fa0/1
   1    0013.f7d2.06d5    DYNAMIC     Fa0/24
   1    0013.f7d2.06e1    DYNAMIC     Fa0/2
Total Mac Addresses for this criterion: 9
Switch#
Switch#show vlan

VLAN Name                             Status    Ports
---- -------------------------------- --------- -------------------------------
1    default                          active    Fa0/1, Fa0/2, Fa0/3, Fa0/4
                                                Fa0/5, Fa0/6, Fa0/7, Fa0/8
                                                Fa0/9, Fa0/10, Fa0/11, Fa0/12
                                                Fa0/13, Fa0/14, Fa0/15, Fa0/16
                                                Fa0/17, Fa0/18, Fa0/19, Fa0/20
                                                Fa0/21, Fa0/22, Fa0/23
```

Figure 4-5. Switch SAT and VLAN output

Another common topology can be seen in Figure 4-6 in which two switches are separated by a router. In this case, a group of nodes are connected to each switch. The nodes on a particular switch share a common IP addressing scheme. There are two networks, 192.168.1.0 and 192.168.2.0.

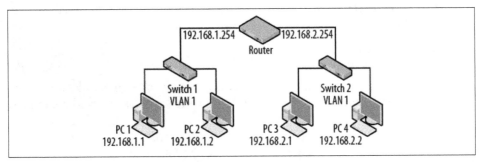

Figure 4-6. Router, switch and VLANs

Note that both of the switches have the same VLAN since, in the absence of any configuration changes, switches from the same vendor will have the same numbering convention. Nonlocal network traffic must be sent to the router for forwarding. Routers will not forward Layer 2 unicast, multicast and broadcast frames. VLANs provide a very similar logical topology in that nodes within a VLAN share a common addressing scheme and that nonlocal traffic (traffic destined for nodes on a different VLAN) must be sent to the router for forwarding. By creating an extra VLAN on one of the switches and removing the other, Figure 4-6 can now be redrawn as shown in Figure 4-7.

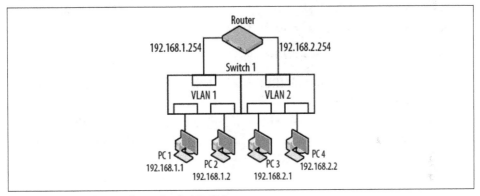

Figure 4-7. Single switch, multiple VLANs

A VLAN operates in the same way as a Layer 3 IP-based network. Thus, nodes on the 192.168.1.0 network must go to the router when trying to communicate with nodes on the 192.168.2.0 network *even though all of the computers are connected to the same switch*. In order to communicate between VLANs, routing functionality must be part of the topology. Layer 2 unicast, multicast and broadcast traffic will not cross VLAN boundaries, therefore traffic generated on VLAN 1 will not be seen by nodes on VLAN 2. Only the switch is aware of the VLANs. The nodes and the router have no idea that VLANs are in use—they are "non VLAN-aware." With the addition of the routing decision, Layer 3 functionality can now be leveraged for additional security settings, problem/traffic containment and load balancing.

The Effect of VLANs

Configuring a switch for multiple VLANs reduces the size of each broadcast domain. Therefore the amount of overhead traffic is lower which reduces bandwidth competition with data traffic. Stated another way, a node in a particular VLAN has less broadcast traffic with which to contend. Since switch forwarding behavior is based on MAC addresses stored in the source address table, the following rules apply:

- For known unicast destinations, the switch will forward the frame to the destination port only.

- For unknown unicast destinations, the switch will forward the frame to all active ports except the originating port. This is called flooding.

- For multicast and broadcast destinations, the switch will forward the frame to all active ports except the originating port.

However, the switch now has the additional requirement of considering the VLAN of the destination node. Referring to Figure 4-7, if PC1 were to issue an ARP request, instead of simply forwarding this frame to every port, the switch determines that the frame originated on VLAN 1. The result is that only PC2 and the leftmost router interface (192.168.1.254) actually see the frame.

Aims and benefits from the 802.1Q standard:

- VLANs are supported over all IEEE 802 LAN MAC protocols, over shared media LANs as well as point-to-point LANs.

- VLANs facilitate easy administration of logical groups of stations that can communicate as if they were on the same LAN. They also facilitate easier administration of moves, adds, and changes in members of these groups.

- Traffic between VLANs is restricted. Switches forward unicast, multicast, and broadcast traffic only on LAN segments that serve the VLAN to which the traffic belongs.

- As far as possible, VLANs maintain compatibility with existing switches and end stations.

- If all switch ports are configured to transmit and receive untagged frames (frames to/from non-VLAN aware devices), switches will work in plug-and-play

ISO/IEC 15802-3 mode. End stations will be able to communicate throughout the Bridged LAN.

VLAN Ports Do Not Need to be Continuous

Since VLANs are logical groupings of nodes that are independent of location, it does not matter where the nodes connect. Figure 4-8 demonstrates this concept. The topology in Figure 4-7 has been redrawn with the IP addresses of network nodes changed. To help with clarity, in this example VLAN 1 is also red and VLAN 2 is blue. Ports 1, 4 and 5 are part of red VLAN 1 while ports 2, 3 and 6 are part of the blue VLAN 2.

It is often the case that network technicians do not wish to rewire the topology every time that a new node is connected. So, a host may simply be connected to any available port and the port is then assigned to a particular VLAN. The critical idea is that the behavior is the same whether or not the ports are right next to each other. Thus, PC1 and PC4 can communicate directly with each other but must use the router to get to PC2 and PC3. Frames issued on red VLAN 1 will not be seen by nodes on blue VLAN 2.

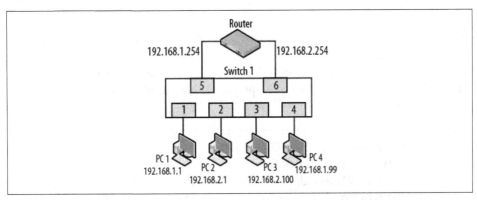

Figure 4-8. Noncontinuous VLANs

Types of VLANs

There are two types of VLANs: static and dynamic. Both of these types can be used to cover small or large geographic areas. The type of VLAN that has been discussed thus far (a single switch divided into multiple VLANs) is called a static VLAN. Membership is largely determined by geographical location and to which port a particular node is connected. Most of the nodes in a particular VLAN are likely to be located in the same building, floor or set of offices. These VLANs can also be thought of as having local membership.

Figure 4-9 depicts an example of how nodes and VLANs might be arranged. PC1 and PC2 are physically located in the same part of the building and so are assigned to the same VLAN. The same is true for PC3 and PC4. It is likely that they serve users from the same department. This type of topology is configured manually by a network administrator who assigns ports on the switch to a particular VLAN. Again, the nodes and router do not have any knowledge about the VLANs.

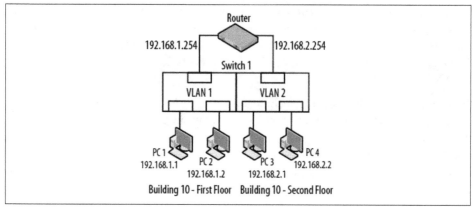

Figure 4-9. Static VLAN, local membership

Most VLANs are configured with static membership. In topologies like those described above, nodes remain connected to the same port and so there is no need to change VLAN membership. The desktop computer is usually associated with an office desk or cubicle assigned to an employee so there is little need to worry that the machine will move.

There are times when nodes do move around. There may be a need to access different resources. Ports may be used by different departments at different times or differing levels of security may be required. Dynamic VLANs are more appropriate for these situations. Dynamic VLANs allow nodes to move around without altering VLAN membership. This means that as they plug into a particular port, the switch automatically configures the port for membership in the correct VLAN. A port that was configured for access in VLAN 1 for node A may now switch to VLAN 2 for node B. Consider the case in Figure 4-10. PC4, now a laptop, is moved from a port in VLAN 2 to a port in VLAN 1.

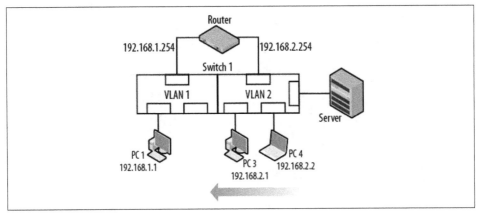

Figure 4-10. Moving from one VLAN to another

Case 1—DHCP

If DHCP has been deployed, when PC4 moves, it will simply obtain a new IP address on the new network, though this is not guaranteed. This may actually be the most common behavior for nodes connecting to a network on a particular VLAN. However, if services or security measures are in place and the organizations' policy is to maintain separation between VLANs, then this configuration may pose a problem—access to the server. Once on the new network, PC4 may no longer be able to reach the correct server or may require additional configuration to support the move.

Case 2—No DHCP

If the IP address of PC4 is statically configured, when it moves to the new location, its IP address will not match the network. It will no longer be able to reach the IP address of the gateway or the server. In this case, the node will not have any connectivity at all.

Solution: Dynamic VLANs

However, if the switch is smart enough to recognize that PC4 has now moved to a new port, it may be able to automatically repair the connection. Once PC4 connects to the new port, it will generate traffic. Upon receipt of a frame from PC4, the switch completes a database look up to determine the VLAN membership and then will assign the port to the proper VLAN. Once this has occurred, PC4 will be able to communicate just as it did before the move. The new topology would look like the one shown in Figure 4-11. The node will not even have to change its IP address.

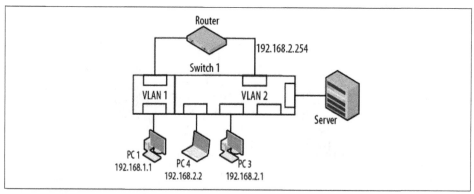

Figure 4-11. New dynamic VLAN topology

But how does the switch know? The most common method of assigning dynamic VLAN membership is via the MAC address. As soon as the node generates a single frame, the switch completes the MAC address query and then assigns the port. The nodes still do not have any knowledge that VLANs are used. VLAN membership can also be based on other criteria or tied to authentication schemes such as 802.1X.

VLANs Between Switches

So far, the VLANs discussed have been deployed on a single switch. The question arises: "What happens if multiple switches are part of the overall network fabric? How does it work?" The answers depend on the switch configurations. A default topology is shown in Figure 4-12 where two switches have simply been powered up and several nodes connected. The default VLAN for both switches (if we assume Cisco devices) will be VLAN 1. This also means that the connections running between the switches will also be in VLAN 1. The router provides the egress point for all nodes.

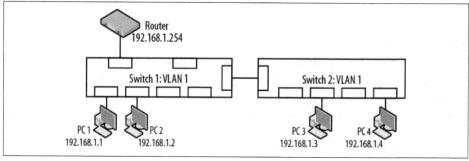

Figure 4-12. Multiple switches, single VLAN

In this default topology, the nodes will not have any trouble connecting to each other because the source address tables on the switches will show that they are all in the same VLAN. This will allow the unicast, multicast and broadcast traffic to flow freely. Note also that the nodes exist on the same IP network. The connection between the switches uses either a crossover cable or an uplink port.

Problems occur when new VLANs are created as shown in Figure 4-13. Since the VLANs create Layer 3 boundaries around the ports connected to the hosts, they are not able to communicate.

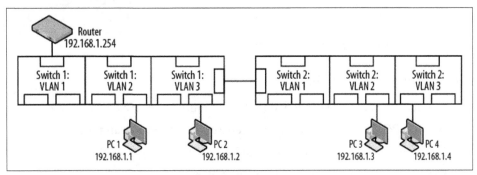

Figure 4-13. Problems with additional VLANs

Examining Figure 4-13, there are a couple of problems. First, the computers are all on the same IP network, despite being connected to different VLANs. Secondly, the router is isolated from all of the nodes because it is in VLAN 1. Lastly, the switches are interconnected via different VLANs. Each of these would create communication difficulties, but taken together, there is little or no communication between network elements.

It is often the case that a switch may be full or that nodes within the same administrative unit are geographically separated from each other. In these cases, a VLAN can be extended to neighboring switches through the use of a trunk line. Trunks will be discussed in greater detail later in this chapter, but for now it is sufficient to say that trunks connecting separate switches can, among other things, convey VLAN information between network devices. Figure 4-14 suggests several changes to repair the items noted in Figure 4-13.

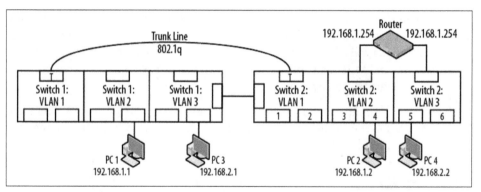

Figure 4-14. Topology repaired with trunking

Repairs to the topology include:

- PC1 and PC2 have been assigned to the 192.168.1.0 network and VLAN 2
- PC3 and PC4 have been assigned to the 192.168.2.0 network and VLAN 3
- The router interfaces are connected to VLANs 2 and 3.
- The switches are interconnected via trunk lines.

Note that while the trunk ports appear to be in VLAN 1, they are not as denoted by the letter T. Trunk ports do not have membership in any particular VLAN. Now that the VLANs persist across multiple switches, the nodes can be physically located anywhere and still be members of the same VLAN. When several switches are configured with VLANs and ports maintain their VLAN membership, the architecture is referred to as "end-to-end" and "static." It is not uncommon to have these switches located in different wiring closets, or even different buildings. Switches in the same closet can also be interconnected via trunk lines.

What is a Trunk?

Generally, there are two ways to look at a trunk line. In telephony, the term trunk refers to connections between offices or distribution facilities. These connections represent an increased number of lines or time division multiplexed connections as shown in Figure 4-15. Examples include 25 pair bundles or T carriers.

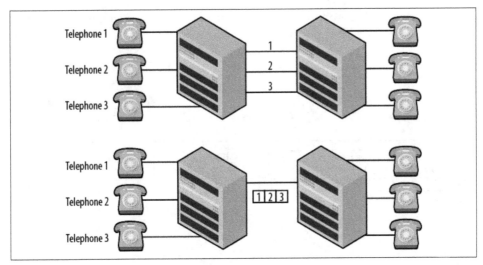

Figure 4-15. Telephone lines and trunks

For data networking, trunks have little to do with increasing the number of connections between switches. The primary use of a trunk line in a data network is to convey VLAN information. The trunk line shown in Figure 4-14 carries VLAN and quality of service information for the participating switch.

When a trunk line is installed, a trunking protocol is used to modify the Ethernet frames as they travel across the trunk line. In Figure 4-14 the ports interconnecting the switches are trunk ports. This also means that there is more than one operational mode for switch ports. By default, all ports are called "access ports." This describes a port used by a computer or other end node to "access" the network. When a port is used to interconnect switches and convey VLAN information, the operation of the port is changed to a trunk. For example, on a Cisco switch the *mode* command would be used to make this change. Other vendors indicate that the port is now "tagged," indicating that a VLAN id will now be inserted into the frames. The 802.1Q standard also includes a provision for "hybrid" ports that understand both tagged and untagged frames. To be clear, nodes and routers are often unaware of the VLANs and use standard Ethernet or "untagged" frames. Trunk lines providing VLAN or priority values will be using "tagged" frames. An example of a tagged frame can be seen in Figure 4-17.

So, on the trunk ports, a trunking protocol is run that allows the VLAN information to be included in each frame as it travels over the trunk line. For configuration, there are generally two steps: converting the port to trunk mode and determining the encapsulation (trunking protocol) to be used.

Using Figure 4-16 we'll go through an example of two nodes communicating over a trunk line. There are several steps to the process (in addition to host routing) so Figure 4-16 is labeled based on the steps listed.

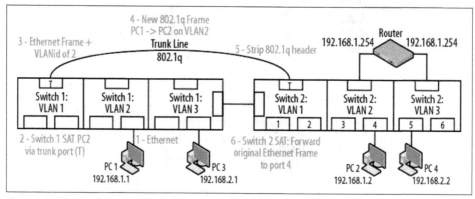

Figure 4-16. Trunking traffic between switches

PC1 sends traffic to PC2 after processing its host routing table. These nodes are in the same VLAN but they are connected to different switches. The basic process:

1. The Ethernet frame leaves PC1 and is received by Switch 1.

2. The Switch 1 SAT indicates that the destination is on the other end of the trunk line.

3. Switch 1 uses the trunking protocol to modify the Ethernet frame by adding the VLAN id.

4. The new frame leaves the trunk port on Switch1 and is received by Switch 2.

5. Switch2 reads the VLAN id and strips off the trunking protocol.

6. The original frame is forwarded to the destination (port 4) based on the SAT of Switch 2.

The packet shown in Figure 4-17 provides detail on this modification. In this particular case, the trunking protocol that has been used is IEEE 802.1Q. This frame is an ICMP echo request from PC1→PC2 and because it traverses the trunk line, the VLAN tag must be included so that Switch 2 knows how to properly forward the packet.

```
Ethernet II, Src: SmcNetwo_d1:dd:3d (00:13:f7:d1:dd:3d), Dst: SmcNetwo_d2:07:98 (00:13:f7:d2:07:98)
802.1Q Virtual LAN, PRI: 0, CFI: 0, ID: 2
    000. .... .... .... = Priority: Best Effort (default) (0)
    ...0 .... .... .... = CFI: Canonical (0)
    .... 0000 0000 0010 = ID: 2
    Type: IP (0x0800)
Internet Protocol, Src: 192.168.1.1 (192.168.1.1), Dst: 192.168.1.2 (192.168.1.2)
Internet Control Message Protocol
```

Figure 4-17. Ethernet frame with 802.1Q trunking

The Ethernet frame is intact but now has several additional fields such as the VLAN ID. In this case, the two computers communicating are on VLAN 2. The binary value of 0000 0000 0010 is shown. Note that the IP and ICMP headers have not been modified. However, because this is a change to the actual frame, the Cyclical Redundancy Check (CRC) at the end of the Ethernet frame must be recalculated. Trunking probably doesn't get as much attention as it should but, as soon as VLANs are configured on the switches, a trunking protocol must be used if the VLANs are to persist from one switch to another. Without a trunk, the nodes will probably all be on the same VLAN which can lead to the problems noted earlier. Trunks and VLANs are a vital part of standard topologies.

Trunking Protocol Standards

There are two trunking protocols used on modern communication networks: Inter-Switch Link (ISL) from Cisco and the aforementioned nonproprietary IEEE 802.1Q. Of the two, IEEE 802.1Q is the industry standard. Even Cisco switches now use IEEE 802.1Q (dot1q) by default.

IEEE 802.1Q

The IEEE 802.1Q standard is actually entitled "IEEE Standards for Local and Metropolitan Area Networks: Virtual Bridged Local Area Networks" and is primarily concerned with VLANs themselves. The trunking protocol or "tagging" of frames is discussed in latter sections of 802.1Q. As a reminder, IEEE 802.1D is the standard for MAC Access Control Bridges upon which Layer 2 networks are constructed. Switch vendors adhere to both of these standards and then add enhancements such as management. The IEEE 802.1Q standard bases much of its language on documents such as the ISO/IEC 15802-3 standard for MAC bridges.

When using IEEE 802.1Q, a 4-byte header is inserted in between the Ethernet and IP headers. Per the 802.1D standard, it is inserted 12 bytes into the frame immediately following the source MAC address. Therefore, frame is actually changed. So, the Ethernet type, which indicates the kind of encapsulated data, must also change. As an example, IP packets have an Ethertype value of 0800 but when running over a trunk it is changed to 8100 as shown in Figure 4-18.

```
Ethernet II, Src: SmcNetwo_d1:dd:3d (00:13:f7:d1:dd:3d), Dst: SmcNetwo_d2:07:98 (00:13:f7:d2:07:98)
⊞ Destination: SmcNetwo_d2:07:98 (00:13:f7:d2:07:98)
⊞ Source: SmcNetwo_d1:dd:3d (00:13:f7:d1:dd:3d)
  Type: 802.1Q Virtual LAN (0x8100)
802.1Q Virtual LAN, PRI: 0, CFI: 0, ID: 2
Internet Protocol, Src: 192.168.1.1 (192.168.1.1), Dst: 192.168.1.2 (192.168.1.2)
Internet Control Message Protocol
```

Figure 4-18. Ethertype for IEEE 802.1Q

The 802.1Q header is straightforward and includes the following fields:

The tag protocol identifier (2-byte TPID)
The value of 8100 can be seen just before the highlighted hexadecimal.
The tag control information (2-byte TCI)

There are three ways that this information can be structured but those used in token ring and FDDI networks will not be covered here. The TCI includes the priority, Canonical Format Indicator and VLAN ID. The 2-byte hexadecimal TCI from Figure 4-18 is *20 65*.

Priority
Used in quality of service implementations, also called class of service. This is a three bit field with values ranging from 000 (0) to 111 (7). The default value is 0 though vendors recommend higher values for certain types of traffic. For example, VoIP traffic is typically set to binary 101 (base 10: 5). Figure 4-18 depicts a slightly elevated priority of 2. Figure 4-19 depicts prioritized traffic from another network. In this case, the priority is set to 111 (7).

Canonical Format Indicator (CFI)
This single bit field was used to indicate bit orders or flags for routing information associated with legacy protocols such as token ring and FDDI. Today, almost all switching is Ethernet. So, the field is almost never used and the value is typically 0.

VLAN ID
The last twelve bits are allocated for the VLAN ID for values ranging from 1 to 4095. The VLAN ID in binary is 1100101. This corresponds to VLAN 101 in base 10 numbers.

```
⊟ Ethernet II, Src: D-Link_b9:5c:15 (00:50:ba:b9:5c:15), Dst: D-Link_53:ff:c2 (00:50:ba:53:ff:c2)
  ⊞ Destination: D-Link_53:ff:c2 (00:50:ba:53:ff:c2)
  ⊞ Source: D-Link_b9:5c:15 (00:50:ba:b9:5c:15)
    Type: 802.1Q Virtual LAN (0x8100)
  ⊟ 802.1Q Virtual LAN
    111. .... .... .... = Priority: 7
    ...0 .... .... .... = CFI: 0
    .... 0000 0110 0101 = ID: 101
    Type: IP (0x0800)
⊞ Internet Protocol, Src: 192.168.16.2 (192.168.16.2), Dst: 192.168.16.1 (192.168.16.1)
⊞ Internet Control Message Protocol
```

Figure 4-19. Tagged frame with priority field

Inter-switch link (ISL)

As this is an older Cisco proprietary protocol, not much time will be spent on its description. Figure 4-20 shows an ISL tagged frame and illustrates a different approach to tagging. IEEE 802.1Q performs what is called "internal tagging" by inserting the VLAN header in between the Ethernet and IP headers. This also forces a recalculation of the frame CRC. ISL prepends the tag. The ISL header is also considerably larger than the 802.1Q header and does not provide for priority handling. Modern Cisco equipment uses IEEE 802.1Q as the default trunking and tagging protocol.

```
ISL
⊞ Destination: ISL-Frame_00 (01:00:0c:00:00:00)
  Source: Cisco_da:55:40 (00:05:32:da:55:40)
  Length: 130
  DSAP: 0xAA
  SSAP: 0xAA
  Control: 0x3
  HSA: 0x00000c
  0000 0000 0000 010. = VLAN ID: 2
  .... .... .... ...0 = BPDU/CDP/VTP: No
  Index: 0
Ethernet II, Src: Cisco_da:55:40 (00:05:32:da:55:40), Dst: Cisco_da:6c:61 (00:05:32:da:6c:61)
Internet Protocol, Src: 192.168.1.1 (192.168.1.1), Dst: 192.168.1.2 (192.168.1.2)
Internet Control Message Protocol
```

Figure 4-20. ISL tagged frame

Pruning

While a particular VLAN may extend well beyond a single switch and may exist throughout much of a topology, it is not necessary to have it persist on every switch.

In Figure 4-21, VLANs 1, and 2 exist on both Switches. But VLAN 3(yellow) only exists on Switch 1. It doesn't make much sense to have the traffic for VLAN 3 forwarded to Switch 2. The benefits include a reduction in trunk line traffic and potential security improvement through this pruning capability, especially with static topologies. Switch 1 *prunes* VLAN 3 traffic (prevents passage) out its trunk port.

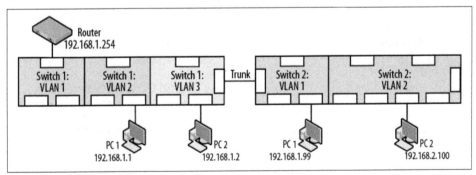

Figure 4-21. Pruning example

Vendors have different approaches to pruning; some permit all VLANs by default (Cisco), others deny all VLANs by default. Regardless of vendor, it is always a good idea to examine the trunking configuration and determine the best approach for tagged frames and untagged frames and pruning.

VLAN Design Considerations

VLANs create boundaries that can isolate nodes or traffic so some thought should go into the design of a multi-VLAN topology. The general question to ask is "Who is talking to whom and what are they trying to get done?" The following list provides some guidelines.

Scaling considerations
How big is the network and how far does the traffic have to go?

Traffic patterns
Over what pathways do packets/frames travel?

Applications
Why is the traffic there? What are the hosts trying to do?

Network management
Is SNMP or some other management protocol running? How will you get to all of the nodes?

Group commonality
What do nodes have in common? Are there shared resources or traffic patterns?

IP addressing scheme
What does the IP address space look like? How many nodes will be in each VLAN?

Physical location
Do the nodes occupy the same office? Floor? Building?

Static versus Dynamic
Are the nodes moving around or are they stationary?

End-to-end versus Local VLANs
Are there nodes outside of a location that should be part of the same VLAN?

80/20 versus 20/80 traffic flow pattern
Is a majority of the flow internal or external? Is this pattern changing?

Common security requirements
Are these nodes servers? End nodes? Wireless? Do the nodes represent vital company resources? Are these public facing machines?

Quality of service
    Are there quality of service concerns?

In addition to these general questions, there are other good practices to follow that will help reduce exposure to security risk and protect vital network resources.

- Wireless should be in its own VLAN. Since wireless is a shared media, all broadcast and much of the multicast traffic coming from the switch will be shared as well. In addition, any flooded unicast traffic will be seen by all wireless nodes. Creating a VLAN for wireless nodes narrows the traffic that they can see. In addition, a potential attack via wireless will have a boundary to cross before reaching other portions of the network.

- VoIP elements should also be in their own VLAN. This is as much for quality of service as it is for protection. Anytime real time voice traffic has to compete for bandwidth, there is the potential for performance degradation. Security concerns are to some extent relieved by the VLANs as well. Tools such as Wireshark can not only capture but decode and play voice traffic so it is important to keep voice traffic separated wherever possible.

- Other important network devices such as servers or even users of sensitive data should be placed in their own VLANs. In addition to the reasons already stated, many vendors have features that allow the creation of VLAN specific security and QoS policies.

Security Considerations

This chapter has discussed the need to isolate traffic. Organizations need not forward data to every single port because this is inefficient and represents a security risk due to potential eavesdroppers. There are several configuration items that should be part of any VLAN deployment checklist. One of the biggest challenges associated with deploying a network device is understanding default behavior. Switches and routers are no different, particularly as the number of features increases.

One of these items is the default configuration mode of the ports on the switch. Most switch ports will wind up connected to computers and so will act as *access* ports. What is not obvious is that on many devices, the default configuration is not *access*, but *dynamic*. This means that the port is willing to negotiate the mode of operation. If two switches are connected together, and one switch is configured with a trunk port, it is often the case that it will generate dynamic trunking protocol messages. Once received, this message may cause the second switch to convert its port to a trunk *automatically*. This is shown in Figure 4-22.

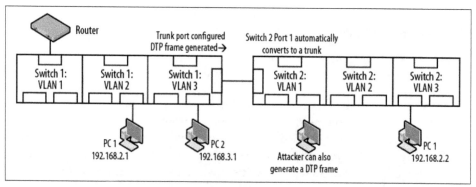

Figure 4-22. Dynamic port configuration security exposure

Initially this auto-configuration sounds convenient but what is to stop an attacker from generating the same message and converting a port in the same way? The attacker's port will then receive broadcast, multicast and flooded unicast traffic for all VLANs not pruned. In addition to allowing the attacker to learn more about the network, it also means that the attacker may be able to generate tagged frames that will be delivered over the entire network. Whenever possible, dynamic configuration should be turned off.

In addition to pruning for proper VLAN boundaries and the default configurations of the ports, it may be prudent to add a couple of additional configuration changes. Unused ports can be collected into a "deadend VLAN" that is not routed and is pruned from the network. Anyone connecting to a port in this VLAN will be isolated. In addition, many vendors offer security enhancements to ports such as authorized MAC addresses and restricting the number of MAC addresses allowed. When invalid MAC addresses are seen on the port, the port will automatically be shutdown or disabled.

Reading

IEEE 802.1Q standard is actually entitled "IEEE Standards for Local and Metropolitan Area Networks: Virtual Bridged Local Area Networks"
ISO/IEC 15802-3 ANSI/IEEE Std 802.1D Information technology—Telecommunications and information exchange between systems—Local and metropolitan area networks—Common specifications—Part 3: Media Access Control (MAC) Bridges

Summary

VLANs are a basic tool for creating network boundaries. While they can create challenges regarding the forwarding of traffic, they can be a powerful tool for handling security and quality of service concerns. This chapter discussed the operation of VLANs and the methods used for propagating VLANs throughout a larger topology. When deploying VLANs and trunks, there are several design considerations to take into account. One must address the basic questions of "Who is talking to whom and why?" As topologies and the VLANs grow, so does the complexity. It is important to review the default operation and configuration of network elements in order to ensure that locally created configurations do not place the network at risk.

Review Questions

1. Broadcast frames will continue to propagate until they reach a routed interface.

   a. TRUE

   b. FALSE

2. Broadcast and multicast traffic will cross VLAN boundaries but unicast traffic will not.

   a. TRUE

   b. FALSE

3. By default, all hosts are connected to the same VLAN.

   a. TRUE

   b. FALSE

4. Hosts do not usually know to what VLAN they are connected.

   a. TRUE

   b. FALSE

5. In a contemporary data network, the primary used of a trunk line is to convey VLAN information.

   a. TRUE

   b. FALSE

6. While they are both part of a switch, the source address table and the VLANs are not integrated in any way.

   a. TRUE

   b. FALSE

7. Which of the following is the industry standard trunking protocol?

a. ISL

b. IEEE 802.1

c. VLANs

8. Pruning is the practice of preventing unauthorized access to trunk lines.

a. TRUE

b. FALSE

9. Dynamic port mode is a security risk because by default attackers can see all unpruned VLAN traffic.

a. TRUE

b. FALSE

10. Services such as VoIP and wireless users should be placed in their own VLANs.

a. TRUE

b. FALSE

Review Answers

1. TRUE

2. FALSE

3. TRUE

4. TRUE

5. TRUE

6. FALSE

7. B

8. FALSE

9. FALSE

10. TRUE

Lab Activities

Activity 1—Setting Up a Local VLANs

Materials: A VLAN capable switch and a router. Note: A home gateway may be used if it can be converted to a router to avoid confusion over the NAT operation.

Note: The goal of this particular activity is simply to understand the basic configuration necessary for routing between VLANs without trunks, as shown in Figure 4-23.

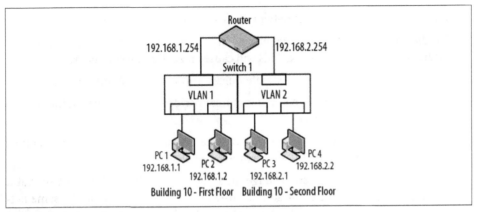

Figure 4-23. Activity 1

1. On the switch create a pair of VLANs.

2. Add a host to teach VLAN and determine the IP addressing scheme. As an example one VLAN might use 192.168.1.0 and the other 192.168.2.0. Handy Cisco command: `switchport access vlan X`.

3. Connect a router interface to each of the VLANs and assign the proper IP addressing. At this point, the nodes on different networks should be able to successfully PING each other.

Activity 2—VLANs and the SAT

Materials: A VLAN capable switch and a router.

1. Once the topology from activity 1 is complete, PING between all of the nodes and router interfaces.

2. On the switch, examine the source address (MAC address) table. Handy Cisco command: show mac-address-table

3. Compare this table to one in which all of the nodes are in the same VLAN.

4. Using the information in the SAT and the routing table of the router, develop a step by step procedure for forwarding packets from one computer to the other.

Activity 3—What Can You See?

Materials: A VLAN capable switch, a router and Wireshark.

During this activity, the goal is to determine how far traffic in one VLAN will travel and if it can be seen on another VLAN on the same switch.

1. Start a capture on one of the network hosts in one of the VLANs.

2. In the other VLAN, generate broadcast traffic by "PINGing" an unused IP address on the same network. This will cause an ARP request to be transmitted.

3. From this same source host, generate unicast traffic by "PINGing" the router.

4. It turns out that Windows-based computers periodically generate multicast traffic as they search for services.

5. Did the capture node in the other VLAN see the unicast, multicast or broadcast traffic that was created by the source host? The answer should be "NO."

6. As an additional experiment, change the IP address of the capture host so that it is on the same network as the source host. They should now be on the same network but in different VLANs. Attempt to PING between these two nodes. This attempt should fail because even though they are on the same network, the switch has separated them and the traffic is not allowed to cross the VLAN boundary.

Activity 4—Basic Trunking

Materials: A second VLAN capable switch, a trunk capable switch and a router.

1. Connect another switch to the topology already constructed.

2. On the new switch create the same VLANs.

3. Move one host into each VLAN. If you have a shortage of computers, it is sufficient to place one in a VLAN on the first switch and a second in the other VLAN on the new switch, as shown in Figure 4-24.

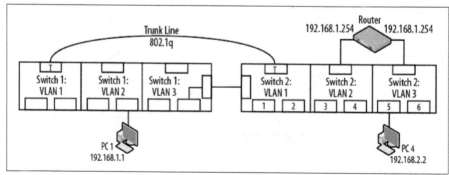

Figure 4-24. Activity 4

4. On each switch, configure as trunks the ports used to interconnect the two switches. Handy Cisco commands: switchport mode trunk, switchport trunk encapsulation dot1q

5. At this point, the network hosts should be able to PING each other.

6. As an additional experiment, explore the capabilities of the switches and attempt to set up a host capable of capturing the traffic running over the trunk. This is typically done with a span, mirror or monitor port. The goal is to examine the IEEE 802.1Q tags used on the trunk. Handy Cisco command: monitor session.

CHAPTER 5

Routing Information Protocol

Of course, in order to define which route is best, we have to have some way of measuring goodness.

—RFC 1058

The Routing Information Protocol, or RIP, is an interior, distance vector protocol for small networks. It is defined in IETF RFCs 1058, 1388 and 1723. It was one of the first routing protocols used on the Internet. This protocol has been through two versions in order to handle classless address spaces. This chapter covers the protocol construction, operation and the content via packet capture. RFCs updating RIP to version 2 are circa 1998. Even at that time it was often held that RIP was an inferior routing protocol that had already had its fifteen minutes of fame. However, RIP still had fans. Quoting from RFC 2453:

> With the advent of OSPF and IS-IS, there are those who believe that RIP is obsolete. While it is true that the newer IGP routing protocols are far superior to RIP, RIP does have some advantages. Primarily, in a small network, RIP has very little overhead in terms of bandwidth used and configuration and management time. RIP is also very easy to implement, especially in relation to the newer IGPs.

> Additionally, there are many, many more RIP implementations in the field than OSPF and IS-IS combined. It is likely to remain that way for some years yet. Given that RIP will be useful in many environments for some period of time, it is reasonable to increase RIP's usefulness. This is especially true since the gain is far greater than the expense of the change.

And this was prior to the implementation of RIPv2. RIP has since been included in other standards such as the High Assurance Internet Protocol Encryptor Interoperability Standard or HAIPE IS. Additionally, with RFCs 2082 and 4822, work has been done to improve the security of RIPv2. These efforts would indicate that RIPv2 has some life left. However, even in the absence of worldwide domination, RIP stands as a pretty good reference and learning environment for routing.

Version 1 Versus Version 2

RIP has been around a long time. While successful, it was not without problems and RIP version 1 has been superseded by RIP version 2. RFC 1923 discusses the applicability, or lack of applicability of RIPv1. The problems with RIPv1 all stem from its classful nature or strict adherence to networks based on Class A, B and C sized networks. RIPv1 messages do not include network masks and so lack the flexibility of modern approaches to managing address space. To summarize RFC 1923, RIPv1:

- RIPv1 assumes the locally used mask is the mask for the entire set of networks.

- RIPv1 cannot be used with variable length subnetting, supernetting and classless interdomain routing.

In addition, RIPv1 is called a "simple distance vector" protocol which means that even with enhancements such as split horizon and poison reverse, it may have to use time consuming techniques such as count to infinity in order to converge. The RFC concludes that if we must use a distance vector protocol, use RIPv2 and consider activating its modest security features. This chapter will discuss both versions of the protocol in terms of packets since RIPv1 is the default. However, the clear recommendation is to use RIPv2. The ideas of split horizon, poison reverse and count to infinity will be covered later in this chapter.

Protocol Description

The story of RIP usually begins with RFC 1058 but the RFC actually an attempt to consolidate ideas that were already in use, one of which (Berkeley Unix "routed" using distance vector) was the defacto standard for routing at the time. But even in 1988 it was generally assumed that RIP would not be appropriate for routing across large internets. Instead, the approach would be that an autonomous system (AS) would use an interior gateway protocol (IGP) such as RIP and then some other routing protocol to communicate with other AS networks. To quote from RFC 1058:

> RIP was designed to work with moderate-size networks using reasonably homogeneous technology. Thus it is suitable as an IGP for many campuses and for regional networks using serial lines whose speeds do not vary widely.

RIP is a distance vector protocol. Distance vector protocols are usually described as implementing the Bellman-Ford algorithm to find the best pathways. But the class of protocols are previously defined in "Flow in Networks" by Ford and Fulkerson. While it has a long lineage dating back to Xerox networks, RIP is designed for IP routing. RIP is a routing protocol that uses table exchange to update neighboring routers. The idea is that each router will send its own routing table out active interfaces via the user datagram protocol (UDP). Figure 5-1 depicts the encapsulation used.

```
⊞ Ethernet II, Src: Cisco_da:5a:a0 (00:05:32:da:5a:a0), Dst: Broadcast (ff:ff:ff:ff:ff:ff)
⊞ Internet Protocol, Src: 192.168.1.254 (192.168.1.254), Dst: 255.255.255.255 (255.255.255.255)
⊞ User Datagram Protocol, Src Port: router (520), Dst Port: router (520)
⊞ Routing Information Protocol
```

Figure 5-1. RIP encapsulation

Routers receiving the information decide whether or not to update their own tables. Routers use the source IP address in the IP packet as the forwarding router. Recall from Chapter 1 that forwarding router IP addresses are critical for the next hop. Information improving either the prefix length or the metric will be saved. This assumes that the administrative distance will be the same on an "all RIP" network. This new network information may be part of future updates. Straight routing table exchange can create as many problems as the move to dynamic routing may solve. For this reason, RIP also includes several mechanisms to speed convergence and avoid loops including the techniques of split horizon, poisoning and count to infinity mentioned above.

RIP internets are limited in size to 15 hops. This means that as far as RIP is concerned, 16 is infinity or unreachable. Each network that is crossed has a value of 1 hop. This hop count is the "metric" used by RIP to measure distance. RIP does not consider any real time data such as cost, utilization or speed. Thus, every pathway is measured using the same standard. Routers receive RIP updates from directly connected neighbor routers. A router receiving an update will in turn send out its own update. Before a router can send an updated routing advertisement, it must increase the metric of all learned routes by 1. The new update will be sent out with the IP address of the new router. This IP address will be the "next hop" router entered into the neighbors' routing table and the metric will be the distance to the destination via that IP address.

Remember that a routing table entry retains information about the age of the information, the destination address, the next hop or gateway from the routers point of view, the local interface used to reach the next hop and the cost of the route. Using this information, a router can make a "distance vector" sort of decision regarding the viability of the route. Because this information is sent to neighboring routers, and any updates are also sent, it is possible to understand the entire collection of networks talking only to adjacent routers.

The administrative distance or protocol value assigned to RIP is 120. This information will appear in the routing table along with the prefix lengths and metrics.

Structure

As can be seen in Figure 5-2, RIPv1 packets have a simple structure. This particular packet was caught in the early configuration stage of the topology used in this chapter. At this point, the network was configured with RIP version 1 only.

```
⊞ Ethernet II, Src: Cisco_da:5a:a0 (00:05:32:da:5a:a0), Dst: Broadcast (ff:ff:ff:ff:ff:ff)
⊞ Internet Protocol, Src: 192.168.1.254 (192.168.1.254), Dst: 255.255.255.255 (255.255.255.255)
⊞ User Datagram Protocol, Src Port: router (520), Dst Port: router (520)
⊟ Routing Information Protocol
    Command: Response (2)
    Version: RIPv1 (1)
  ⊟ IP Address: 192.168.2.0, Metric: 1
      Address Family: IP (2)
      IP Address: 192.168.2.0 (192.168.2.0)
      Metric: 1
  ⊟ IP Address: 192.168.3.0, Metric: 2
      Address Family: IP (2)
      IP Address: 192.168.3.0 (192.168.3.0)
      Metric: 2

0000  ff ff ff ff ff ff 00 05  32 da 5a a0 08 00 45 c0   ........ 2.Z...E.
0010  00 48 00 00 00 00 02 11  f5 3f c0 a8 01 fe ff ff   .H...... .?......
0020  ff ff 02 08 02 08 00 34  b0 76 02 01 00 00 00 02   .......4 .v......
0030  00 00 c0 a8 02 00 00 00  00 00 00 00 00 00 00 00   ........ ........
0040  00 01 00 02 00 00 c0 a8  03 00 00 00 00 00 00 00   ........ ........
0050  00 00 00 00 00 02                                  ......
```

Figure 5-2. RIPv1 packet

Command

A 1-byte field that describes the message type. A request asks for a routing table and a response contains the routing table of the router. There are a couple of other messages defined but these are now obsolete.

Version

This is also a single byte allocated to the flavor of RIP being used.

Zero

Following the version field and the address family identifier, there are "must-be-zero fields." These are 2 bytes in length. An 8 byte must-be-zero field follows the actual IP address of the destination network.

Each entry in the routing table is given space for information about the network and its metric. The hex for the 192.168.2.0 network is shown in Figure 5-3.

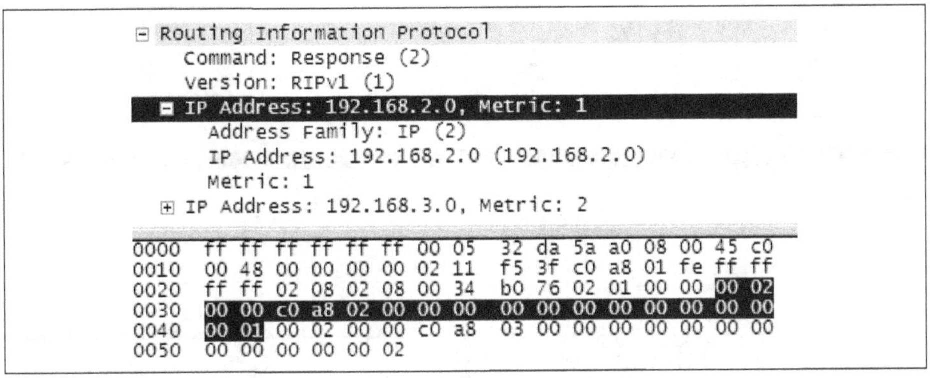

```
☐ Routing Information Protocol
    Command: Response (2)
    Version: RIPv1 (1)
  ☐ IP Address: 192.168.2.0, Metric: 1
      Address Family: IP (2)
      IP Address: 192.168.2.0 (192.168.2.0)
      Metric: 1
  ⊞ IP Address: 192.168.3.0, Metric: 2

0000  ff ff ff ff ff ff 00 05  32 da 5a a0 08 00 45 c0
0010  00 48 00 00 00 00 02 11  f5 3f c0 a8 01 fe ff ff
0020  ff ff 02 08 02 08 00 34  b0 76 02 01 00 00 00 02
0030  00 00 c0 a8 02 00 00 00  00 00 00 00 00 00 00 00
0040  00 01 00 02 00 00 c0 a8  03 00 00 00 00 00 00 00
0050  00 00 00 00 00 02
```

Figure 5-3. Hex example for network 192.168.2.0

Address Family ID (AFI)

This value indicates that type communication protocol used on the current network. While there is room for other protocols to be listed, no other values were defined in RFC 1058. The AFI for IP is 2.

IP address

This is the IP address for the destination network in the routing table. In the hexadecimal example, the 192.168.2.0 network is c0 a8 20 00.

Metric

This is the distance to the destination network by hop count. In the example, the hop count is 1. This is a 4-byte field.

RIPv1 packets are limited to 512 bytes in total length. In the event of large routing tables, entries can be divided into multiple packets.

The structure of the RIPv2 packet shown in Figure 5-4 is similar, with the addition of a couple of fields for subnets. For consistency, this packet examines the same network address.

```
⊞ Ethernet II, Src: Cisco_da:5a:a0 (00:05:32:da:5a:a0), Dst: IPv4mcast_00:00:09 (01:00:5e:00:00:09)
⊞ Internet Protocol, Src: 192.168.1.254 (192.168.1.254), Dst: 224.0.0.9 (224.0.0.9)
⊞ User Datagram Protocol, Src Port: router (520), Dst Port: router (520)
⊟ Routing Information Protocol
     Command: Response (2)
     Version: RIPv2 (2)
     Routing Domain: 0
   ▣ IP Address: 192.168.2.0, Metric: 1
       Address Family: IP (2)
       Route Tag: 0
       IP Address: 192.168.2.0 (192.168.2.0)
       Netmask: 255.255.255.0 (255.255.255.0)
       Next Hop: 0.0.0.0 (0.0.0.0)
       Metric: 1
   ⊞ IP Address: 192.168.3.0, Metric: 2
   ⊞ IP Address: 192.168.4.0, Metric: 3

0000  01 00 5e 00 00 09 00 05  32 da 5a a0 08 00 45 c0   ..^.....2.Z...E.
0010  00 5c 00 00 00 00 02 11  15 22 c0 a8 01 fe e0 00   .\......."......
0020  00 09 02 08 02 08 00 48  0e 93 02 02 00 00 00 02   .......H........
0030  00 00 c0 a8 02 00 ff ff  ff 00 00 00 00 00 00 00   ................
0040  00 01 00 02 00 00 c0 a8  03 00 ff ff ff 00 00 00   ................
0050  00 00 00 00 00 02 00 02  00 00 c0 a8 04 00 ff ff   ................
0060  ff 00 00 00 00 00 00 00  00 03                     .......... ..
```

Figure 5-4. RIPv2 packet

The message format of the two versions is essentially the same with fields defined in RFC1058 remaining unchanged. Comparing the hexadecimal portion of the packets seen in Figure 5-3 and Figure 5-4 we can see that the same number of bytes has been assigned in each version. Changes to the global packet in RIPv2 include the version value and the routing domain field.

Routing domain

Along with the route tag for individual destinations, the RIP routing domain differentiates the current RIP set of networks from those learned from external protocols.

For the individual networks, netmask, route and next hop fields have been added.

Netmask

This is the mask of the destination network. There is some concern that this field may be misinterpreted by routers running RIPv1 so some care should be taken in a mixed version environment. Or, simply use RIPv2.

Route tag

The route tag field is an attribute used to identify a route that has been learned from an external source such as another IGP. The route did not originate from the current RIP set of networks.

Next hop

Normally a router receiving a RIP message uses the source IP address as the next hop for routing table entries. If this field has a value of 0.0.0.0, the router will use the source IP of the update for the next hop. There are times that there will be more than one pathway to the destination, in which case the source IP address and the next hop may not match. In all cases, the next hop address must be reachable from the network to which it was advertised.

A final note on the address family ID for RIPv2: RIPv2 allows for authentication of RIPv2 messages. Should the AFI be set to a value of FFFF, then the space allocated for the network destination (20 bytes) will be used for the authentication information. It will include a 2-byte authentication type and 16 bytes of authentication data.

Basic Operation

As discussed earlier, RIP uses table exchange to update its neighboring regarding reachable networks. The topology shown in Figure 5-5 will be used to step through the basic operation of RIP and some of the techniques used to optimize RIP for performance. Since RIPv1 should not be used, all of the examples discussed will use RIPv2. This topology has four networks. The IP addresses of the router interfaces are included. You probably recognize it from Chapter 1 and this discussion will start out the same way.

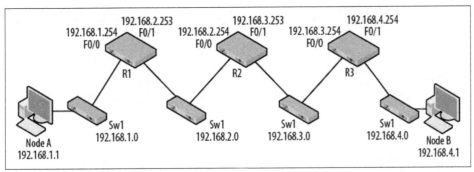

Figure 5-5. RIP topology

Initially the routers have been configured with their IP addresses but RIP is not currently running. The routing tables of the routers will only contain the directly connected routes. Each router is aware of the two networks for which is has interfaces. As a side note, the term "directly connected route" appears in the early RFCs and so is not necessarily a Cisco thing.

Table 5-1. Initial routing tables

R1	R2	R3
C 192.168.1.0 F0/0	C 192.168.2.0 F0/0	C 192.168.3.0 F0/0
C 192.168.2.0 F0/1	C 192.168.3.0 F0/1	C 192.168.4.0 F0/1

Moving from left to right, RIPv2 is configured on the routers. The Cisco commands are straightforward and in the case of R1 they would be as follows:

```
router rip
    version 2
    network 192.168.1.0
    network 192.168.2.0
```

Once these commands have been issued, RIP packets are sent from both interfaces on R1. However, even though R2 will see these packets, it will not update its routing table yet because it is not running RIP.

 Current versions of the Cisco IOS include the auto-summary command for RIP. This command is on by default and "summarizes subprefixes to the classful network boundary when crossing classful network boundaries." When routing between disconnected subnets, this command should be disabled to advertise the subnets.

The packets generated by R1 have a sequence and obey the split horizon rule as we will see. The first packets are shown in **Figure 5-6** and were captured on the 192.168.1.0 network.

12 192.168.1.254	224.0.0.9	RIPV2	9.996674	Request
57 192.168.1.254	224.0.0.9	RIPv2	17.821149	Response
58 192.168.1.254	224.0.0.9	RIPv2	18.041530	Response
71 192.168.1.254	224.0.0.9	RIPv2	47.610498	Response
78 192.168.1.254	224.0.0.9	RIPv2	75.023898	Response
83 192.168.1.254	224.0.0.9	RIPv2	102.317097	Response
89 192.168.1.254	224.0.0.9	RIPv2	129.021237	Response
95 192.168.1.254	224.0.0.9	RIPv2	154.547572	Response
102 192.168.1.254	224.0.0.9	RIPv2	180.903084	Response

Figure 5-6. RIPv2 startup exchange

For this output, packets for RIP were filtered so it looks like some packets were left out. The first packet sent is a request. This type of message asks for the neighboring router to provide its routing table. All of the packets came from R1 meaning that no response was received. Once R1 has been given a network to advertise, it generates the Response which contains R1s' routing table. These messages are depicted in Figure 5-7 and Figure 5-8.

```
Ethernet II, Src: Cisco_da:5a:a0 (00:05:32:da:5a:a0), Dst: IPv4mcast_00:00:09 (01:00:5e:00:00:09)
Internet Protocol, Src: 192.168.1.254 (192.168.1.254), Dst: 224.0.0.9 (224.0.0.9)
User Datagram Protocol, Src Port: router (520), Dst Port: router (520)
Routing Information Protocol
  Command: Request (1)
  Version: RIPv2 (2)
  Routing Domain: 0
⊞ Address not specified, Metric: 16
```

Figure 5-7. RIP request

```
Ethernet II, Src: Cisco_da:5a:a0 (00:05:32:da:5a:a0), Dst: IPv4mcast_00:00:09 (01:00:5e:00:00:09)
Internet Protocol, Src: 192.168.1.254 (192.168.1.254), Dst: 224.0.0.9 (224.0.0.9)
User Datagram Protocol, Src Port: router (520), Dst Port: router (520)
Routing Information Protocol
  Command: Response (2)
  Version: RIPv2 (2)
  Routing Domain: 0
⊞ IP Address: 192.168.2.0, Metric: 1
```

Figure 5-8. RIP response

Request messages can ask for all or part of a routing table and are processed entry by entry. In the event that there is only one destination entry with an AFI of 0 and a metric of 16, it is a request for the entire routing table. Response messages are sent whenever a request is received, during an update and during normal steady state operations.

Upon receipt of the response message, a router should validate the content of the message since this is information that may find its way into the routing table. For example, the source IP and format of the entries may be examined. At this point, the metrics and prefix lengths will be checked. If similar entries do not exist or if the response values are better, these routes will be installed. Timers will be updated (discussed below) and an update will be sent after increasing the metrics.

As R2 and R3 are configured with a similar set of commands (the networks will be different), the routing tables will be updated based on the received information. In addition, similar packets will be generated between routers. There is one variation from the traffic seen so far: once routers are aware of neighbors that are also running RIPv2, messages may be addresses directly to the neighboring router as shown in Figure 5-9.

No.	Time	Source	Destination	Protocol	Info
8	24.819831	192.168.2.253	224.0.0.9	RIPv2	Request
9	26.645505	192.168.2.253	224.0.0.9	RIPv2	Response
19	56.615399	192.168.2.253	224.0.0.9	RIPv2	Response
28	82.342309	192.168.2.253	224.0.0.9	RIPv2	Response
36	107.876897	192.168.2.253	224.0.0.9	RIPv2	Response
40	111.708452	192.168.2.254	224.0.0.9	RIPv2	Request
41	111.710017	192.168.2.253	192.168.2.254	RIPv2	Response
48	126.018395	192.168.2.253	224.0.0.9	RIPv2	Response
51	136.785207	192.168.2.253	224.0.0.9	RIPv2	Response
57	150.014075	192.168.2.254	224.0.0.9	RIPv2	Response
63	166.078039	192.168.2.253	224.0.0.9	RIPv2	Response
66	178.717430	192.168.2.254	224.0.0.9	RIPv2	Response

Figure 5-9. Packet exchange between R2 and R3

This set of packets starts from the beginning of our configuration with the first request (packet 8) sent after R1 was initially configured for RIP. Note the source IP address for this packet. Packet 40 was issued when R2 was configured for RIP. The resulting response packet (41) is addressed not to the RIPv2 multicast address but to the address of R3. Unicast IP addresses are used in association with the command/

response flags. Once this exchange has been completed, the routers return to the multicast address that will be read by routers that might be added to the network.

After R3 has also been configured for RIPv2, the routing tables will be fully populated with via the request/response packets as shown in Table 5-2.

Table 5-2. Routing tables fully populated after RIP

R1	R2	R3
C 192.168.1.0 F0/0	C 192.168.2.0 F0/0	C 192.168.3.0 F0/0
C 192.168.2.0 F0/1	C 192.168.3.0 F0/1	C 192.168.4.0 F0/1
R 192.168.3.0 [120/1] via 192.168.2.254	R 192.168.1.0 [120/1] via 192.168.2.253	R 192.168.1.0 [120/2] via via 192.168.3.253
R 192.168.4.0 [120/2] via 192.168.2.254	R 192.168.4.0 [120/1] via 192.168.3.254	R 192.168.2.0 [120/1] via via 192.168.3.253

All of the details in the routing tables are important but there are a couple of items worth pointing out. The administrative distance (AD) and metric are included in the brackets. RIP has an administrative distance of 120 and the metric is hop count. In our small network, the largest metric is 2. This information can be tracked to the source RIP packets like the ones seen in Figure 5-2 through Figure 5-4.

Another important detail is the forwarding router or next hop. In the routing table this is the "via" address. This address is learned from the source IP in the RIP packet. As can be seen, some of the RIP learned routes have the same forwarding address. For example, R3 sends traffic to 192.168.3.253 for both the 192.168.1.0 and 192.168.2.0 networks. This is as it should be this topology, but as we discussed in the Chapter 1 static routing section, this might be a candidate for a default route. The actual routing table for R1 is shown in Figure 5-10.

```
R1#
R1#show ip route
Codes: C - connected, S - static, I - IGRP, R - RIP, M - mobile, B - BGP
       D - EIGRP, EX - EIGRP external, O - OSPF, IA - OSPF inter area
       N1 - OSPF NSSA external type 1, N2 - OSPF NSSA external type 2
       E1 - OSPF external type 1, E2 - OSPF external type 2, E - EGP
       i - IS-IS, su - IS-IS summary, L1 - IS-IS level-1, L2 - IS-IS level-2
       ia - IS-IS inter area, * - candidate default, U - per-user static route
       o - ODR, P - periodic downloaded static route

Gateway of last resort is not set

R    192.168.4.0/24 [120/2] via 192.168.2.254, 00:00:13, FastEthernet0/1
C    192.168.1.0/24 is directly connected, FastEthernet0/0
C    192.168.2.0/24 is directly connected, FastEthernet0/1
R    192.168.3.0/24 [120/1] via 192.168.2.254, 00:00:13, FastEthernet0/1
R1#
```

Figure 5-10. R1 actual routing table

This output is obtained via the *show ip route* command. The router also applies a time to each dynamic entry. This helps keep track of the learned route age.

Timers

Like many protocols, RIP has a collection of timers that govern advertisements and the removal of old or bad routing information.

Response or Update timer
   During normal operations the routing process sends an unsolicited response message every 30 seconds in an effort to keep routing information fresh.

Route timeout or invalid timer
   After 180 seconds, any route that has not been refreshed via a response packet is considered bad and will be removed from the routing table. After this timer expires, the neighboring routers are informed that the route is bad via updates and the garbage collection timer is set. In the updates, the metric will be set to 16 for that destination.

Garbage collection or flush timer
   Upon the expiration of this timers, the route is finally expunged from the routing table. This is where implementations can be a little tricky. RFC 2453 specifies that this time should be set to 120 seconds. Cisco uses 60 seconds from the time that the timeout timer expires or 240 seconds in total age for the route entry. Cisco refers to a hold down timer which describes this time difference. However the documentation gives a 180 second value.

Addressing

Another important detail lies not in the routing table but in the addressing in the headers containing the RIP packet. Figure 5-11 depicts both RIPv1 and RIPv2 packets.

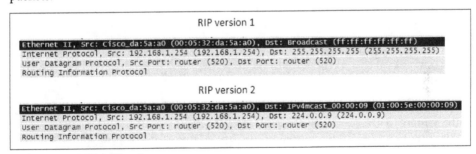

Figure 5-11. RIP addressing

Both packets have a source IP address that matches the transmitting interface of the router. However, RIP version 1 uses a limited broadcast address (255.255.255.255) as the destination while version 2 uses the reserved multicast address of 224.0.0.9. Layer 2 addressing often follows the Layer 3 addressing and so the RIPv1 packet uses a broadcast address for the Ethernet frame. The RIPv2 packet uses a multicast MAC address in the Layer 2 frame which is based on the Layer 3 IP multicast address.

While this chapter is not about multicast addressing, it is helpful to have a little background. Table 5-3 provides the general multicast addressing is outlined in RFC 3171:

Table 5-3. RFC 3171 multicast addressing

Address	Purpose
224.0.0.0 - 224.0.0.255	Local Network Control Block
224.0.1.0 - 224.0.1.255	Internetwork Control Block
224.0.2.0 - 224.0.255.0	AD-HOC Block
224.1.0.0 - 224.1.255.255	ST Multicast Groups
224.2.0.0 - 224.2.255.255	SDP/SAP Block
224.252.0.0 - 224.255.255.255	DIS Transient Block
225.0.0.0 - 231.255.255.255	RESERVED
232.0.0.0 - 232.255.255.255	Source Specific Multicast Block
233.0.0.0 - 233.255.255.255	GLOP Block
234.0.0.0 - 238.255.255.255	RESERVED
239.0.0.0 - 239.255.255.255	Administratively Scoped Block

Within the Local Network Control Block, there are several addresses that are near and dear to our hearts:

224.0.0.1
   All hosts multicast

224.0.0.2
   All routers multicast

224.0.0.5
   OSPF

224.0.0.9
   RIPv2

This address is assigned to RIPv2 by the RFC. Since routers are the only devices typically running RIPv2, other devices do not commonly process these packets. Multicasting can be an interesting challenge for network administrators because routers do not forward multicast packets, at least not without the help of protocol independent multicast (PIM) and Interior Group Management Protocol (IGMP). Fortunately RIPv2 packets are not actually forwarded. They are modified and retransmitted.

The last piece of addressing seen in the packet is actually the Layer 4 UDP port number. Both RIPv1 and RIPv2 use port 520. It is sometimes fun to watch new network administrators configuring access control lists or firewall rules. They are often so concerned with blocking unwanted UDP/TCP traffic, that RIP sometimes get filtered out, leaving the administrator to wonder why there are so many ICMP destination unreachable messages.

Advanced Operation

The basic operation of RIP can be understood by looking inside the packets. RIP packets can also be very instructive because of what they *do not* contain. In this section we will explore some of the extra rules built into the protocol to help avoid problems.

Split Horizon

If you were to observe two people introducing themselves for the first time, the conversation would probably go something like:

> Person 1: "Hi my name is Bob."
> Person 2: "Hi my name is Sally."

You would NOT expect to see:

> Person 1: "Hi my name is Bob."
> Person 2: "Hi your name is Bob."

Bob is already aware that his name is Bob, and so it is silly for Sally to tell Bob something that he just told her. The same is true for routers. Thus, routers should not tell their neighbors about networks the neighbor just advertised. Stated another way: do not advertise something out the same interface through which you learned it. There is also no reason to advertise the availability of a network to that network.

In Figure 5-12, R1 is directly connected to 192.168.1.0 and 192.168.2.0. R1 will not advertise the 192.168.1.0 network to the 192.168.1.0 network. The same rule applies to the R2 advertisement on 192.168.2.0 network.

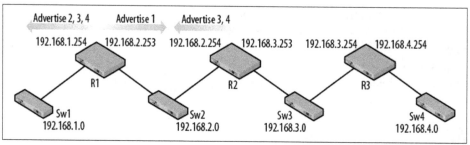

Figure 5-12. Split horizon advertising

We can continue to diagram the behavior seen between R1 and R2. R1 advertises network 192.168.1.0 to the right and networks 192.168.2.0, 192.168.3.0 and 192.168.4.0 to the left. R2 receives information about the 192.168.1.0 network from R1 and is directly connected to the 192.168.2.0 network. So, the advertisement going back to R1 contains only the 192.168.3.0 and 192.168.4.0 networks. Split horizon operation can be seen in the packets. Figure 5-13 displays the packets from R2 and R3, as seen on the 192.168.2.0 network.

```
Ethernet II, Src: Cisco_da:5a:a1 (00:05:32:da:5a:a1), Dst: IPv4mcast_00:00:09 (01:00:5e:00:00:09)
Internet Protocol, Src: 192.168.2.253 (192.168.2.253), Dst: 224.0.0.9 (224.0.0.9)
User Datagram Protocol, Src Port: router (520), Dst Port: router (520)
Routing Information Protocol
   Command: Response (2)
   Version: RIPv2 (2)
   Routing Domain: 0
⊞ IP Address: 192.168.1.0, Metric: 1

Ethernet II, Src: Cisco_28:02:80 (00:05:5e:28:02:80), Dst: IPv4mcast_00:00:09 (01:00:5e:00:00:09)
Internet Protocol, Src: 192.168.2.254 (192.168.2.254), Dst: 224.0.0.9 (224.0.0.9)
User Datagram Protocol, Src Port: router (520), Dst Port: router (520)
Routing Information Protocol
   Command: Response (2)
   Version: RIPv2 (2)
   Routing Domain: 0
⊞ IP Address: 192.168.3.0, Metric: 1
⊞ IP Address: 192.168.4.0, Metric: 2
```

Figure 5-13. Split horizon packet comparison

The IP addresses in these packets shows that they originate from R2 and R3. As we can see, the routers are obeying the rules of split horizon thus minimizing the size of the packets. But the real advantage to split horizon is to speed convergence because pathways to the destinations are clear.

What happens split horizon is not used? It turns out that there are some WAN connections that do not use it, but this is unusual. Turning off split horizon is usually bad. Using the same topology, let us assume that the routers are advertising all networks out every interface as shown in Figure 5-14. To help illustrate the scope of the problem, another router has been inserted but the same networks are used.

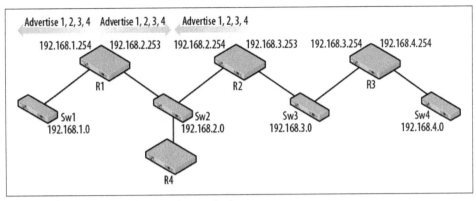

Figure 5-14. Advertisements without split horizon

Assume that R1 fails. R1 was the only path to the 192.168.1.0 network. However, R2 is advertising the availability of the 192.168.1.0 network. In fact, if R4 is not obeying split horizon, it will advertise the network as well. Remember that the 192.168.1.0 network is no longer available. So all of the routers in this topology will continue to believe that this network is still available and will keep it in their routing tables. One other possible scenario is that instead of losing R1, only the 192.168.1.254 interface failed. Again, R1 would cease to advertise the 192.168.1.0 network but upon hearing the advertisement from R2, would believe that the network was available from the opposite side of the topology. Split horizon is on by default to help prevent these convergence problems.

Poisoning

One of the other protections is route poisoning. In the event that a router configuration has changed or if equipment has failed, a router can poison a route so that the other routers know that the network(s) is no longer available. In order to poison a route, the router simply inserts a metric that is the equivalent of infinity. For RIP, this is 16.

What would happen if, in the same topology, 192.168.3.253 were to lose connectivity to the192.168.3.0 network? As long as R2 is still connected via 192.168.2.254, it could poison the 192.168.3.0 network? Routers receiving a poisoned packet know immediately that the pathway is bad and will remove it from their routing tables more quickly. A poisoned packet is shown in Figure 5-15.

```
Ethernet II, Src: Cisco_28:02:80 (00:05:5e:28:02:80), Dst: IPv4mcast_00:00:09 (01:00:5e:00:00:09)
Internet Protocol, Src: 192.168.2.254 (192.168.2.254), Dst: 224.0.0.9 (224.0.0.9)
User Datagram Protocol, Src Port: router (520), Dst Port: router (520)
Routing Information Protocol
  Command: Response (2)
  Version: RIPv2 (2)
  Routing Domain: 0
⊟ IP Address: 192.168.3.0, Metric: 16
    Address Family: IP (2)
    Route Tag: 0
    IP Address: 192.168.3.0 (192.168.3.0)
    Netmask: 255.255.255.0 (255.255.255.0)
    Next Hop: 0.0.0.0 (0.0.0.0)
    Metric: 16
```

Figure 5-15. Poisoned packet

If R2 had failed completely, the other routers in the topology would have to rely on
their timers to solve the problem. Poisoning of routes is done by default.

Poison Reverse

Poison reverse builds on the idea of poisoning but it is used during steady operation
to ensure that a no attempt is made to reach a network via an unsuitable or undesira-
ble path. In the same topology, with R1 advertising the availability of the 192.168.1.0
network, R2 will advertise the unreachability of the same network back to R1. The
effect is that if something were to happen to R1, the other routers have explicitly stated that they do not have a pathway to the lost networks as seen in Figure 5-16.

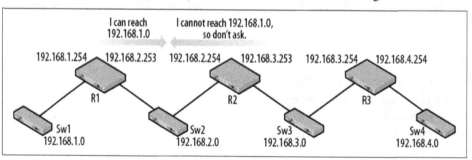

Figure 5-16. Poison reverse messaging

Poison reverse is not on by default so it has to be enabled on the router. However,
some routing implementations use poison reverse during the "discover your neighbors" phase. Figure 5-17 depicts the request and response packets flowing between R2
and R3 over the 192.168.2.0 network. While not part of normal RIP traffic, we can see
that immediately after learning of the 192.168.3.0 and 192.168.4.0 networks from R2,
R1 (192.168.2.253) uses poison reverse to inform R2 that it knows no other pathway
to these destinations. After this exchange, the RIP packets return to normal.

```
No.      Source              Destination       Protocol  Time         Info
    6 192.168.2.253      255.255.255.255      RIPv1     2.770111     Request
   11 192.168.2.253      255.255.255.255      RIPv1     7.452966     Response
   12 192.168.2.254      255.255.255.255      RIPv1     8.454928     Request
   25 192.168.2.254      255.255.255.255      RIPv1    11.567494     Request
   26 192.168.2.253      192.168.2.254        RIPv1    11.569164     Response
   32 192.168.2.254      255.255.255.255      RIPv1    19.131660     Response
   39 192.168.2.253      255.255.255.255      RIPv1    36.657248     Response

⊞ Frame 26: 106 bytes on wire (848 bits), 106 bytes captured (848 bits)
⊞ Ethernet II, Src: Cisco_da:5a:a1 (00:05:32:da:5a:a1), Dst: Cisco_28:02:80 (00:05:5e:28:02:80)
⊞ Internet Protocol, Src: 192.168.2.253 (192.168.2.253), Dst: 192.168.2.254 (192.168.2.254)
⊞ User Datagram Protocol, Src Port: router (520), Dst Port: router (520)
⊟ Routing Information Protocol
    Command: Response (2)
    Version: RIPv1 (1)
  ⊟ IP Address: 192.168.1.0, Metric: 1
      Address Family: IP (2)
      IP Address: 192.168.1.0 (192.168.1.0)
      Metric: 1
  ⊟ IP Address: 192.168.3.0, Metric: 16
      Address Family: IP (2)
      IP Address: 192.168.3.0 (192.168.3.0)
      Metric: 16
  ⊟ IP Address: 192.168.4.0, Metric: 16
      Address Family: IP (2)
      IP Address: 192.168.4.0 (192.168.4.0)
      Metric: 16
```

Figure 5-17. Poison reverse packet exchange

Triggered Updates

Whenever information regarding a routing table entry is changed, the router sends
out a RIP packet with just the new information immediately without waiting for the
update timer to expire. This quick RIP packet is called a triggered update. The rationale is that bad or changed information can propagate through the network much
faster than it would if the routers waited for the standard update timer to expire. In
addition, routers receiving a triggered update may in turn send out their own triggered updates. In this way a wave of fresh information will reach all points of the network. This helps speed up convergence time.

A couple of examples of triggered updates can be seen when the timers expire.
Assume that the link between R3 and S3 is lost which means that R2 will no longer
receive updates from R3 regarding the 192.168.4.0 network. After 180 seconds, the
route will be listed as possibly down in the routing table (shown in Figure 5-18) and a
triggered update will be sent advertising the 192.168.4.0 network with a metric of 16.
These triggered updates will propagate almost immediately across the entire network.
When another 60 seconds has passed, the route will be flushed from the routing table.
Another example is if the 192.168.4.254 interface were to be shutdown. In this case an
update would be sent immediately.

```
Gateway of last resort is not set

R    192.168.4.0/24 is possibly down, routing via 192.168.3.254, FastEthernet0/1
R    192.168.1.0/24 [120/1] via 192.168.2.253, 00:00:26, FastEthernet0/0
C    192.168.2.0/24 is directly connected, FastEthernet0/0
C    192.168.3.0/24 is directly connected, FastEthernet0/1
R2#
```

Figure 5-18. The 192.168.4.0 is possibly down

Triggered updates are also sent for improvements. When the 192.168.4.254 interface is brought back up, triggered updates are immediately sent and then propagated through the entire network. The routing tables of the neighboring routers are also updated immediately.

Count to Infinity

Count to infinity is another tool used to get the network out of a bind if there are no updates or poisoned routes. It is a last resort for times when there is a loss of connectivity or a device failure. For example, in Figure 5-16, if the link connecting R3 to Switch 3 were lost, R2 would be unaware of the problem since the link pulse would still be present for 192.168.3.253.

Figure 5-19 depicts a slightly more complex topology. A loop has been installed which results in routing information flowing in two directions. R4 advertises the availability of the 192.168.4.0 network and states that it is 1 hop away.

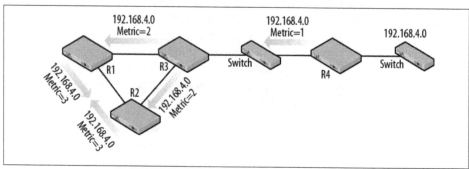

Figure 5-19. Count to infinity problem

R3 then advertises the same network after increasing the hop count by 1. Since R3 is connected to downstream routers R1 and R2, the same RIP information goes to both of them, though from different interfaces. Not to be undone, R1 and R2 both advertise the same network to each other after increasing the hop count. Upon receipt of these RIP packets, R1 and R2 discard the information because it is inferior to the routes they already possess.

But what happens upon catastrophic loss of R4? Even if we assume that split horizon, poisoning and triggered updates are all working fine, they are of little use to us. R3 has no idea that R4 is gone and so can only go by the information that it already learned and the RIP timers. Eventually R3 will purge the route and stop advertising. Once this happens, downstream routers R1 and R2 no longer have to worry about split horizon and *start advertising that the 192.168.4.0 network is available.* But the metric will have increased. R3 starts advertising the route to the other side of the network after increasing the hop count by 1. Originally R1 and R2 learned about the 192.168.4.0 from R3. From their perspective, the distance to the destination (metric) may have changed, but the source IP address (vector) did not. So they increment to hop count and send the RIP packets around again. This continues until the RIP packet contains a hop count of 16 and the path is considered unusable.

The hope is that poisoning expired routes and triggered updates will solve this problem and network administrators will never have to rely on this time consuming process. But RFC 2453 warns:

> If the system could be made to sit still while the cascade of triggered updates happens, it would be possible to prove that counting to infinity will never happen. Bad routes would always be removed immediately, and so no routing loops could form. Unfortunately, things are not so nice. While the triggered updates are being sent, regular updates may be happening at the same time. Routers that haven't received the triggered update yet will still be sending out information based on the route that no longer exists. It is possible that after the triggered update has gone through a router, it might receive a normal update from one of these routers that hasn't yet gotten the word. This could reestablish an orphaned remnant of the faulty route.

How Do I Get Off of My Network?

Up to this point, RIP has been used to reach destinations within the collection of RIP-based networks or what the RFC calls the autonomous system. But, the traffic is unable to go anywhere else. So, how does a network topology transition from the interior gateway protocol to the rest of the world? Chapter 1 discussed general routing and included a section on gateways of last resort or the default route. Since the topology used in this chapter was the exact same one, the same rules apply. A default route candidate usually appears several times in the routing tables of other routers. Modifying the topology a little, there is a clear pathway off this set of networks as shown in Figure 5-20.

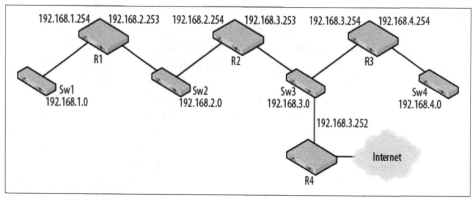

Figure 5-20. RIP default route topology

Even with the addition of R4, the topology is still straightforward. On one hand the network administrator could simply install default routes on all of the routers. However, the network would be unprotected against changes to the topology or downed connections.

Another strategy that can be used with RIP is the idea of redistribution. As the pathway out, R4 can install a default route pointing to the Internet. By running RIP on the 192.168.3.0 side, this default route can be communicated to the downstream routers (R1, R2, R3) by using the command *redistribute static*. The basic configuration of R4 follows:

```
router rip
    version 2
    redistribute static
    network 192.168.3.0
ip route 0.0.0.0 0.0.0.0 10.101.100.254
```

Once the redistribute command is issued, RIP packets flow downstream with the default route included. R1, R2 and R3 update their routing tables to include the new information. This packet is shown in Figure 5-21.

```
⊞ Ethernet II, Src: Cisco_28:1c:a0 (00:05:5e:28:1c:a0), Dst: IPv4mcast_00:00:09 (01:00:5e:00:00:09)
⊞ Internet Protocol, Src: 192.168.3.252 (192.168.3.252), Dst: 224.0.0.9 (224.0.0.9)
⊞ User Datagram Protocol, Src Port: router (520), Dst Port: router (520)
⊟ Routing Information Protocol
    Command: Response (2)
    Version: RIPv2 (2)
    Routing Domain: 0
  ⊟ IP Address: 0.0.0.0, Metric: 1
      Address Family: IP (2)
      Route Tag: 0
      IP Address: 0.0.0.0 (0.0.0.0)
      Netmask: 0.0.0.0 (0.0.0.0)
      Next Hop: 0.0.0.0 (0.0.0.0)
      Metric: 1
```

Figure 5-21. Default route RIP packet

Figure 5-22 depicts the changes to the routing tables downstream. Note that R2 and R3 are connected to the same network as R4 and point directly to R4 as their default route with a hop count of 1. However, the RIP packet was updated by R2 and R1 now uses R2 as its default gateway with an increased hop count.

```
Gateway of last resort is 192.168.2.254 to network 0.0.0.0

R    192.168.4.0/24 [120/2] via 192.168.2.254, 00:00:06, FastEthernet0/1
C    192.168.1.0/24 is directly connected, FastEthernet0/0
C    192.168.2.0/24 is directly connected, FastEthernet0/1
R    192.168.3.0/24 [120/1] via 192.168.2.254, 00:00:06, FastEthernet0/1
R*   0.0.0.0/0 [120/2] via 192.168.2.254, 00:00:06, FastEthernet0/1
R1#


Gateway of last resort is 192.168.3.252 to network 0.0.0.0

R    192.168.4.0/24 [120/1] via 192.168.3.254, 00:00:09, FastEthernet0/1
R    192.168.1.0/24 [120/1] via 192.168.2.253, 00:00:25, FastEthernet0/0
C    192.168.2.0/24 is directly connected, FastEthernet0/0
C    192.168.3.0/24 is directly connected, FastEthernet0/1
R*   0.0.0.0/0 [120/1] via 192.168.3.252, 00:00:05, FastEthernet0/1
R2#


Gateway of last resort is 192.168.3.252 to network 0.0.0.0

C    192.168.4.0/24 is directly connected, FastEthernet0/1
R    192.168.1.0/24 [120/2] via 192.168.3.253, 00:00:24, FastEthernet0/0
R    192.168.2.0/24 [120/1] via 192.168.3.253, 00:00:24, FastEthernet0/0
C    192.168.3.0/24 is directly connected, FastEthernet0/0
R*   0.0.0.0/0 [120/1] via 192.168.3.252, 00:00:00, FastEthernet0/0
R3#
```

Figure 5-22. Routing tables with default routes installed

RIP and Loops

Routing loops can be created by physical connections or by misconfiguration. Looped architectures can severely hamper transmission. Most routing protocols, including RIP, apply techniques to limit the effect of loops on IP packets such as those discussed earlier in this chapter. But what happens if a loop is introduced into the topology? Figure 5-23 depicts R1, R2 and R3 connected in a loop. The 192.168.1.0 network has been removed and R1 given an address on the 192.168.4.0 network. In a topology like this, RIP packets flow exactly as they do in the topologies already discussed.

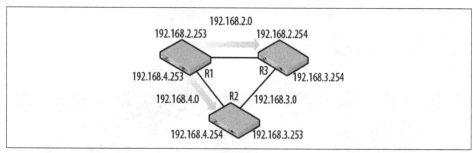

Figure 5-23. Looped topology

Examining the topology from the perspective of R1, it is directly connected to the 192.168.2.0 and 192.168.4.0 networks. It is also one hop away from the 192.168.3.0 network. But this network can be reached from two different directions. The advantage is that should one pathway be lost, the other will automatically take over. The actual routing table from R1 is shown in Figure 5-24.

```
Gateway of last resort is not set

C    192.168.4.0/24 is directly connected, FastEthernet0/0
C    192.168.2.0/24 is directly connected, FastEthernet0/1
R    192.168.3.0/24 [120/1] via 192.168.2.254, 00:00:06, FastEthernet0/1
                    [120/1] via 192.168.4.254, 00:00:15, FastEthernet0/0
R1#
```

Figure 5-24. R1 routing table

Packet captures on the two directly connected networks reveal that if traffic is sent to the 192.168.3.0 network, R1 load balances sending half of the traffic via 192.168.2.254 and half via 192.168.4.254.

Security

Good network security design has many aspects including the security of the network devices and the protocols running on the network. Routing protocols are notoriously simple to disrupt. As the triggered updates demonstrated, when a router receives new or better information regarding destinations, it does not question the information but quickly assimilates it into the routing table. Thus, traffic can be redirected, good information can be supplanted or traffic can be sent down nonexistent pathways. Consider that an intruder gaining access to the network can not only capture traffic running on that network, but inject traffic as well. Routers receiving information from the attacker would not be able to differentiate between that and authentic information from neighboring routers.

The problem can be addressed in several ways. The management of routers can be restricted to particular segments or interfaces. In addition, traffic heading for the routers can be filtered. So, routers will not listen to routing updates from a particular direction and may not respond to ICMP messages or other requests for information. Another valuable tool in the network administrator's toolbox is the loopback interface. Loopbacks are software interfaces that are not tied to any particular physical interface. This means that the loopback is always available even if some of the physical ports are shutdown. Loopbacks can also be given IP addresses that are separate from the data network so that an attacker will not have access to the management interface on the device. Lastly, routing protocols can run on the loopback interfaces. Together these techniques can effectively isolate the management network from the data network.

RIPv2 has one additional capability that makes life a little more difficult on the attacker: authentication of RIP messages. As mentioned previously, when the RIP AFI is set to FFFF, the message is actually used for authentication of the remaining information in the RIP response. Authentication credentials are configured on each router within the AS topology. RFC 2453 specified that the authentication would be a simple plaintext password with RFC 2082 suggesting MD5-based authentication. These were both updated with RFC 4822 which supports additional keying algorithms. One of major differences in the update is that the RIPv2 packet is modified to include authentication information at the end of the packet rather than simply placing it in fields allocated for a network destination.

RIP and IPv6

There is a deployment model for IPv6 RIP. IPv6 RIP is also known as RIPng or RIP next generation. RFC 2080 reveals that the structure and operation of the protocol do not vary much from the IPv4 configuration. Some of the modifications are noted here. Figure 5-25 depicts a topology similar to the one used earlier in this chapter. The router interfaces have been reconfigured with IPv6 addresses. For an explanation of static routing on this same IPv6 topology, see Chapter 1.

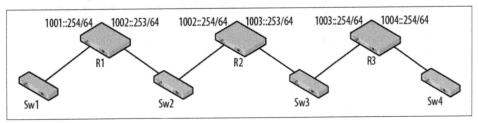

Figure 5-25. IPv6 topology

The basic configuration of the router for IPv6 RIP is straightforward with one significant difference: the RIP commands are tied to the interface. The word "book" is simply a keyword for this instance of the RIP process.

```
ipv6 unicast-routing
interface FastEthernet0/0
    ipv6 address 1001::254/64
    ipv6 rip book enable
!
interface FastEthernet0/1
    ipv6 address 1002::253/64
    ipv6 rip book enable
ipv6 router rip book
```

Figure 5-26 depicts the routing table for R1. IPv6 adds the link routes and the 1001 and 1002 networks are directly connected. Both the 1003 and 1004 networks are leaned via RIP. Note that the administrative distance and the hop counts are utilized in the same way.

```
C    1001::/64 [0/0]
       via FastEthernet0/0, directly connected
L    1001::254/128 [0/0]
       via FastEthernet0/0, receive
C    1002::/64 [0/0]
       via FastEthernet0/1, directly connected
L    1002::253/128 [0/0]
       via FastEthernet0/1, receive
R    1003::/64 [120/2]
       via FE80::219:2FFF:FE8E:DB48, FastEthernet0/1
R    1004::/64 [120/3]
       via FE80::219:2FFF:FE8E:DB48, FastEthernet0/1
L    FF00::/8 [0/0]
       via Null0, receive
```

Figure 5-26. IPv6 RIP routing table

Operationally, IPv6 RIP is about the same although the packets had to be modified slightly to accommodate the different Layer 3 protocol. In addition there is a behavior change for split horizon. While IPv6 RIP obeys split horizon, it does advertise the local network. The packet shown in Figure 5-27 displays a packet captured on the 1001::/64 network. IPv6 has a different view of the network and makes use of link local addressing instead of the globally scoped IP address.

This packet advertises all four of the known networks as opposed to just those learned from the opposite side of the router. The destination is an IPv6 reserved multicast address (FF02::9) and the port number is 521. As can be seen, the structure is very similar and even though this is called version 1, it includes the mask or prefix length information.

```
Ethernet II, Src: Cisco_f6:a9:10 (00:1c:58:f6:a9:10), Dst: IPv6mcast_00:00:00:09 (33:33:00:00:00:09)
Internet Protocol Version 6, Src: fe80::21c:58ff:fef6:a910 (fe80::21c:58ff:fef6:a910), Dst: ff02::9 (ff02::9)
User Datagram Protocol, Src Port: ripng (521), Dst Port: ripng (521)
RIPng
   Command: Response (2)
   version: 1
 ⊟ IP Address: 1002::/64, Metric: 1
     IP Address: 1002::
     Tag: 0x0000
     Prefix length: 64
     Metric: 1
 ⊟ IP Address: 1001::/64, Metric: 1
     IP Address: 1001::
     Tag: 0x0000
     Prefix length: 64
     Metric: 1
 ⊟ IP Address: 1003::/64, Metric: 2
     IP Address: 1003::
     Tag: 0x0000
     Prefix length: 64
     Metric: 2
 ⊟ IP Address: 1004::/64, Metric: 3
     IP Address: 1004::
     Tag: 0x0000
     Prefix length: 64
     Metric: 3
```

Figure 5-27. IPv6 RIP packet on the 1001 network

Reading

RFC 1058: Routing Information Protocol

RFC 1112: Host Extensions for IP Multicasting

RFC 1256: ICMP Router Discovery Messages

RFC 1812: Requirements for IP Version 4 Routers

RFC 1923: RIPv1 Applicability Statement for Historic Status

RFC 2080: RIPng for IPv6

RFC 2453: RIP Version 2 (obsoletes 1723, 1388)

RFC 3171: IANA Guidelines for IPv4 Multicast Address Assignments

RFC 4822: RIPv2 Cryptographic Authentication (obsoletes 2082 RIP-2 MD5 Authentication)

Summary

RIP and distance vector routing have been in use since the early days of internet communication. Due to its slow convergence time, RIP has an administrative distance of 120. This makes routing updates from RIP less desirable than those from other protocols. Using a metric of hop count and because it was designed for a small collection of networks, RIP has a maximum network size of 15. RIP has survived largely due to a series of techniques such as split horizon, poisoning, poison reverse, count to infinity and triggered updates. Support for authentication adds security to the aging protocol perhaps continuing to breathe life into RIP.

Review Questions

1. The key difference between RIPv1 and RIPv2 is support for subnets.
   a. TRUE
   b. FALSE

2. What is the metric used for RIP?
   a. Cost
   b. Hop count
   c. Utilization

3. What is the administrative distance for RIP?
   a. 90
   b. 100
   c. 110
   d. 120

4. Both RIPv1 and RIPv2 use a multicast destination address.
   a. TRUE
   b. FALSE

5. What is the Update timer value?

6. What is the Route Timeout value?

7. What is the Garbage Collection timer value based on the RFC?

8. Split horizon encourages routers to forward the entire routing table in all directions.
   a. TRUE
   b. FALSE

9. In a poisoned packet, the metric is set to 16.
   a. TRUE
   b. FALSE

10. RIP cannot be used in topologies containing loops.
    a. TRUE
    b. FALSE

Review Answers

1. TRUE

2. B. Hop count

3. D. 120

4. FALSE

5. 30 sec

6. 180 sec

7. 120 sec

8. FALSE

9. TRUE

10. FALSE

Lab Activities

Activity 1—Build the Topology Depicted in Figure 5-28

Materials: 2 routers, 2 computers, optional switches (or VLANs) for each network

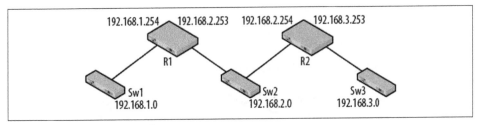

192.168.1.254   192.168.2.253   192.168.2.254   192.168.3.253

R1   R2

Sw1   Sw2   Sw3
192.168.1.0   192.168.2.0   192.168.3.0

Figure 5-28. Activity 1topology

1. Cable the topology and configure the IP addresses on the router interfaces.

2. Connect a computer to the 192.168.1.0 and 192.168.2.0 networks.

3. Manually configure the IP addresses and gateways for the computers.

4. For the computer on the 192.168.2.0 network, does it matter which default gateway is used? Why? What about after RIP is running?

5. Examine the routing tables on the routers. What do they contain? Handy Cisco command: show ip route.

Activity 2—Enable RIP on the Routers

Materials: Activity 1 topology, Wireshark

1. On each router configure the router to use RIP. Use RIP version 2.
2. Handy Cisco commands: router rip, network _____, version
3. Capture traffic on both computers and watch as the RIP packets begin to flow. Once the configuration is complete, examine the routing tables of the routers again.
4. What has changed in the router routing tables? What are the values in the brackets? Why?
5. Does the fact that RIP is running in the network have anything to do with the host routing tables?

Activity 3—Split Horizon

Materials: Activity 1 topology, Wireshark

1. What is split horizon? Split horizon with poison reverse?
2. Examine the packets captured on these networks and find evidence that either shows split horizon is active or inactive.

Activity 4—Loss of a Route

Materials: Activity 1 topology, Wireshark

1. With the Wireshark captures running, disconnect the link to the 192.168.3.0 network from R2.
2. What traffic is generated as a result? How quickly were the packets seen?
3. Examine the content of the packets. Is there anything significant about the information for the 192.168.3.0 network?
4. Recover the topology for the next activity.

Activity 5—Timers

Materials: Activity 1 topology, Wireshark, a switch between R1 and R2

1. Monitor the rate at which RIP packets are sent by the routers. Does this match the timer value in this chapter?

---

2. With the Wireshark captures running, disconnect the link to the 192.168.2.0 network from R2. From the perspective of R1, what are the differences between this action and the previous activity?

3. Monitor the routing table of R1. How long does it take for the 192.168.3.0 network entry to be lost?

4. Was there any change to the packets as a result of this disconnect? Hint: Does R2 think that the 192.168.3.0 network is gone?

5. What are the actual timers associated with R1? Handy Cisco command: show ip protocol.

CHAPTER 6

Open Shortest Path First

Open Shortest Path First (OSPF) and the Routing Information Protocol (RIP) are both interior routing protocols designed for networks within a single autonomous system, but the similarities end there. OSPF uses a completely different algorithm and is a link state protocol while RIP is a distance vector protocol. In the last chapter, RIP was shown to be a simple but reliable protocol. However, the limitations regarding overall network size and its slow convergence speed have restricted RIP deployments. When network topologies grow beyond fifteen hops or the topologies become more complex, protocols like OSPF not only become more attractive but a requirement.

This chapter will continue the tradition of building the sample topologies on Cisco equipment, exploring the ideas, packets and operation of OSPF. Like most protocols, getting OSPF up and running requires a small number of commands. However, OSPF can easily grow to significant complexity. OSPF has a lengthy specification and a number of RFCs that expand the original protocol. To keep the chapter readable, the commonly deployed features will be discussed here.

Protocol Description

The Open Shortest Path First specification was first described in the 1989 RFC 1131 but was quickly surpassed by RFC 1247 two years later which covered OSPF version 2. This version of the protocol has also been updated several times. For the purposes of this chapter, RFC 2328 (and packet captures) will form the basis of the discussion. Unlike RIP, OSPF messages are encapsulated directly into IP packets. The IP protocol ID for OSPF is 89 so filtering out UDP streams doesn't create the same problem as it did for RIP. The encapsulation and IP protocol ID are shown in Figure 6-1.

```
Ethernet II, Src: Cisco_da:5a:a0 (00:05:32:da:5a:a0), Dst: IPv4mcast_00:00:05 (01:00:5e:00:00:05)
Internet Protocol, Src: 192.168.2.253 (192.168.2.253), Dst: 224.0.0.5 (224.0.0.5)
   Version: 4
   Header length: 20 bytes
⊞ Differentiated Services Field: 0xc0 (DSCP 0x30: Class Selector 6; ECN: 0x00)
   Total Length: 64
   Identification: 0x3a50 (14928)
⊞ Flags: 0x00
   Fragment offset: 0
   Time to live: 1
   Protocol: OSPF IGP (89)
⊞ Header checksum: 0xdaaa [correct]
   Source: 192.168.2.253 (192.168.2.253)
   Destination: 224.0.0.5 (224.0.0.5)
Open Shortest Path First
```

Figure 6-1. OSPF encapsulation and IP protocol ID

Distance vector protocols generally operate by sending periodic updates that contain all or part of a routers' routing table. These advertisements are enhanced through techniques such as split horizon, poisoning, triggered updates and count-to-infinity. Link state protocols take a different approach in that they send "link state advertisements" everywhere via multicast flood but once the topology has stabilized, the updates cease. Instead, a Hello message is sent which indicates that nothing has changed. Hello messages have very little useable content. Routers engaging in OSPF develop a picture of the topology and this is stored in the link state database or LSDB for each router.

OSPF networks are organized around the idea of areas. An area is a collection of routers forwarding traffic for a group of networks. An OSPF autonomous system (AS) is a group of OSPF areas. Another way of looking at this is to think of OSPF as having smaller topologies within the AS topology. Routers inside an area do not know very much about the world outside the area. This basic idea is depicted in Figure 6-2.

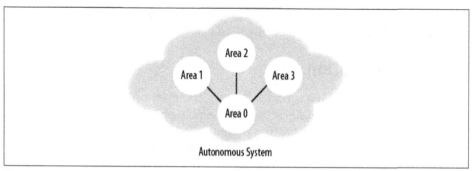

Figure 6-2. Autonomous system with areas

Each area has its own instance of the link state protocol running and eventually develops its own tree of shortest paths and router routing tables. Areas are given a numerical value and the numerical area ID can be formatted in either a single number or the dotted quad notation like that of an IP address. From the captures in this chapter, area 51 becomes 0.0.0.51. Networks of any size have a "backbone" section. The backbone is always assigned to area 0. Areas must be physically contiguous but they do not have to be virtually contiguous. This means that an area can live on either side of a virtual link such as a virtual private network connection. Packets traveling between nonbackbone areas flows over the backbone. Traffic is either intra-area (source to destination in one area) or inter-area in which the traffic flows from an area to the backbone and then to another area. Per RFC 2328:

> Looking at this another way, inter-area routing can be pictured as forcing a star config-
> uration on the Autonomous System, with the backbone as hub and each of the non-
> backbone areas as spokes.

An OSPF topology includes several different types of routers:

- Area border routers (ABR)—interconnects areas
- Internal routers (IR)—routers within an area
- Backbone routers (BR)—routers that have an interface on the backbone, can be an ABR
- AS boundary router (ASBR)—exists at the edge of the AS and exchanges routing information with other ASBRs. This router will also advertise external routes on the local OSPF topology.

Adding these routers, the diagram from Figure 6-2 can be modified as shown in Figure 6-3.

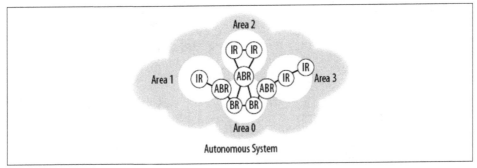

Figure 6-3. Modified AS diagram

From Figure 6-3 it can be seen that the individual area topologies can vary. Routing within an autonomous system is resolved via OSPF link state advertisements or LSAs. In the case of stub areas (areas having one pathway out), the ABR will typically adver-tise a default route. In addition, externally derived LSAs are not advertised into stub areas because there is no need. OSPF supports routing to externally derived destinations (leaves on the OSPF tree) and classless inter-domain routing or CIDR. The externally derived routes will be advertised throughout the autonomous system.

Being Link State

A router's "state" describes its location in the topology. The state consists of the router's connected interfaces and the neighbors' reachable via those interfaces. From RFC 2328:

> From the Link-state database, each router constructs a tree of shortest paths with itself as root. This shortest-path tree gives the route to each destination in the Autonomous System.

Link state protocols are also referred to as shortest path first protocols or at least are based on shortest path first algorithms. Like distance vector protocols, they have been around for decades. Essentially, the network is envisioned as a graph. The routers are the vertices or points on the graph and the links between them are called edges. Edges can also connect a router to a network. In OSPF, the networks are either transit or stub. Transit network traffic differs from that on a stub network because it can carry traffic that is "neither locally generated or locally destined" In addition, a network can have one or more routers attached to it, no matter its type. The cost of a particular route or link is associated with the output side of the router interface. Lower costs are better. From the collection of network types, costs and IP-based connections, a graph can be drawn depicting the connectivity. A very simple example is shown in Figure 6-4. This diagram was taken from RFC 2328 and modified with a sample cost based on slow speed output links.

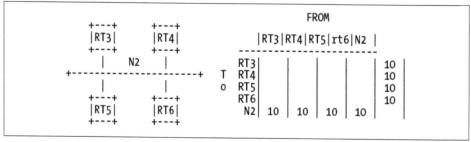

Figure 6-4. Sample graph

The diagram on the left shows four routers connected to network N2. On the right is a graphical depiction of this network connectivity and the speed on the connections. The cost or metric for a particular destination is a single "dimensionless" metric that is a factor of network conditions. This is different from RIP which uses a simple hop count as a metric.

As the routers send out link state advertisements (LSAs), a link state database (LSDB) can be built that contains information about the routers' neighborhood. The LSAs are flooded to the entire network with each router adding more and more detail. *Without different areas, each router would eventually learn about the entire autonomous system topology and they all would have the same LSDB.* With the LSDB in hand, the routers develop their own tree of shortest paths to each destination. So, while the LSDBs might be the same, the trees that come out of it will not. Connectivity to destinations external to the OSPF AS can be reached by simply advertising the routes internally. Metrics for the advertisements are called Type I and Type II. Type I metrics convert the external cost to OSPF and add the two together.

- Type I = cost to the advertising router + cost to the external destination
- Type II does not convert, but just advertises the smallest external cost to the destination

Once a set of contiguous networks is organized into an area, they will run a separate copy of the link state algorithm, develop their own LSDB and trees of shortest paths. As stated earlier, routers inside an area do not know very much about the entire AS or other areas. In the topology shown in Figure 6-2, there would be at least four different instances on the link state algorithm running. This reduces overall routing traffic since individual routers do not need to advertise everywhere. Routers rely on an area border router (ABR) to forward traffic to destinations external to the area.

OSPF routers communicate quite a bit in order to develop the LSDB. In next section will utilize a small topology to explain the messages and fields used to accomplish this.

Structure and Basic Operation

The section will cover the content and structure of the five OSPF messages. The small topology shown in Figure 6-5 will provide the environment for the messages. Initially the topology is configured like the others seen in this book; IP addresses are given to the interfaces and the interfaces are activated. Once the cabling is connected, the routing tables for R1 and R2 will contain the entries seen in Table 6-1.

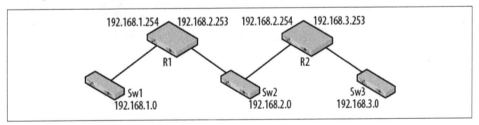

Figure 6-5. Small OSPF topology

Table 6-1. Initial routing tables

R1	R2
C 192.168.1.0/24	C 192.168.2.0/24
C 192.168.2.0/24	C 192.168.3.0/24

After the topology is built and the routing tables established, the routers must be configured to run OSPF. The following commands were issued on R1 and R2:

```
R1
    router ospf 10
    network 192.168.1.0 255.255.255.0 area 51
    network 192.168.2.0 255.255.255.0 area 51
R2
    router ospf 20
    network 192.168.2.0 255.255.255.0 area 51
    network 192.168.3.0 255.255.255.0 area 51
```

The first command establishes the process and the process number for the router. The process ID identifies the instance of OSPF running. A router can have more than one OSPF process running. Routers within the same OSPF AS do not have to use the same process ID. The network command describes the network to be advertised and assigns the network to an area.

Hello

Moving from left to right, as commands are entered and networks are added to the list for advertisement, the routers begin to send out their first OSPF message: Hello. For example, once R1 is given the command "network 192.168.1.0 255.255.255.0 area 51" command, it immediately issues a "Hello" message to that network. An example of a Hello message is shown in Figure 6-6.

The Hello message allows a router to advertise itself and learn about other OSPF neighbors. The idea of a "neighbor" is an important one to OSPF. Since the router is learning about the environment, Hello messages use the OSPF specific multicast address of 224.0.0.5. A collection of routers that can learn this way are said to be operating in an OSPF broadcast network. Once the neighbors are discovered, the Hello message is used to maintain this relationship. Routers establish adjacencies with neighboring routers. Routers connected to the same network will be neighbors. However, only adjacent routers will exchange routing information. Adjacency is desired when the routers can exchange Hello messages and the OSPF options are compatible. Once established, neighbor addresses appear in the Hello message, database information can be exchanged and the information can be kept up-to-date.

```
Ethernet II, Src: Cisco_28:02:81 (00:05:5e:28:02:81), Dst: IPv4mcast_00:00:05 (01:00:5e:00:00:05)
Internet Protocol, Src: 192.168.2.254 (192.168.2.254), Dst: 224.0.0.5 (224.0.0.5)
Open Shortest Path First
⊟ OSPF Header
    OSPF version: 2
    Message Type: Hello Packet (1)
    Packet Length: 44
    Source OSPF Router: 192.168.3.253 (192.168.3.253)
    Area ID: 0.0.0.51
    Packet Checksum: 0x37c6 [correct]
    Auth Type: Null
    Auth Data (none)
⊟ OSPF Hello Packet
    Network Mask: 255.255.255.0
    Hello Interval: 10 seconds
    ⊟ Options: 0x02 (E)
        0... .... = DN: DN-bit is NOT set
        .0.. .... = O: O-bit is NOT set
        ..0. .... = DC: Demand Circuits are NOT supported
        ...0 .... = L: The packet does NOT contain LLS data block
        .... 0... = NP: NSSA is NOT supported
        .... .0.. = MC: NOT Multicast Capable
        .... ..1. = E: External Routing Capability
        .... ...0 = MT: NO Multi-Topology Routing
    Router Priority: 1
    Router Dead Interval: 40 seconds
    Designated Router: 0.0.0.0
    Backup Designated Router: 0.0.0.0
```

Figure 6-6. OSPF hello

The OSPF hello message is straightforward for a simple configuration such as this one:

Version
> This 1-byte field will almost always be set to 2.

Message type
> This is a 1-byte field that provides the numeric code for the message. A hello message has a code of 1.

Packet length
> This is the length of the OSPF packet alone.

Source OSPF router
> This is a configurable value I for the IP address of the source router.

Area ID
> These 4 bytes describe the area configured for the network.

Packet Checksum
> This is the 16 bit one's compliment checksum of the OSPF packet

Authentication Type and Data
> The RFC calls for OSPF packets to be authenticated via the type specified in this field. In the absence of a configuration, the fields will be null as shown above.

Network mask
  Mask of the network specified in the router configuration.

Hello interval
  Rate that Hello messages are generated, 2 bytes.

Options
  A 1-byte field describing the operational characteristics of the OSPF router. For the most part, the options do not change very much with a basic configuration. The key idea is that options between neighbors should match. The critical option is the E bit. The options field is included in several packet types and is commonly used to indicate if routing advertisements are transmitted to the local network. Five bits of this field are defined in RFC 2328, though more were added by later RFCs.

  DN
    Indicates that this route should not be used in OSPF calculations per RFC 2547.

  O
    Support for opaque LSAs as defined in RFC 2370.

  DC
    Indicates support for demand circuits as defined in RFC 3883 (1793).

  L
    Indicates support for link local signaling for additional routing data. See RFC 5613.

  NP
    Handling of Type 7 Not-so-stubby-areas (NSSA) LSAs. See RFC 1587.

  MC
    Indicates whether multicast forwarding is per RFC 1584.

  E
    Describes the flooding method for LS advertisements.

  MT
    Provides support for different types of topologies or traffic such as quality of service,

Router priority
  A 1-byte field used to select the designated router for the network.

Router dead interval
  Indicates how often a router must heard in order to still be considered a live neighbor.

Designated router
Router specified to advertise the state of the network.

Backup designated router
Takes over in the absence of the designated router.

As the commands continue to be entered, R1 and R2 will exchange Hello messages, establishing that they are neighbors. Once this occurs, the routers will exchange routing information via the Link State Updates. The conversation can be seen in Figure 6-7 which displays the standard set of OSPF message types.

53 192.168.2.253	224.0.0.5	OSPF	84.257834	Hello Packet
57 192.168.2.254	224.0.0.5	OSPF	88.795019	Hello Packet
60 192.168.2.253	224.0.0.5	OSPF	94.258557	Hello Packet
61 192.168.2.254	192.168.2.253	OSPF	94.259601	DB Description
62 192.168.2.253	192.168.2.254	OSPF	94.260585	DB Description
63 192.168.2.253	192.168.2.254	OSPF	94.261230	DB Description
64 192.168.2.254	192.168.2.253	OSPF	94.262474	DB Description
65 192.168.2.254	192.168.2.253	OSPF	94.262477	LS Request
66 192.168.2.253	192.168.2.254	OSPF	94.263597	DB Description
67 192.168.2.253	192.168.2.254	OSPF	94.263978	LS Request
68 192.168.2.253	192.168.2.254	OSPF	94.263981	LS Update
69 192.168.2.254	192.168.2.253	OSPF	94.264987	DB Description
70 192.168.2.254	192.168.2.253	OSPF	94.265694	LS Update
71 192.168.2.253	192.168.2.254	OSPF	94.266069	DB Description
72 192.168.2.253	224.0.0.5	OSPF	94.791544	LS Update
73 192.168.2.254	224.0.0.5	OSPF	94.972350	LS Update
75 192.168.2.254	224.0.0.5	OSPF	96.763368	LS Acknowledge
76 192.168.2.253	224.0.0.5	OSPF	96.766709	LS Acknowledge
77 192.168.2.254	224.0.0.5	OSPF	98.794559	Hello Packet
79 192.168.2.253	192.168.2.254	OSPF	99.551290	LS Update
80 192.168.2.254	192.168.2.253	OSPF	99.908307	LS Update
81 192.168.2.254	224.0.0.5	OSPF	102.051871	LS Acknowledge
82 192.168.2.253	224.0.0.5	OSPF	102.407911	LS Acknowledge
83 192.168.2.253	224.0.0.5	OSPF	104.259093	Hello Packet
95 192.168.2.254	224.0.0.5	OSPF	108.794843	Hello Packet
101 192.168.2.253	224.0.0.5	OSPF	114.259578	Hello Packet

Figure 6-7. OSPF conversation between R1 and R2

DB Description

The database description packets (OSPF type 2) are exchanged as a beginning to the adjacency decision. Examining one of the last Hello messages before the DB description packets (packet 60), a field has been added—Active Neighbor. The active neighbor hello is shown in Figure 6-8 and the DB description is shown in Figure 6-9.

```
Ethernet II, Src: Cisco_da:5a:a0 (00:05:32:da:5a:a0), Dst: IPv4mcast_00:00:05 (01:00:5e:00:00:05)
Internet Protocol, Src: 192.168.2.253 (192.168.2.253), Dst: 224.0.0.5 (224.0.0.5)
Open Shortest Path First
⊞ OSPF Header
⊟ OSPF Hello Packet
    Network Mask: 255.255.255.0
    Hello Interval: 10 seconds
  ⊞ Options: 0x02 (E)
    Router Priority: 1
    Router Dead Interval: 40 seconds
    Designated Router: 192.168.2.253
    Backup Designated Router: 0.0.0.0
    Active Neighbor: 192.168.3.253
```

Figure 6-8. Active neighbor hello

At this point, one or more DB description packets will be sent between the routers. The conversation is controlled by the designated router and occurs in a poll/response procedure with one router acting as the master. The DB description exchange can be followed by examining the R, I, M and MS bits in addition to the DD sequence numbers.

R

Resynchronize bit. Allows vendor specific implementations to recalculate the link state database (LSDB) without a topology change. Described in RFC 4811.

I

Init bit, indicates the start of the exchange.

M

More, indicates whether the DB description is complete.

MS

Master/Slave, indicates the router in control of the exchange. Note that in Figure 6-9, the DB description packet came from 192.168.2.254 (R2) and the master bit is set.

DD

This is the sequence number of a particular message. With the init flag set, this packet is the first. The DD values will increment until the DB description is complete.

The last section of the packet(s) is governed by the LSA header and contains information about the link state database (LSDB).

Link state advertisement (LSA) header

There are several types of LSA defined in the RFC. Of these, the two most common are the *router-LSA* (used by all routers) and the *network-LSA* (designated router). Other types include summary and external. The LSA headers can change based on the LSA type. In Figure 6-9, the LSA type is a router-LSA. This message is part of the conversation between R1 and R2 so the IP addressing is between R1 and R2. Other LSAs will be flooded via multicast throughout the topology via the OSPF multicast addresses. Taken together, the LSAs constitute the link state database (LSDB). Once the routers possess the LSDB, they can construct (or reconstruct) the tree of shortest paths. Recall that every router pictures itself as the root of the tree. The tree results in the routing table.

```
Ethernet II, src: Cisco_28:02:81 (00:05:5e:28:02:81), Dst: Cisco_da:5a:a0 (00:05:32:da:5a:a0)
Internet Protocol, Src: 192.168.2.254 (192.168.2.254), Dst: 192.168.2.253 (192.168.2.253)
Open Shortest Path First
⊞ OSPF Header
⊟ OSPF DB Description
    Interface MTU: 1500
    ⊟ Options: 0x42 (O, E)
        0... .... = DN: DN-bit is NOT set
        .1.. .... = O: O-bit is SET
        ..0. .... = DC: Demand Circuits are NOT supported
        ...0 .... = L: The packet does NOT contain LLS data block
        .... 0... = NP: NSSA is NOT supported
        .... .0.. = MC: NOT Multicast Capable
        .... ..1. = E: External Routing Capability
        .... ...0 = MT: NO Multi-Topology Routing
    ⊟ DB Description: 0x03 (M, MS)
        .... 0... = R: OOBResync bit is NOT set
        .... .0.. = I: Init bit is NOT set
        .... ..1. = M: More bit is SET
        .... ...1 = MS: Master/Slave bit is SET
    DD Sequence: 4235
⊟ LSA Header
    LS Age: 4 seconds
    Do Not Age: False
    ⊟ Options: 0x22 (DC, E)
        0... .... = DN: DN-bit is NOT set
        .0.. .... = O: O-bit is NOT set
        ..1. .... = DC: Demand Circuits are supported
        ...0 .... = L: The packet does NOT contain LLS data block
        .... 0... = NP: NSSA is NOT supported
        .... .0.. = MC: NOT Multicast Capable
        .... ..1. = E: External Routing Capability
        .... ...0 = MT: NO Multi-Topology Routing
    Link-State Advertisement Type: Router-LSA (1)
    Link State ID: 192.168.3.253
    Advertising Router: 192.168.3.253 (192.168.3.253)
    LS Sequence Number: 0x80000001
    LS Checksum: 0xc32e
    Length: 36
```

Figure 6-9. DB description message

The options field represents the capabilities of the networks. The link state ID is either the IP address of the designated router or the source interface. The LS sequence number helps detect duplicates. The checksum is for the LSA but excludes the LS age field.

Link State Request

An LS request is shown in Figure 6-10. This is OSPF message type 3. As the simplest OSPF message, it does not contain any information not already discussed. This is used to request information when the router wishes to update its LSDB. In this case, the router does not have any information in the LSDB, but it understands the structure and options of the routing domain. Note that the addressing is between the established neighbors.

```
Ethernet II, Src: Cisco_28:02:81 (00:05:5e:28:02:81), Dst: Cisco_da:5a:a0 (00:05:32:da:5a:a0)
Internet Protocol, Src: 192.168.2.254 (192.168.2.254), Dst: 192.168.2.253 (192.168.2.253)
Open Shortest Path First
⊟ OSPF Header
     OSPF Version: 2
     Message Type: LS Request (3)
     Packet Length: 36
     Source OSPF Router: 192.168.3.253 (192.168.3.253)
     Area ID: 0.0.0.51
     Packet Checksum: 0xb3b1 [correct]
     Auth Type: Null
     Auth Data (none)
⊟ Link State Request
     Link-State Advertisement Type: Router-LSA (1)
     Link State ID: 192.168.1.254
     Advertising Router: 192.168.1.254 (192.168.1.254)
```

Figure 6-10. LS request message

Link State Update

The LS update shown in Figure 6-11 is in response to an LS Request. The LS Update is message type 4 for OSPF. The purpose of the packet is to flood LSAs throughput the topology. LS Updates forward information 1 hop. In this way, the information eventually propagates everywhere.

The packet shown in Figure 6-11 has an example of Wireshark trying to be helpful in deciphering the packet but it can be a little confusing. Under each link entry there appears to be much more information than is actually included in the packet. To clarify what is actually sent, I've included the hexadecimal values below the packet and examples in the field descriptions. Each LSA entry is only 12 bytes and starts with the network address.

Beginning with the Flags field the LSA construction follows:

V

Indicates that the router is an endpoint for a virtual link. Value from Figure 6-11: 0

E

External, the router is positioned as an AS boundary router. Value from Figure 6-11: 0

B

This router is an area border router. Value from Figure 6-11: 0

Number of links

Total number of links possessed by the router. In this topology, the routers each have 2.

```
Ethernet II, Src: Cisco_da:5a:a0 (00:05:32:da:5a:a0), Dst: Cisco_28:02:81 (00:05:5e:28:02:81)
Internet Protocol, Src: 192.168.2.253 (192.168.2.253), Dst: 192.168.2.254 (192.168.2.254)
Open Shortest Path First
⊞ OSPF Header
⊟ LS Update Packet
    Number of LSAs: 1
  ⊟ LS Type: Router-LSA
      LS Age: 50 seconds
      Do Not Age: False
    ⊞ Options: 0x22 (DC, E)
      Link-State Advertisement Type: Router-LSA (1)
      Link State ID: 192.168.1.254
      Advertising Router: 192.168.1.254 (192.168.1.254)
      LS Sequence Number: 0x80000004
      LS Checksum: 0xef85
      Length: 48
    ⊟ Flags: 0x00
        .... .0.. = V: NO virtual link endpoint
        .... ..0. = E: NO AS boundary router
        .... ...0 = B: NO Area border router
      Number of Links: 2
      ⊟ Type: Stub      ID: 192.168.2.0     Data: 255.255.255.0   Metric: 1
          IP network/subnet number: 192.168.2.0
          Link Data: 255.255.255.0
          Link Type: 3 - Connection to a stub network
          Number of TOS metrics: 0
          TOS 0 metric: 1
      ⊟ Type: Stub      ID: 192.168.1.0     Data: 255.255.255.0   Metric: 1
          IP network/subnet number: 192.168.1.0
          Link Data: 255.255.255.0
          Link Type: 3 - Connection to a stub network
          Number of TOS metrics: 0
          TOS 0 metric: 1
```

```
 00   00 05 5e 28 02 81 00 05   32 da 5a a0 08 00 45 c0   ..^(....  2.Z...E.
 10   00 60 3a 5f 00 00 01 59   f6 da c0 a8 02 fd c0 a8   .`:_...Y ........
 20   02 fe 02 04 00 4c c0 a8   01 fe 00 00 33 9b 42   .....L.. ....3.B
 30   00 00 00 00 00 00 00 00   00 00 00 00 00 01 00 32   ........ .......2
 40   22 01 c0 a8 01 fe c0 a8   01 fe 80 00 00 04 ef 85   "....... ........
 50   00 30 00 00 00 02 c0 a8   02 00 ff ff ff 00 03 00   .0...... ........
 60   00 01 c0 a8 01 00 ff ff   ff 00 03 00 00 01   ...... .......
```

Figure 6-11. LS Update message

Link ID

This value depends on the type of link (Table 6-2) but in Figure 6-11, it is the network ID of 192.168.2.0. Hex: c0 a8 02 00

Table 6-2. OSPF LSA Link IDs

Type	Link ID
1	Neighboring router's router ID
2	IP address of designated router
3	IP network or subnetwork
4	Neighboring router's router ID

Data

This also depends on the link type but in this case it is the mask of 255.255.255.0. Hex: ff ff ff 00

Link Type

There are four link types defined as shown in Table 6-3. In this particular packet, R1 initially believes that both networks are stub networks meaning that they do not have another pathway out. So both have a value of 3 and use the IP network as the Link ID.

Table 6-3. OSPF LSA link types

1	Point-to-point
2	Connection to a transit network
3	Connection to a stub network
4	Virtual link

Number of ToS metrics

Type of Service or ToS is a priority or quality setting describing the treatment of packets. IP ToS values are used infrequently and have largely been replaced by Differentiated Services. If no metrics are specified, the field is set to 0, as in this case.

Metric

RFC 2328 simply states this as the cost of using the link, although speed of the link is a critical factor.

The IP addressing in Figure 6-11 is due to the conversation between R1 and R2. Figure 6-12 depicts another LS Update from the same conversation (packet 72) but it can be seen that R1 been elected as the designated router for this segment.

```
Ethernet II, Src: Cisco_da:5a:a0 (00:05:32:da:5a:a0), Dst: IPv4mcast_00:00:05 (01:00:5e:00:00:05)
Internet Protocol, Src: 192.168.2.253 (192.168.2.253), Dst: 224.0.0.5 (224.0.0.5)
Open Shortest Path First
 OSPF Header
 LS Update Packet
     Number of LSAs: 2
   LS Type: Router-LSA
     LS Age: 1 seconds
     Do Not Age: False
    Options: 0x22 (DC, E)
     Link-State Advertisement Type: Router-LSA (1)
     Link State ID: 192.168.1.254
     Advertising Router: 192.168.1.254 (192.168.1.254)
     LS Sequence Number: 0x80000005
     LS Checksum: 0xf815
     Length: 48
    Flags: 0x00
     Number of Links: 2
    Type: Transit  ID: 192.168.2.253   Data: 192.168.2.253   Metric: 1
       IP address of Designated Router: 192.168.2.253
       Link Data: 192.168.2.253
       Link Type: 2 - Connection to a transit network
       Number of TOS metrics: 0
       TOS 0 metric: 1
    Type: Stub      ID: 192.168.1.0     Data: 255.255.255.0   Metric: 1
       IP network/subnet number: 192.168.1.0
       Link Data: 255.255.255.0
       Link Type: 3 - Connection to a stub network
       Number of TOS metrics: 0
       TOS 0 metric: 1
   LS Type: Network-LSA
     LS Age: 1 seconds
     Do Not Age: False
    Options: 0x22 (DC, E)
     Link-State Advertisement Type: Network-LSA (2)
     Link State ID: 192.168.2.253
     Advertising Router: 192.168.1.254 (192.168.1.254)
     LS Sequence Number: 0x80000001
     LS Checksum: 0xa3ef
     Length: 32
     Netmask: 255.255.255.0
     Attached Router: 192.168.1.254
     Attached Router: 192.168.3.253
```

Figure 6-12. LS Update from Designated Router

There are some other significant changes to the LS Update packet. One of the links has been identified as a *transit network* because advertisements were seen from another router on that network. So, the link type, ID and data fields have all been updated. The 192.168.1.0 network is still a stub network. Lastly, because this update came from a designated router, the LSA is a network-LSA. The destination IP addressing in this packet has returned to the "SPF all routers address."

Link State ACK

For reliability, each LS update packet is acknowledged by routers attached to the same network via the type 5 LS ACK message. The LS ACK contains the LS sequence number. More than one LS update can be acknowledged by a single LS ACK message.

```
Ethernet II, Src: Cisco_28:02:81 (00:05:5e:28:02:81), Dst: IPv4mcast_00:00:05 (01:00:5e:00:00:05)
Internet Protocol, Src: 192.168.2.254 (192.168.2.254), Dst: 224.0.0.5 (224.0.0.5)
Open Shortest Path First
⊞ OSPF Header
⊟ LSA Header
      LS Age: 50 seconds
      Do Not Age: False
   ⊟ Options: 0x22 (DC, E)
         0... .... = DN: DN-bit is NOT set
         .0.. .... = O: O-bit is NOT set
         ..1. .... = DC: Demand Circuits are supported
         ...0 .... = L: The packet does NOT contain LLS data block
         .... 0... = NP: NSSA is NOT supported
         .... .0.. = MC: NOT Multicast Capable
         .... ..1. = E: External Routing Capability
         .... ...0 = MT: NO Multi-Topology Routing
      Link-State Advertisement Type: Router-LSA (1)
      Link State ID: 192.168.1.254
      Advertising Router: 192.168.1.254 (192.168.1.254)
      LS Sequence Number: 0x80000004
      LS Checksum: 0xef85
      Length: 48
⊟ LSA Header
      LS Age: 1 seconds
      Do Not Age: False
   ⊟ Options: 0x22 (DC, E)
         0... .... = DN: DN-bit is NOT set
         .0.. .... = O: O-bit is NOT set
         ..1. .... = DC: Demand Circuits are supported
         ...0 .... = L: The packet does NOT contain LLS data block
         .... 0... = NP: NSSA is NOT supported
         .... .0.. = MC: NOT Multicast Capable
         .... ..1. = E: External Routing Capability
         .... ...0 = MT: NO Multi-Topology Routing
      Link-State Advertisement Type: Network-LSA (2)
      Link State ID: 192.168.2.253
      Advertising Router: 192.168.1.254 (192.168.1.254)
      LS Sequence Number: 0x80000001
      LS Checksum: 0xa3ef
      Length: 32
```

Figure 6-13. LS ACK

Once the exchange of information has been completed, the routers return to steady state operations with Hello messages. At this point, the routing tables in our topology are fully populated. The routing tables for R1 and R2 are shown in Figure 6-14.

```
Gateway of last resort is not set

C    192.168.1.0/24 is directly connected, FastEthernet0/1
C    192.168.2.0/24 is directly connected, FastEthernet0/0
O    192.168.3.0/24 [110/2] via 192.168.2.254, 03:43:11, FastEthernet0/0
R1#

Gateway of last resort is not set

O    192.168.1.0/24 [110/2] via 192.168.2.253, 03:44:38, FastEthernet0/1
C    192.168.2.0/24 is directly connected, FastEthernet0/1
C    192.168.3.0/24 is directly connected, FastEthernet0/0
R2#
```

Figure 6-14. Updated routing tables

These routing tables reflect the topology shown in Figure 6-4 with R1 and R2 directly connected to a pair of networks, but neither of them can connect to all destinations. OSPF was started and the packet exchange from Figure 6-6 was completed. The routing tables show the additional dynamic entries learned from OSPF. Each of these entries contains the destination network and the next hop information for that network. The table also depicts the OSPF specific administrative distance and metric which appear in the brackets: [110/2]. The administrative distance is an evaluation of the quality of OSPF information relative to other routing protocols. OSPF has an administrative distance of 110. RIP has an administrative distance of 120. The metric is derived from a number of factors and is not a simple hop count.

Timers

OSPF defines two general types of timers: single shot and interval. Single shot timers are for events such as the LS updates and routing changes. Interval timers govern items such as the Hello message. The Hello packets contain some of these values:

- Hello interval: details how often OSPF hello messages are sent. The current value is 10 seconds.
- Router dead interval: when this timer expires, a router will exit the wait state. It also describes the time after which a router will be considered "dead" (no Hello message received). The current value is 40 seconds and after this time, routes derived from the neighbor will be removed from the routing table.

Advanced Operation

The first topology used in this chapter is very simple containing a single area. If you have been reading through the text thus far, you probably realized that there is little point in running a routing protocol on a network that small. Now that the packet types and fields are out of the way, and the terminology hurdle has been cleared, let's move on to some more complex ideas and Figure 6-15.

Figure 6-15 depicts another OSPF topology and at first glance it might seem a little complex. But a closer look reveals that there are only three areas: 1, 2 and the backbone (0). Two of the areas (0 and 2) have some loops built in for redundancy. In backbone sections of a network loops are a common response to resiliency concerns. All of the devices pictured are running OSPF except for the hosts.

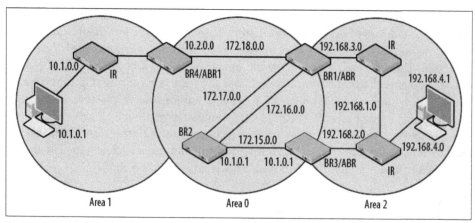

Figure 6-15. OSPF topology with three areas

Area 1 has a very simple topology and would be considered a stub area. The 10.0.0.0 networks are restricted to Area 1. On the right, Area 2 contains all of the 192.168.0.0 subnets and has a greater number of connections. In this case, there is more than one path out of the area and is conceivable traffic in this area might simply be passing through rather than having a destination address on one of the 192.168.0.0 subnets. This makes Area 2 a transit area. Both Area 1 and Area 2 have area border routers (ABR) connecting them to the center backbone area. In the case of Area 2, there are two routers serving as ABRs. The backbone routers (BR1-4) exist in the backbone area but three of them also serve as ABRs.

Figure 6-16 displays a routing table from BR4 once the topology has converged. There are a total of ten networks in this topology. Two of these (10.2.0.0 and 172.18.0.0) are directly connected to BR4. This is reflected in both the topology diagram and the routing table.

```
O       172.15.0.0/16 [110/3] via 172.18.0.253, 00:19:55, FastEthernet0/0
O       172.17.0.0/16 [110/2] via 172.18.0.253, 00:19:55, FastEthernet0/0
O       172.16.0.0/16 [110/2] via 172.18.0.253, 00:19:55, FastEthernet0/0
C       172.18.0.0/16 is directly connected, FastEthernet0/0
O IA 192.168.4.0/24 [110/4] via 172.18.0.253, 00:19:55, FastEthernet0/0
        10.0.0.0/16 is subnetted, 2 subnets
C          10.2.0.0 is directly connected, FastEthernet0/1
O          10.1.0.0 [110/2] via 10.2.0.254, 00:08:38, FastEthernet0/1
O IA 192.168.1.0/24 [110/3] via 172.18.0.253, 00:19:56, FastEthernet0/0
O IA 192.168.2.0/24 [110/4] via 172.18.0.253, 00:08:39, FastEthernet0/0
O IA 192.168.3.0/24 [110/2] via 172.18.0.253, 00:19:56, FastEthernet0/0
```

Figure 6-16. Large topology routing table

BR4 is a member of two different OSPF areas. In the configuration for this particular router, the following commands were issued:

```
interface FastEthernet0/0
    ip address 172.18.0.254 255.255.0.0
interface FastEthernet0/1
    ip address 10.2.0.253 255.255.0.0
router ospf 10
    log-adjacency-changes
    network 10.2.0.0 0.0.255.255 area 1
    network 172.18.0.0 0.0.255.255 area 0
```

As was seen earlier in the chapter, the LSA messages between the routers carry not only the network information but the areas as well. All of the networks in Areas 0 and 2 arrive via the next hop of 172.18.0.253 which happens to be BR1. All of these routes were learned via OSPF and thus have the letter O leftmost in the entry. Another indication that these are OSPF routes is that the bracketed values all list an administrative distance of 110. For example, the administrative distance and metric for the 172.15.0.0 network are [110/3]. All of the routes to the networks beginning with 192 are from Area 2. BR4 does not have an interface on Area 2. So, these are "inter-area" routes as indicated by the IA near the left side.

Moving to the backbone area, the routing table for BR1 is depicted in Figure 6-17. Notice that the inter-area routes are now the routes from Area 1. One other difference is that these routes are not tied to interfaces but VLANs. This actually has nothing to do with OSPF. This particular device is a multilayer switch rather than a straightforward router.

One of the most important things to notice is that because of the position change, there are several destinations that can be reached by more than one path. This brings up the whole question of loops in OSPF. The very first entry indicates that there are two pathways to the 172.15.0.0 network. The topology in Figure 6-15 actually provides a third pathway but it is through Area 2. The router has discarded that pathway in favor of the smaller metric. Recall that OSPF uses a dimensionless metric that is a factor of network conditions meaning that the metric does not have a "unit." The two variables that most affect this routing table entries are hop count and speed of the link. The packets earlier in this chapter indicated that there were no ToS metrics being used. See Figure 6-12. So, how is the metric for this entry derived? From BR1, the 172.15.0.0 network is one hop away. Per Cisco, the cost of these links are all based on the following formula: cost = 100,000,000 / link bandwidth in bps. For a 100Mbps link (100,000,000bps) the cost would be 1. Since there are two links used to get to the destination (BR1 output and BR2 output) the cost is 2.

```
O       172.15.0.0/16 [110/2] via 172.17.0.253, 00:39:11, Vlan17
                      [110/2] via 172.16.0.253, 00:39:11, Vlan16
C       172.17.0.0/16 is directly connected, Vlan17
C       172.16.0.0/16 is directly connected, Vlan16
C       172.18.0.0/16 is directly connected, Vlan18
O       192.168.4.0/24 [110/3] via 192.168.3.253, 23:15:59, Vlan2
        10.0.0.0/16 is subnetted, 2 subnets
O IA      10.2.0.0 [110/2] via 172.18.0.254, 00:27:54, Vlan18
O IA      10.1.0.0 [110/3] via 172.18.0.254, 00:27:55, Vlan18
O       192.168.1.0/24 [110/2] via 192.168.3.253, 23:16:00, Vlan2
O       192.168.2.0/24 [110/3] via 192.168.3.253, 23:16:00, Vlan2
C       192.168.3.0/24 is directly connected, Vlan2
```

Figure 6-17. Backbone routing table

In a RIP topology, 50/50 load balancing is accomplished when two pathways to the same destination have the same hop count. RIP does not consider the quality of the links. In this case, OSPF would do the same thing for traffic heading to the 172.15.0.0 network because the metrics are the same. Figure 6-18 depicts a LS Update packet with an increased metric. In this case, the metric was changed due to a speed configuration on the router port. The corresponding routing table entry would show [110/12] in brackets.

```
Ethernet II, Src: Cisco_aa:1b:42 (00:0a:b8:aa:1b:42), Dst: IPv4mcast_00:00:05 (01:00:5e:00:00:05)
Internet Protocol, Src: 172.16.0.253 (172.16.0.253), Dst: 224.0.0.5 (224.0.0.5)
Open Shortest Path First
⊞ OSPF Header
⊟ LS Update Packet
    Number of LSAs: 1
  ⊟ LS Type: Summary-LSA (IP network)
      LS Age: 2 seconds
      Do Not Age: False
    ⊟ Options: 0x22 (DC, E)
          0... .... = DN: DN-bit is NOT set
          .0.. .... = O: O-bit is NOT set
          ..1. .... = DC: Demand Circuits are supported
          ...0 .... = L: The packet does NOT contain LLS data block
          .... 0... = NP: NSSA is NOT supported
          .... .0.. = MC: NOT Multicast Capable
          .... ..1. = E: External Routing Capability
          .... ...0 = MT: NO Multi-Topology Routing
      Link-State Advertisement Type: Summary-LSA (IP network) (3)
      Link State ID: 192.168.3.0
      Advertising Router: 192.168.2.254 (192.168.2.254)
      LS Sequence Number: 0x80000001
      LS Checksum: 0x1b3f
      Length: 28
      Netmask: 255.255.255.0
      Metric: 12
```

Figure 6-18. LS update—increased metric due to link speed change

If you read the RIP chapter and have a handle on its operation, compare it to the behavior of OSPF. When discussing routing protocols it is sometimes said that OSPF is fairly aggressive when it comes to discovering pathways and removing dead routes. So, OSPF topologies converge and recover more quickly than RIP topologies. On the other hand OSPF updates can be large and the Hello packets take up network resources. Hello packets in OSPF are generated more often than steady state RIP updates. Given the improvements, many administrators consider these drawbacks worth the cost.

But just because OSPF uses a different approach does not mean that it ignores the lessons learned from other routing protocols. For example, OSPF has its own version of split horizon in that it will not advertise area routes back to the area. External routes may not be advertised to every area either. Additionally, if a route metric exceeds the OSPF infinity value, it will not continue to be advertised. This value can be seen at the bottom of Figure 6-19. OSPF quickly moves to adjust topologies with its own triggered updates. For example, if a link leading to an area were to be lost or if there were configuration changes necessitating a recalculation of the LSDB, some destinations might not be able to be reached. Like RIP, OSPF may advertise these routes as no longer available through the use of a large metric as shown in Figure 6-19.

```
Ethernet II, Src: Cisco_aa:1b:42 (00:0a:b8:aa:1b:42), Dst: IPv4mcast_00:00:05 (01:00:5e:00:00:05)
Internet Protocol, Src: 172.16.0.253 (172.16.0.253), Dst: 224.0.0.5 (224.0.0.5)
Open Shortest Path First
⊞ OSPF Header
⊟ LS Update Packet
     Number of LSAs: 1
  ⊟ LS Type: Summary-LSA (IP network)
       LS Age: 3600 seconds
       Do Not Age: False
    ⊟ Options: 0x22 (DC, E)
         0... .... = DN: DN-bit is NOT set
         .0.. .... = O: O-bit is NOT set
         ..1. .... = DC: Demand Circuits are supported
         ...0 .... = L: The packet does NOT contain LLS data block
         .... 0... = NP: NSSA is NOT supported
         .... .0.. = MC: NOT Multicast Capable
         .... ..1. = E: External Routing Capability
         .... ...0 = MT: NO Multi-Topology Routing
       Link-State Advertisement Type: Summary-LSA (IP network) (3)
       Link State ID: 192.168.1.0
       Advertising Router: 192.168.2.254 (192.168.2.254)
       LS Sequence Number: 0x80000002
       LS Checksum: 0xb6b0
       Length: 28
       Netmask: 255.255.255.0
       Metric: 16777215
```

Figure 6-19. OSPF infinity metric

OSPF and IPv6

OSPF for IPv6 is similar to its IPv4 version. The behavior and packet traffic remain the same. The database description is a bit more complex and the packets have been expanded to include additional options and LSA types. The topology in Figure 6-20 depicts the IPv6 topology for this section.

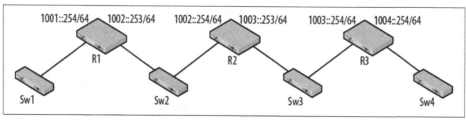

Figure 6-20. IPv6 topology

As demonstrated in the last chapter, when configuring the routing protocol for IPv6, many of the commands reside on the interface. A basic IPv6 OSPF configuration follows:

```
ipv6 unicast-routing
interface FastEthernet0/0
    ipv6 address 1001::254/64
    ipv6 ospf 1 area 51
interface FastEthernet0/1
    ipv6 address 1002::253/64
    ipv6 ospf 1 area 51
ipv6 router ospf 1
    router-id 1.1.1.1
```

The router id is used to identify the router in the event that IPv4 addresses are not present on the router. Once all of the routers have been given their configurations, the routing tables will have been updated with the OSPF learned routes are seen in Figure 6-21. To reduce complexity for this example, only one area was configured.

```
C    1001::/64 [0/0]
        via FastEthernet0/0, directly connected
L    1001::254/128 [0/0]
        via FastEthernet0/0, receive
C    1002::/64 [0/0]
        via FastEthernet0/1, directly connected
L    1002::253/128 [0/0]
        via FastEthernet0/1, receive
O    1003::/64 [110/2]
        via FE80::219:2FFF:FE8E:DB48, FastEthernet0/1
O    1004::/64 [110/3]
        via FE80::219:2FFF:FE8E:DB48, FastEthernet0/1
L    FF00::/8 [0/0]
        via Null0, receive
```

Figure 6-21. IPv6 OSPF routing table

Like the previous IPv6 examples in this book, the directly connected and link routes are independent of the routing protocol. The OSPF routes have been installed and depict nearly the same information as their IPv4 counterparts with the network address, mask, administrative distance and metric standard.

While wading through all of the IPv6 packet types is a little beyond this chapter, it is worth taking a look at a sample packet. Figure 6-22 depicts a LS Update captured between R1 and R2. The IPv6 LS Updates can get quite large so much of the header has been collapsed. The open fields show the network prefix, mask length and the use of the router-id. As mentioned previously, additional options (such as a flag for IPv6) and LSA types have been added.

```
Ethernet II, Src: Cisco_f6:a9:11 (00:1c:58:f6:a9:11), Dst: Cisco_8e:db:48 (00:19:2f:8e:db:48)
Internet Protocol Version 6, Src: fe80::21c:58ff:fef6:a911 (fe80::21c:58ff:fef6:a911), Dst: fe80::219:2fff:fe8e:db48 (fe80::219:2fff:fe8e:db48)
Open Shortest Path First
+ OSPF Header
= LS Update Packet
    Number of LSAs: 5
  + Router-LSA (Type: 0x2001)
  + Network-LSA (Type: 0x2002)
  + Link-LSA (Type: 0x0008)
  = Intra-Area-Prefix-LSA (Type: 0x2009)
    LS Age: 28 seconds
    Do Not Age: False
    LSA Type: 0x2009 (Intra-Area-Prefix-LSA)
    Link State ID: 0.0.0.0
    Advertising Router: 1.1.1.1 (1.1.1.1)
    LS Sequence Number: 0x80000003
    LS Checksum: 0x70d9
    Length: 56
    # prefixes: 2
    Referenced LS type 0x2001 (Router-LSA)
    Referenced Link State ID: 0.0.0.0
    Referenced Advertising Router: 1.1.1.1
    PrefixLength: 64
  + PrefixOptions: 0x00
    Metric: 1
    Address Prefix: 1002::
    PrefixLength: 64
  + PrefixOptions: 0x00
    Metric: 1
    Address Prefix: 1001::
  + Intra-Area-Prefix-LSA (Type: 0x2009)
```

Figure 6-22. IPv6 OSPF LS Update

In this case, one of the new LSA types (Intra-Area-Prefix-LSA) can be seen. Per RFC 5340:

This LSA carries all IPv6 prefix information that in IPv4 is included in router-LSAs and network-LSAs.

This also means that the network and router LSAs have been changed in IPv6 and no longer carry address information.

Reading

RFC 1584: Multicast Extensions to OSPF
RFC 1587: The OSPF NSSA Option
RFC 1793: Extending OSPF to Support Demand Circuits
RFC 2328: OSPF version 2 (obsoletes RFCs 2178, 1583, 1247)
RFC 2370: The OSPF Opaque LSA Option
RFC 2547: Using an LSA Options Bit to Prevent Looping in BGP/MPLS IP VPNs
RFC 3883: Detecting Inactive Neighbors over OSPF Demand Circuits (DC)
RFC 4811: OSPF Out-of-Band Link State Database (LSDB) Resynchronization
RFC 4915: Multi-Topology (MT) Routing in OSPF
RFC 5340: OSPF for IPv6 (obsoletes RFC 2740)
RFC 5613: OSPF Link Local Signaling (obsoletes RFC 4813)

Summary

As a link state protocol, OSPF operation has many important changes when compared to RIP. Hello messages, link state updates, database descriptions, additional metrics and rapid dissemination of routing information all serve to improve performance. OSPF also operates in a hierarchical fashion with routers understanding more and more of the topology as they become area border or backbone routers. Routers within the areas understand very little of the overall autonomous system.

It takes quite a bit of experience to become an expert on OSPF. While getting the protocol up and running is straightforward, OSPF can offer significant complexity when compared to distance vector protocols. However, through the packet captures, definitions and operational discussion, the reader is well equipped to configure and troubleshoot OSPF topologies.

Review Questions

1. Pick the set of terms that best describe OSPF.

   a. Link state, flat

   b. Link state, hierarchical

   c. Distance vector, flat

   d. Distance vector, hierarchical

2. What is the destination IP address used for OSPF?

3. OSPF topologies begin with each router believing it is the root.

   a. TRUE

   b. FALSE

4. OSPF area zero is known as the external route.

   a. TRUE

   b. FALSE

5. In OSPF, routers within an area did not know anything about the AS topology.

   a. TRUE

   b. FALSE

6. What is the value of the OSPF hello timer?

7. The network-LSA is used by all routers?

   a. TRUE

   b. FALSE

8. Which of the following is OSPF message type 4?

---

a. DB description

b. LS update

c. LS ACK

d. LS request

9. What is the administrative distance for OSPF?

10. The default metric of OSPF is comprised of what two values?

Review Answers

1. B. link state, hierarchical

2. 224.0.0.5

3. TRUE

4. FALSE

5. TRUE

6. 10 seconds

7. FALSE

8. LS Update

9. 110

10. Speed of the link and hop count

Lab Activities

Activity 1—Build the Topology Depicted in Figure 6-23

Materials: 2 routers, 2 computers, optional switches (or VLANs) for each network

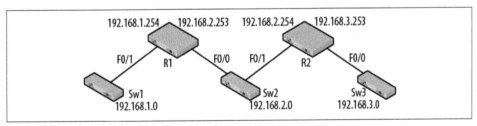

Figure 6-23. Activity 1 topology

1. Cable the topology and configure the IP addresses on the router interfaces.

2. Connect a computer to the 192.168.1.0 and 192.168.2.0 networks.

3. Manually configure the IP addresses and gateways for the computers.

4. For the computer on the 192.168.2.0 network, does it matter which default gateway is used? Why? What about after OSPF is running?

5. Examine the routing tables on the routers. What do they contain? Handy Cisco command: show ip route

Activity 2—Enable OSPF on the Routers

Materials: Activity 1 topology, Wireshark

1. On each router configure the router to use OSPF.

2. Handy Cisco commands: router ospf *process-id*, network _____ area _____

3. Capture traffic on both computers and watch as the OSPF packets begin to flow. Once the configuration is complete, examine the routing tables of the routers again.

4. What has changed in the router routing tables? What are the values in the brackets? Why?

Activity 3—Tracing the Packet Flow

Materials: Activity 1 topology, Wireshark

1. Disconnect the router interfaces from the topology.

2. Make sure that the Wireshark capture is running on the 192.168.2.0 network.

3. Examine the packets captured and trace the packet exchange. Can you identify the order of the packets and reasons for each?

4. Select a link state update that includes route information. Can you identify the fields described in this chapter?

Activity 4—Changing Network Conditions

Materials: Activity 1 topology, Wireshark

1. Predict what would happen if the IP address for F0/0 on R2 was changed. Include packets that might be generated and changes to routing tables.

2. With the Wireshark captures running, change the IP address to 192.168.4.253. Make the necessary changes to the OSPF configuration as well.

3. What traffic is generated as a result? What were the changes to your routing tables? How close were your predictions?

4. Recover the topology for the next activity.

Activity 5—A Loop

Materials: Activity 1 topology, Wireshark, a switch between R1 and R2

1. Change the IP address of F0/0 on R2 to 192.168.1.253.

2. Connect the interface to Switch 1 which creates a loop.

3. What are the changes to the routing tables?

4. With the loops constructed and Wireshark running, ping the addresses on the 192.168.1.0 network from R2. Over what links does the traffic pass? How does OSPF handle load sharing?

CHAPTER 7

Network Address Translation

The world has run out of IPv4 address space. Of course, this is not really news. In 2011 it was announced that some of the last five /8s of publicly available IPv4 address space were being allocated (*https://www.nro.net/news/ipv4-free-pool-depleted*).

Since then, IPv4 address space depletion has been a continuing concern. Trends such as the Internet of Things (IoT) promise to add IP addresses to everything from cars to refrigerators. The simple truth is that there are not enough addresses to go around (and this has been the case for several years).

Many believe that IPv6, with its vast 128-bit addressing, will save the Internet. To date there have been a series of IPv6 days in which organizations are challenged and encouraged to transition from IPv4 to IPv6. Given these factors, the world should be running on IPv6. But it is not. One of the biggest reasons for this is network address translation (NAT).

NAT is described in RFC 1631as a technique by which a single IPv4 public address can be used by several computers. This is because the computers actually use private addresses (also known as RFC 1918 addresses) which are translated into the public address. The effect is that the number of IPv4 public addresses needed is smaller than the number of computers. It works so well that in all likelihood, we will continue to rely on NAT.

NAT describes the process of converting traffic coming from private, inside IPv4 addresses to traffic that appears to have come from a globally unique outside address. The information describing this conversion is stored in a translation table. The effect is that someone on the outside cannot tell that the network traffic originated from an inside private network. But be careful—often touted as a security tool, network address translation is primarily an address management technique and it is the reason why so many of us have the same IP addresses on our home networks. This chapter will discuss and demonstrate NAT operation, table traversal, and the addressing associated with NAT-based topologies.

Description

In order to truly understand the structure and operation of network address translation there are a couple of aspects that we need to explore: addressing, table construction, and operation.

As illustrated in Figure 7-1, the basic idea of NAT is that some collection of addresses will be used on the "inside" network and another set of addresses will be used on the "outside" network.

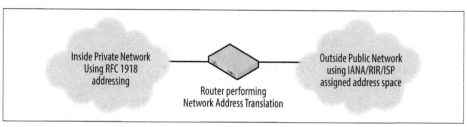

Figure 7-1. A rough sketch of how NAT works

The inside network will use the private addressing as defined in RFC 1918 and the outside network will typically use public addresses, though there are exceptions. Most public address space comes to an organization via its Internet Service Provider (ISP). This allocation can eventually be traced back to a Regional Internet Registry (RIR) and then on to the Internet Assigned Numbers Authority (IANA).

An important idea to keep in mind when working with NAT is that it is not only a question of addressing, but about addresses that are reachable and able to be resolved. So, there is a connection between private addressing and the Domain Name System.

Problem Overview

In 1994, RFC 1631 outlined the problem that NAT is trying to tackle. To quote:

> The two most compelling problems facing the IP Internet are IP address depletion and scaling in routing.

> This memo proposes another short-term solution, address reuse, that complements CIDR or even makes it unnecessary. The address reuse solution is to place Network Address Translators (NAT) at the borders of stub domains.

It is interesting to note that while this was originally intended as a short-term solution, its success is such that it is still widely used today. And despite the growing support for IPv6, NAT is likely to be around for some time to come.

Routing Tables

Core Internet routers have very large routing tables because they have knowledge of so many destinations. At the time of this writing, it is common to see routing table size approaching 500,000 entries. Parsing a table of this size is time consuming and is part of the rationale for protocols such as Multi-Protocol Label Switching (MPLS).

Routing table size and growth can be managed via aggregation. Routing tables are largely controlled through the hierarchical assignment of IP addresses from IANA to the regional registries to the ISPs. Blocks of address are given to ISP customers based on the number of public addresses needed. The use of Classless Inter-Domain Routing (CIDR) notation and Variable Length Subnet Masks (VLSMs) allows administrators to collapse several entries into entries with shorter prefixes. Remember that an address prefix refers to the network portion of the address. Shorter prefixes represent larger chunks of address space and therefore fewer entries are needed in the routing table. This is also known as aggregation or summarization. But even this approach cannot survive forever.

IPv4 Address Space Exhaustion

A central concept with network address translation is the idea that addresses are separated into inside (private) and outside (public) addresses. This concept is described in RFC 1918 Address Allocation for Private Internets.

In RFC 1918, hosts might be categorized three ways: those not needing any access to the public Internet, those needing occasional access, and those requiring a globally unique (unambiguous) IPv4 address. According to RFC 1918, hosts in the first two categories could use private addresses and thus do not impact public router routing table size or use up public IPv4 addresses. A really important idea is that these same addresses can be used by many different organizations and end hosts at the same time.

Within the networking world, we have many addresses that are reserved. For example, the 224.0.0.0–239.255.255.255 range is used for multicast and 127.0.0.0–127.255.255.255 is for the local host and testing. And you would never assign an address ending in 0 or 255 to an end host. RFC 1918 is another series of IPv4 addresses reserved for a particular purpose:

10.0.0.0–10.255.255.255	(10/8 prefix)
172.16.0.0–172.31.255.255	(172.16/12 prefix)
192.168.0.0–192.168.255.255	(192.168/16 prefix)

If we take another look at our basic network topology, we can now see where the addresses fit in (Figure 7-2).

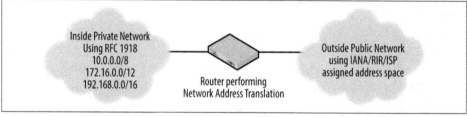

Figure 7-2. NAT internal and external addressing

By adding a network address translator, we can use these addresses and still communicate with the outside. There are some other problems that a NAT box can help address: What would we do with hosts or organizations that were not connected to the public Internet but now wish to be? Where could we obtain the necessary addresses? Because addresses come from the ISP, the organization would use a particular address range that would require renumbering of the IPv4 host addresses. Would they be available? Similarly, what happens when an organization changes ISPs or connections?

Today, smaller organizations and home networks need not assign globally unique addresses to any of their hosts. Instead, private addresses are assigned to every host within the networks, which is the answer to many of these questions.

Structure

Let's examine this connectivity from a broader viewpoint. If we consider several homes or businesses connected to an ISP, we might wind up with a topology like the one seen in Figure 7-3.

Here, three homes or small organizations have a connection to their ISP and the ISP is then connected to the Internet. Each of the three small networks uses the exact same addressing internally: the 192.168.1.0/24 network, which is part of the RFC 1918 address space. Each of the routers (remember that they still have the task of routing IP packets) is performing network address translation and has as an outside IP address, which is a globally unique IPv4 address from the space controlled by the ISP. The job of the NAT router is to convert the inside private addresses to the globally unique public address.

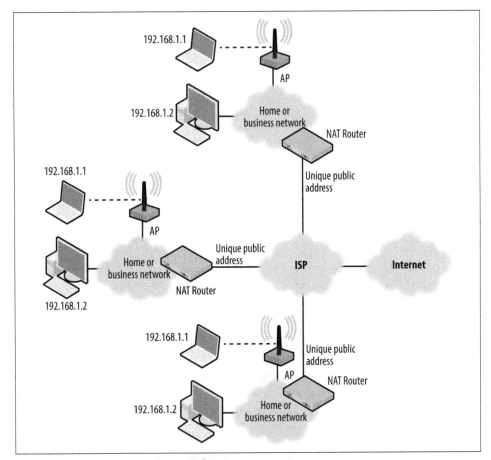

Figure 7-3. NAT use in an ISP topology

Operation

In a nutshell, the NAT router builds a translation table for outgoing transmissions. In one part of the table are the original source and destination addresses. In another location, the new or translated addresses are stored. The new source addressing is the outside interface of the router itself. In the outgoing direction, the NAT box makes a substitution. It keeps track of the transmission information and when the transmission comes back to the router, resubstitutes the original addressing and forwards the traffic to the original sender.

We now have to extend this idea of translation to include what we might call the inside socket and the outside socket. In other words, once the packets reach the router performing NAT, the addresses change. But because we are tracking a transmission or conversation, we also have to follow the Layer 4 ports. A socket is comprised of four numbers: source and destination IP addresses and ports. That is, the Transmission Control Protocol (TCP) and the User Datagram Protocol (UDP) ports. We can see an example in Figure 7-4.

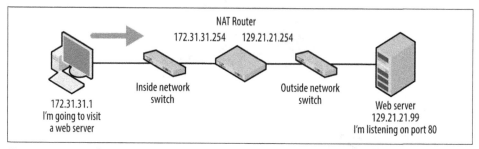

Figure 7-4. Sample NAT topology

In this example, a transmission originates from the node on the left: 172.31.31.1. Note that this node address resides in a block of private address space. The destination is a web server seen on the right: 129.21.21.99. A transmission of this sort can only be completed if the node connects to the correct port. In this case, it will be port 80. But the source host also has a source port. These four numbers make up the connection. Some network address translation tables contain a fifth value which is the protocol. In this case, it would be TCP.

When the packets reach the NAT box, it will substitute itself as the source in order to make it seem like the transmission came from the external interface of the router: 129.21.21.254. The original information and the substitution are stored in the translation table:

Original information	Substitution
172.31.31.1:64843 →129.21.21.99:80	129.21.21.254:2000 → 129.21.21.99:80

When the transmission returns from the web server to the outside interface of the NAT router, the router modifies the packets again in order to send them back to the original source: 172.31.31.1.

Now let's take a look at the actual traffic and tables resulting from a connection like this one. Without NAT, the traffic on either side of the router will look the same, at least at Layer 3, and this is shown in Figure 7-5.

```
 30  00:0c:85:a2:70:01      01:80:c2:00:00:00         STP
 31  172.31.31.1            129.21.21.99             TCP        80
 32  129.21.21.99           172.31.31.1              TCP        64843
 33  172.31.31.1            129.21.21.99             TCP        80
```
```
▷ Frame 31: 74 bytes on wire (592 bits), 74 bytes captured (592 bits) on interface 0
▷ Ethernet II, Src: 3c:97:0e:1b:81:33, Dst: 00:0c:ce:42:38:60
▷ Internet Protocol Version 4, Src: 172.31.31.1, Dst: 129.21.21.99
▷ Transmission Control Protocol, Src Port: 64843 (64843), Dst Port: 80 (80), Seq: 0, Len: 0
```

Figure 7-5. Packets seen on the inside network

As described before, the transmission begins (packet 31) and uses the source and destination values of 172.31.31.1:64843 and 129.21.21.99:80, respectively. Normally these values would not change as the packet traverses the path through the Internet. Once network address translation is implemented, the source values will change to those shown in Figure 7-6. These packets were captured on a separate machine and on the outside interface of the NAT router.

```
 28 24.612817    129.21.21.254    129.21.21.99     TCP     64843 → 80 [SYN] Seq=0
 29 24.613428    129.21.21.99     129.21.21.254    TCP     80 → 64843 [SYN, ACK] S
 30 24.614998    129.21.21.254    129.21.21.99     TCP     64843 → 80 [ACK] Seq=1
```

Figure 7-6. Packets seen on the external network

Looking back at Figure 7-4, these two captures represent the traffic from the lefthand (inside) and righthand (outside) sides.

As we can see, the new source IP address is 129.21.21.254 though the source port has remained the same. It is important to realize that the port numbers sometimes change depending on availability and implementation. As long as the values are stored in the translation table, the conversion can be completed successfully. The packet number has changed because while the timing is close (they came from the same event) this is not the original packet and has been captured on a different network. The translation table used by the router is shown in Figure 7-7.

```
Router#sh ip nat translations
Pro Inside global      Inside local      Outside local      Outside global
tcp 129.21.21.254:64843 172.31.31.1:64843 129.21.21.99:80    129.21.21.99:80
icmp 129.21.21.254:1    172.31.31.1:1     129.21.21.99:1     129.21.21.99:1
```

Figure 7-7. Router translation table

This was obtained from a Cisco router after issuing the command show ip nat translations.

In this case, the translated fields are the first two that depict the actual inside source (inside local) and the one used by the router on the outside (inside global). When the packets come back in, the router simply does a table lookup and resubstitutes for the original values. This example is straightforward because the router and web server share the outside network. However, this basic operation works no matter where the destination resides.

The router configuration for this example:

```
interface FastEthernet0/0
 ip address 172.31.31.254 255.255.255.0
 ip nat inside
!
interface FastEthernet0/1
 ip address 129.21.21.254 255.255.255.0
 ip nat outside
!
ip nat inside source list 1 interface FastEthernet0/1 overload
!
access-list 1 permit any
```

The `ip nat inside source list 1 interface FastEthernet0/1 overload` command tells us that the source addresses indicated by the access list (any) will be translated to the addressing used on interface f0/1. In addition, because of the "overload" keyword, all of the translated traffic will use the same address of 129.21.21.254.

What about ICMP?

If you have been following closely, you probably noticed that this entire structure and operation is predicated on knowing all four values used in the transmission: src IP, dest IP, src port, and dest port. The reason that this is important is that these four numbers uniquely identify every single transmission on the Internet. This is also used to describe a connected pair of sockets. Different transmissions will always modify at least one of these numbers in order to be unique. Even if we were to open several browser pages to the same destination, making the source IP, destination IP, and destination port the same, the source port would be different. This is shown in Figure 7-8.

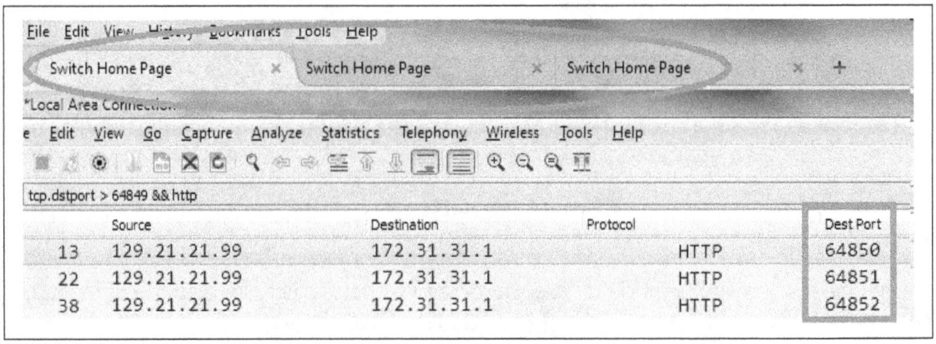

Figure 7-8. Packets using different ports but accessing the same website

At the top the browser tabs are open to the same webpage. Overlaid is the Wireshark capture depicting the different ports. All of the other values are the same. This is the only parameter that facilitates the delivery of the data to the correct process on the source machine.

But what happens when we do not have the port numbers available to us? It turns out that ICMP does not have a Layer 4 header but somehow, the delivery still succeeds, even with multiple nodes behind the NAT box. The ICMP table entry is shown in Figure 7-9.

```
Router#sh ip nat translations
Pro Inside global     Inside local       Outside local      Outside global
icmp 129.21.21.254:1  172.31.31.1:1      129.21.21.99:1     129.21.21.99:1
```

Figure 7-9. Router translation table with ICMP entries

It also looks as though there is another value associated with each entry. You can see the *:1* after each IP address. For ICMP, at least in this Cisco implementation, the ICMP ID field value is used instead of the TCP port. This is shown is Figure 7-10.

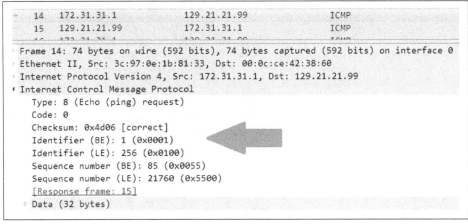
```
   14   172.31.31.1            129.21.21.99            ICMP
   15   129.21.21.99          172.31.31.1            ICMP

Frame 14: 74 bytes on wire (592 bits), 74 bytes captured (592 bits) on interface 0
Ethernet II, Src: 3c:97:0e:1b:81:33, Dst: 00:0c:ce:42:38:60
Internet Protocol Version 4, Src: 172.31.31.1, Dst: 129.21.21.99
Internet Control Message Protocol
    Type: 8 (Echo (ping) request)
    Code: 0
    Checksum: 0x4d06 [correct]
    Identifier (BE): 1 (0x0001)
    Identifier (LE): 256 (0x0100)
    Sequence number (BE): 85 (0x0055)
    Sequence number (LE): 21760 (0x5500)
    [Response frame: 15]
    Data (32 bytes)
```

Figure 7-10. ICMP packet identifier

Within Wireshark the Identifier BE and LE (big endian, little endian) fields refer to the same octet.

Modes

In the chapter configuration example, there are a couple of items worth examination. The first is that the NAT commands were used in conjunction with an access control list (ACL). An ACL is simply a collection of rules that make up a container. We see them used most often with security where they permit or deny traffic based on matching criteria. In this case, the ACL indicates traffic that should be translated. Anything not matching the rule is simply routed.

The other item to note is the keyword "overload" which means that all of the nodes in the inside network will use the same outside address when translated. This is shown in Figure 7-11.

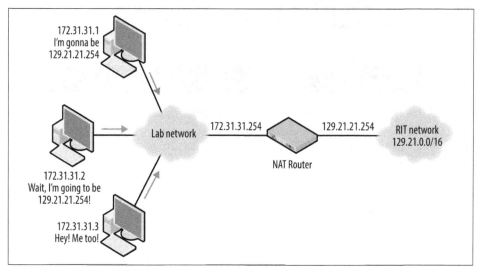

Figure 7-11. NAT overload example

If this many-to-1 mapping is not desired, individual nodes can have their own outside address and be mapped to this; although this doesn't do much for address conservation. The command would be modified to give each node a static translation as follows:

```
ip nat inside source static 172.31.31.1 129.21.21.55 extendable
```

This will cause the outbound traffic to use the specified address (129.21.21.55) rather than the IP address of the router interface. The extendable keyword allows multiple static translations of this type. The new translation table would reflect the changes as shown in Figure 7-12.

```
Router#sh ip nat translations
Pro Inside global      Inside local       Outside local      Outside global
tcp 129.21.21.55:65334 172.31.31.1:65334  129.21.21.99:80    129.21.21.99:80
icmp 129.21.21.55:1    172.31.31.1:1      129.21.21.99:1     129.21.21.99:1
--- 129.21.21.55       172.31.31.1        ---                ---
```

Figure 7-12. Router translation table after static configuration

Figure 7-13 shows that the traffic captured on the outside network also follows the updated translation rules.

```
 8 9.925567      129.21.21.55        129.21.21.99        ICMP
 9 9.925886      129.21.21.99        129.21.21.55        ICMP
10 9.999872      CiscoInc_a2:74:15   Spanning-tree-(for…  STP
11 10.927452     129.21.21.55        129.21.21.99        ICMP
12 10.927784     129.21.21.99        129.21.21.55        ICMP
```

Figure 7-13. Traffic resulting from static configuration

Another common approach is to use pools when configuring translations. The idea is that a range of addresses will be allocated for those needing to be translated. A sample command would look like this:

```
ip nat pool oreilly-pool 129.21.21.41 129.21.21.44 netmask 255.255.255.0
ip nat inside source list 1 pool nat-chapter overload
access-list 1 permit any
```

where "oreilly-pool" is the name of the pool and the addresses 129.21.21.41 through 129.21.21.44 inclusive mark the boundaries of the pool. The access list is still used. Figure 7-14 depicts the new translation table.

```
Router#sh ip nat translations
Pro Inside global     Inside local     Outside local     Outside global
tcp 129.21.21.41:65338 172.31.31.1:65338 129.21.21.99:80  129.21.21.99:80
icmp 129.21.21.41:1    172.31.31.1:1    129.21.21.99:1    129.21.21.99:1
Router#
```

Figure 7-14. Router translation table after pool configuration

Again, we can see the effect as Figure 7-15 shows the change to traffic.

```
25 13.041895     129.21.21.41        129.21.21.99        ICMP
26 13.042228     129.21.21.99        129.21.21.41        ICMP
27 14.042314     129.21.21.41        129.21.21.99        ICMP
28 14.042623     129.21.21.99        129.21.21.41        ICMP
```

Figure 7-15. Traffic resulting from pool configuration

Remember that all of these different modes are accomplishing the same task—controlling address use on the public side of the router by changing the inside address to a smaller number of outside addresses seen on the network. As an administrator, you would pick the method best suited to organizational needs.

Performance and Servers

There are a couple of things to consider when deploying a router running NAT. For small or home office networks (SOHO), there are many factors that can affect the quality of your Internet performance. This includes the type of connection you have and the distance from the ISP aggregation point. The number of different connections (each Internet node can have several) can also affect performance because like any other networking device table, the entries must be processed. In addition, all of the packets must be rewritten because of the address changes. Even a large router can have trouble if the translation table gets too large. Lastly, NAT can also degrade performance in the header checksum calculation. Figure 7-16 shows an example.

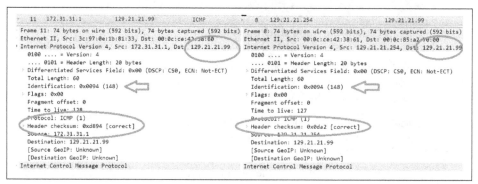

Figure 7-16. IP packet depicting changed addresses and calculated checksums

If we examine the transmission on both sides of the NAT router we can see that they are the same ICMP transmission (they also have the same ICMP ID although that is not shown here), have the same IP identification field value, and have the same destination IP address. But because the source IP address is different, the header is rewritten and the header checksum must be recalculated. This can greatly impact performance because of the additional processing.

Running a server behind a NAT box can be challenging because many NAT routers prevent unsolicited incoming traffic. Stated another way—if the conversation did not originate from inside, it is not permitted to pass. This means that a server is not publicly accessible unless we make some configuration changes. By altering the command we saw earlier, we can port forward to the correct destination:

```
ip nat inside source static tcp 172.31.31.1 22 129.21.21.100 22
```

This command means that incoming traffic is forwarded to the specified inside destination based on the Layer 4 TCP or UDP port. Implemented properly, this is the only port permitted through.

This example is a static entry that would allow an external host to connect to 129.21.21.100 so that it could SSH into 172.31.31.1—the router forwards port 22 based on this rule. Running more than one server of the same type can be problematic if you wish to use the same port.

Security

Most people believe that Network Address Translation is a security tool because it makes hosts and the network invisible. While this idea is mentioned in both RFC

3022 and the original RFC 1631, it is clearly not the main focus of the RFCs. In fact, the entire discussion in RFC 3022 is limited to the following:

> Traditional NAT can be viewed as providing a privacy mechanism as sessions are unidirectional from private hosts and the actual addresses of the private hosts are not visible to external hosts.

> The same characteristic that enhances privacy potentially makes debugging problems (including security violations) more difficult. If a host in private network is abusing the Internet in some way (such as trying to attack another machine or even sending large amounts of spam) it is more difficult to track the actual source of trouble because the IP address of the host is hidden in a NAT router.

There are several reasons to avoid relying on this invisibility for your security, as there are several techniques that can be used to find out something about your network.

First, a router that runs NAT is different from a home gateway because the home gateway is also implementing a firewall for you. An example can be seen in the common "block anonymous outside requests" and "do not allow this device to be managed from outside" options, as shown in Figure 7-17.

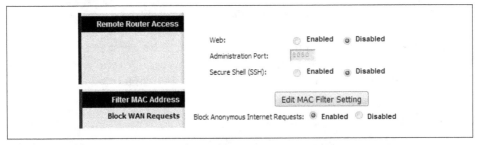

Figure 7-17. Home gateway security settings

While a router such as the one configured for this chapter can be configured with similar rules, by default your home gateway is more secure than a standard router, at least from a NAT perspective.

Because all of the private networks draw upon the same address space for their hosts, the number of targets to choose from is small, allowing the attacker to guess a few of the common address ranges. For example, many home networks are configured for the 192.168.0.0/24 network. After that it is a matter of trying to get traffic to be passed to the internal network. It turns out that many routers will forward traffic to internal IP addresses via static routes, routing protocols, and even ICMP redirects. This is because the router knows where the destination is even though it is a private address.

Second, some applications and protocols include the IP address in the application layer conversation. This means that the IP address appears above Layer 4. For example, HTTP has the ability to query the client for the client IP address. Many of these can be prevented but another example can be seen in Figure 7-18.

```
 8742  129.21.25.155          10.160.100.109          SIP          5060

Frame 8742: 597 bytes on wire (4776 bits), 597 bytes captured (4776 bits) on interface 0
Ethernet II, Src: 3c:97:0e:1b:81:33, Dst: 00:00:0c:07:ac:01
Internet Protocol Version 4, Src: 129.21.25.155, Dst: 10.160.100.109    <===
User Datagram Protocol, Src Port: 52836 (52836), Dst Port: 5060 (5060)
Session Initiation Protocol (REGISTER)
   Request-Line: REGISTER sip:10.160.100.109 SIP/2.0
 ⊿ Message Header
     Via: SIP/2.0/UDP 129.21.25.155:52836;branch=z9hG4bK-524287-1---a03d2750b3ffa329;rport
     Max-Forwards: 70
     Contact: <sip:5740003@129.21.25.155:52836;rinstance=2b0f28e8c73c1d97>
     To: "Bruce-sip-1"<sip:5740003@10.160.100.109>
     From: "Bruce-sip-1"<sip:5740003@10.160.100.109>;tag=b61e4021
     Call-ID: 76589ZGY1NWFjZWZmZWUxNzM1MjZjYmY2MmY3NjJmZTM4N2U
     CSeq: 1 REGISTER
     Expires: 3600
     Allow: SUBSCRIBE, NOTIFY, INVITE, ACK, CANCEL, BYE, REFER, INFO, MESSAGE
     User-Agent: X-Lite 4.8.4 76589-aebb73eb-W6.1
     Content-Length: 0
Session Initiation Protocol (SIP as raw text)
```

Figure 7-18. IP addresses exposed in application header

In this packet, the server IP address (10.160.100.109) can be seen but also the current IP address (129.21.25.155) that the host is attempting to use. The arrow indicates Layer 3. Clearly this information is not hidden by the NAT router.

Traversal

As noted in RFC 3022, NAT connections can actually make life more difficult for applications and security. An example can be found in virtual private networks (VPNs). IPSec (RFC 4301) is the standard protocol for encapsulating and encrypting VPN traffic. The trouble is that IPSec is a Layer 3 VPN, which means that the Layer 4 port information is encrypted or hidden. For this reason, many home gateways use the "VPN pass-through" option, which simply forwards traffic to the VPN client on the internal network. The downside is that it is difficult to run more than one VPN client simultaneously. This is similar to the "multiple servers of the same type" problem.

But problems do not end here. As soon as network address translation is involved, things can become challenging for the end hosts wishing to connect. Because of these application difficulties, there have been several traversal techniques developed to cope with the problem. Some of the problems faced by applications traveling through a NAT box include:

- Dealing with different NAT types (this leads to a misunderstanding with how the translation is handled)
- Communicating with another node that is also behind a NAT box
- Handling offer/answer protocols such as the Session Descriptor protocol in which port numbers are negotiated for later use
- Translation table entries timing out

We know that a socket is comprised of the source and destination ip:port pairs. NAT operation can hide or obfuscate the ports to be used and when this happens the connection fails. Each traversal technique seeks to address this problem and keep sessions alive. This is commonly accomplished via an outside service to which the endpoints connect. To quote RFC 5766 (Traversal Using Relays for NAT):

> If a host is located behind a NAT, then in certain situations it can be impossible for that host to communicate directly with other hosts (peers). In these situations, it is necessary for the host to use the services of an intermediate node that acts as a communication relay.

To date there have been several attempts to solve these problems including ICE (Interactive Connectivity Establishment), TURN (Traversal Using Relays around NAT), and STUN (Session Traversal Utilities) for NAT but none of these is a panacea.

NAT Behind NAT

There are alternative configurations that we have not discussed, including the NAT behind NAT implementation pictured in Figure 7-19.

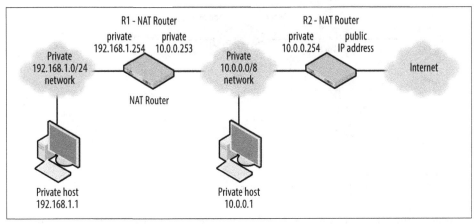

Figure 7-19. NAT behind NAT topology

It may look a little strange but it works for the exact same reason as the previous topologies. The private host (192.168.1.1) sends traffic to the Internet via R1. But to the host on the 10.0.0.0/8 net, it appears as though the traffic came from 10.0.0.253. From then on, it is just as before with traffic appearing to come from the public IP address on the R2-NAT Router. Traffic traveling back into the 192.168.1.0/24 network is simply processed by two translation tables.

A Note on DNS

The Domain Name System serves the purpose of mapping IP addresses to human-readable names. This is the reason we do not have to use IP addresses in browsers or in connections to servers. We now know that the addresses used in association with NAT are private. That is, they do not appear on the public Internet address space. This means that public DNS servers do not use these addresses. Users wishing to connect to a server name (HTTP, FTP, SSH, etc.) that maps to a private IP address cannot if they are connecting from the public Internet space. There are a couple of exceptions. If they are connecting to the outside interface of a NAT box that forwards traffic to the inside, they can communicate with the server. In this case, the public DNS record would not point to a private address. This is not to say that servers cannot have private IP addresses. Examine Figure 7-20.

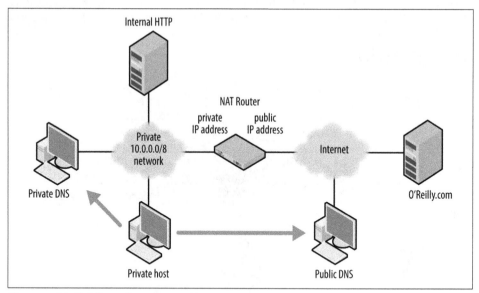

Figure 7-20. Public and private DNS servers

As noted previously, we can map to internal addresses but we can also create private DNS servers. It is not uncommon for an organization to have public- and private-facing servers that are reached or resolved by different systems. So the private host on the left might use the private DNS lookup to find the internal HTTP server. To reach *oreilly.com*, the external DNS might be queried. A private DNS server can also refer queries to another server.

Summary

The problem of IPv4 address depletion has been a concern for more than two decades. RFC 1631 first discussed the problem in 1994. That document also discussed the problem of excessive routing table size. The IP Network Address Translator (NAT) was to be part of a collection of short-term solutions. The IPv6 long-term solution should have been an end to the problem of address depletion. However, NAT has been an extremely successful technology, and combined with the slow rollout of IPv6, NAT will continue to be with us for years to come.

This chapter covered the IPv4 address depletion problem addressed by NAT. The operation and structure of NAT architectures were also discussed and demonstrated. Included were various configuration options, such as overload and pools. NAT does present some challenges for applications and this chapter discussed security and traversal operations for NAT deployments. These were illustrated by system output and packet captures.

Reading

RFC 1631: The IP Network Address Translator (NAT)—obsoleted by 3022
RFC 1918: Address Allocation for Private Internets
RFC 3022: Traditional IP Network Address Translator (Traditional NAT)
RFC 5245: Interactive Connectivity Establishment (ICE): A Protocol for Network Address Translator (NAT) Traversal for Offer/Answer Protocols
RFC 5389: Session traversal Utilities for NAT
RFC 5508: NAT Behavioral Requirements for ICMP
RFC 6314: Traditional IP Network Address Translator (Traditional NAT)

More information regarding masking, prefixes, IPv4, IPv6, TCP, and UDP can be found in the *Packet Guide to Core Network Protocols*.

Review Questions

1. Which RFC governs the addressing used in NAT topologies?
2. What are the three ranges of address used in conjunction with NAT?
3. The address used for translation is typically the inside address of the edge router.
   a. TRUE
   b. FALSE

4. All of the home networks sharing an ISP-supplied network could use the same internal IP addressing when NAT is deployed.

   a. TRUE

   b. FALSE

5. What numeric socket fields are used by NAT?

6. NAT boxes always use the same source port as the originating client machine.

   a. TRUE

   b. FALSE

7. What is the term describing the technique used to allow outside users to connect to a server sitting behind a NAT box?

8. Traversal techniques are used whenever a host establishes a connection to an outside server.

   a. TRUE

   b. FALSE

9. The other important issue specifically addressed by RFC 3022 is internal host and network security.

   a. TRUE

   b. FALSE

10. For traversal operations it is common to see an outside service used to help discover the ports to be used.

    a. TRUE

    b. FALSE

Review Answers

1. 1918

2. 10.0.0.0–10.255.255.255 (10.0.0.0/8), 172.16.0.0–172.31.255.255 (172.16.0.0/12), 192.168.0.0–192.168.255.255 (192.168.0.0/16)

3. FALSE

4. TRUE

5. Source IP address, source port, destination IP address, destination port

6. FALSE

7. Port forwarding

8. FALSE

9. FALSE

10. TRUE

Lab Activities

Activity 1—SOHO Network Discovery

Materials: home network, home gateway, network host

1. On your home or lab provided gateway, open a web browser and browse to the internal IP address of the gateway. This will also be the default gateway for your nodes.

2. Using the web interface, see if you can discover the network parameters and NAT settings for the gateway.

   a. What is the ISP network?

   b. What address has been given to the gateway?

   c. What network are you running internally? Can this be changed? Would it impact the operation of the network?

   d. Does your gateway have a viewable translation table? If so, what is in it? Explain any entries you find.

3. What security features protect your network from external traffic?

Activity 2—SOHO Network Traffic

Materials: home network, home gateway, network host, Wireshark, hub or switch, second PC to capture traffic

1. Using Wireshark, capture traffic on a host sitting in the private network. Does this match the settings from the previous activity?

2. Insert a hub or switch with a monitor session between your home gateway's outside interface and the external network.

3. Start a capture there.

4. Generate traffic from the inside host.

5. Most home gateways do not give us the ability to see the translation table. However, we can now see the traffic on both sides.

6. See if you can trace the flow of traffic from inside to outside. Try this with ping and an application such as web browsing.

Activity 3—NAT Build

Materials: router, network hosts

1. Using the configuration provided in the chapter, build the sample topology. You may adjust the addressing for your environment.
2. Ensure that you can ping all of the addresses from the private host.
3. Take a look at your translation table. Can you explain the entries?

Activity 4—NAT Build Traffic

Materials: router, network hosts

1. Using Wireshark, capture traffic on a host sitting in the private (inside) network.
2. Using Wireshark, capture traffic on a host sitting in the public (outside) network.
3. Generate traffic from the inside host to the outside.
4. See if you can trace the flow of traffic from inside to outside. Try this with ping and an application such as web browsing. If you are building an isolated network, as a substitution for web browsing you may set up a simple file share or FTP server such as Filezilla.

Activity 5—Running a Server on the Private Network

Materials: router, network hosts

1. On the private (inside) network set up a server or file share of some kind. A good example is Filezilla. Do not forget necessary user accounts and permissions.
2. Test your server from another inside host.
3. Attempt to connect to the server from the outside host. Does it work? Specifically, why/why not?
4. To fix this we need to make two adjustments. First, configure the router to allow port forwarding as discussed in this chapter. You must configure the proper ports for your application.
5. Second, try to connect to the outside interface of the router rather than the IP address of the server. Why do we need to do this?
6. See if you can explain the operation. What appears in the translation table?

CHAPTER 8

Multicast

Most of the host-based traffic seen on IPv4 networks is the result of unicast (node-to-node) or broadcast (node-to-everyone) frames or packets. The third type of traffic is called multicast, which is used to contact a subset of the nodes on the network or to create a one-to-many transmission. Perhaps the most famous use of multicast comes to us from the MBone, the Multicast Backbone project. While interest in the MBone project is somewhat quiescent, multicast still has its uses in networks today, including video streams, protocols such as spanning tree, and vendor-specific communication. With IPv6, we also see much greater dependence on multicast as broadcast addressing is no longer used. Thus, it becomes important for a network administrator to know something of multicast operation and its impact on the network.

Multicast has two parts: that which occurs between devices on the same network and a component that enables multicast over a collection of networks. Routers handle traffic traveling between networks and by default, routers do not forward multicast traffic. They have to be configured to forward multicast and like most destinations, the routers also have to be given instructions for the multicast transmissions. This is accomplished via Protocol Independent Multicast (PIM).

As we will later in this chapter, another way to think of multicast traffic is traffic that goes to a "host group." Locally, end hosts signal their interest in a multicast transmission via the Internet Group Management Protocol (IGMP). Because multicast traffic is similar to broadcast traffic in its ability to leak all over the network, some effort is put into preventing multicast traffic from leaking everywhere.

This chapter will cover both PIM and IGMP in terms of their operation and integration. The sample topologies will be supported with packet captures and configuration lines as we examine the structure and operation of the multicast architecture. Examples will include the most recent protocol versions with supporting discussion from previous popular versions.

Protocol Description

As mentioned previously, there are two parts to a multicast deployment: local, which is handled by the Internet Group Management Protocol (IGMP), and network, which is handled by Protocol Independent Multicast (PIM). A topology like the one seen in Figure 8-1 will have a multicast source and some nodes interested in the multicast content.

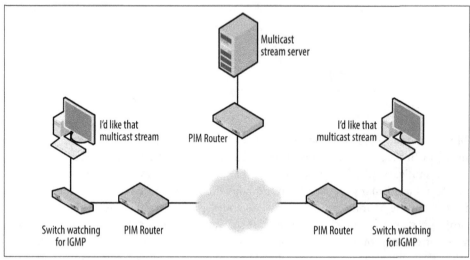

Figure 8-1. Sample topology for this chapter

Nodes interested in the multicast stream will signal their interest via the network by trying to connect using IGMP. By default, switches forward multicast traffic throughout the Layer 2 broadcast domain. If we remember our TCP/IP model, IGMP is similar to the Internet Control Message Protocol (ICMP) in that it is encapsulated in an IP packet and is considered part of Layer 3. This encapsulation is shown in Figure 8-2.

```
Ethernet II, Src: 10:8c:cf:57:20:c0, Dst: 01:00:5e:00:00:01
Internet Protocol Version 4, Src: 129.21.25.252, Dst: 224.0.0.1
Internet Group Management Protocol
```

Figure 8-2. Layer 2 IGMP encapsulation

In this example, the IGMP message came from host 129.21.25.252. As the encapsulation shows, IGMP resides inside of the IP packet. As we can see, the "all hosts" destination multicast address of 224.0.0.1 being used. This is one of the many reserved multicast addresses we see used in networks today. This along with the IGMP packet types and operation will be explained later in this chapter.

In order to support IGMP, all hosts are already a part of the 224.0.0.1 multicast group.

The importance of PIM is to facilitate the transmission of the Layer 3 multicast packets in the routing domain. Routers are configured for multicast and exchange information regarding the processing of multicast packet. PIM encapsulation can be seen in Figure 8-3.

```
Ethernet II, Src: 00:09:11:2a:b8:00, Dst: 01:00:5e:00:00:0d
Internet Protocol Version 4, Src: 10.6.4.254, Dst: 224.0.0.13
Protocol Independent Multicast
    0010 .... = Version: 2
    .... 0000 = Type: Hello (0)
    Reserved byte(s): 00
    Checksum: 0xe059 [correct]
  ◢ PIM Options: 5
    ▷ Option 1: Hold Time
      Holdtime: 1
    ▷ Option 20: Generation ID: 4
    ▷ Option 19: DR Priority: 1
    ▷ Option 21: State Refresh Capable: Version = 1, Interval = 0s
    ▷ Option 65004: Unknown: 65004
```

Figure 8-3. Layer 3 PIM encapsulation

In this example, a testbed router (10.6.4.254) sent this PIMv2 HELLO message, which uses another reserved multicast address: 224.0.0.13. We will cover PIM in greater detail in subsequent sections.

Consider the problem of routing multicast traffic. Remember that by default routers do not forward multicast traffic. Routing protocols and static routes provide pathways to unicast destinations. So, routers do not know how far multicast traffic should be forwarded. A typical unicast routing table is shown in Figure 8-4.

```
      172.29.0.0/24 is subnetted, 1 subnets
S       172.29.29.0 [1/0] via 172.30.30.253
      172.31.0.0/24 is subnetted, 1 subnets
C       172.31.31.0 is directly connected, FastEthernet0/0
      172.30.0.0/24 is subnetted, 1 subnets
C       172.30.30.0 is directly connected, FastEthernet0/1
Router-A#
```

Figure 8-4. Router IPv4 unicast routing table

All of the destinations listed (172.29.0.0, 172.30.0.0, and 172.31.0.0) are specific to a single unicast address space: an address space comprised on unicast hosts. Standard Internet traffic travels from a unicast host address to another unicast host address.

The process of handling these transmissions is unicast routing. This means that a router given a message with a destination like those shown previously (224.0.0.1 and 2240.0.0.13) would have no idea how to process the information or forward packets. At this point, the router would not understand multicast routing.

Thus hosts on opposite sides of the same router would not be able to access a multicast stream. The problem is even more challenging when the topology grows larger and traffic must cross several routers. We can see this problem in Figure 8-1. Nodes on opposite sides of a routed topology might be interested in the multicast stream. But how would nodes from all over the topology signal to the stream sources that they were interested in the traffic? How would multicast packets be forwarded throughout the topology? Unicast transmissions are tied to a single source location and an individual network will reside in exactly one location. All routers will eventually learn how to get to this destination or what router can help them find it. But multicast destinations are not part of the routing tables and we must have a mechanism for discovery of multicast sources and signaling in order to join and leave multicast streams.

To answer this, multicast-enabled routers are aware of the IGMP messaging and can answer host queries. In this way they become aware of hosts interested in receiving or transmitting multicast packets regardless of how many and their location. Routers also use PIM to communicate with neighboring routers about multicast sources.

Multicast Addressing

Although we distinguish between Layer 2 and Layer 3 addressing, it is often true that these addresses go together. This is certainly the case with multicast. We can also make a distinction between IPv4 multicast and IPv6 multicast. The addresses typically used for these are shown in the following table:

	Layer 2	Layer 3
IPv4	Begins with 01	224.0.0.0–239.255.255.255 (RFC 1112), the high order bits are set to 1110
IPv6	Begins with 33:33	Begins with FF

When a multicast IP packet is created, it is wrapped up in a multicast frame at Layer 2. What is more, the Layer 2 address is based on the Layer 3 address. Examples are shown in Figure 8-5.

```
IPv4
  Ethernet II, Src: 60:67:20:2c:5c:ca, Dst: 01:00:5e:7f:ff:fa  ⇦
  Internet Protocol Version 4, Src: 10.249.100.48, Dst: 239.255.255.250  ⇦
  User Datagram Protocol, Src Port: 58880 (58880), Dst Port: 1900 (1900)
  Hypertext Transfer Protocol

IPv6
  Ethernet II, Src: 60:67:20:2c:5c:ca, Dst: 33:33:00:01:00:02
  Internet Protocol Version 6, Src: fe80::a817:35db:400:4988, Dst: ff02::1:2
  User Datagram Protocol, Src Port: 546 (546), Dst Port: 547 (547)
  DHCPv6
```

Figure 8-5. IPv4 and IPv6 multicast packets

In this example, the IPv4 packet on the top has a destination address of 239.255.255.250. Remember that 239 is part of the Class D multicast IP address range. The destination MAC address begins with 01 and is tied to the Layer 3 address through the partial conversion of this address to hexadecimal. The values 255 and 250 convert to FF and FA respectively. From RFC 1112:

> An IP host group address is mapped to an Ethernet multicast address by placing the low-order 23-bits of the IP address into the low-order 23 bits of the Ethernet multicast address 01-00-5E-00-00-00 (hex). Because there are 28 significant bits in an IP host group address, more than one host group address may map to the same Ethernet multicast address.

This is all very well and good, but a bit difficult to parse—let's do a conversion example to help explain. Figure 8-5 depicts a typical multicast frame. This conversion process modifies the MAC address based on the destination IP address: 239.255.255.250. We will begin by expanding the IP address into binary. Organizing the bits in groups of four indicates the hexadecimal character boundaries. The low order 23 bits are highlighted bold italic:

```
1110 1111 . 1111 1111 . 1111 1111 . 1111 1010
```

Per RFC 1112, we will convert these 23 bits to hexadecimal and insert them into the MAC address:

```
1110 1111 . 1 111 1111 . 1111 1111 . 1111 1010
              7  F      F    F    F    A
```

Adding these to the reserved prefix we have:

```
01 00 5E 7F FF FA
```

This gives us the final MAC address used in this particular frame. To continue, if the low order 23 bits are the same between addresses, they will map to the same Ethernet multicast address. In this example we saw 239.255.255.250 converted. But the same conversion would occur for 224.255.255.250.

IPv4 has a number of reserved multicast addresses. These address are reserved to prevent accidental use of an address used by the infrastructure for a particular purpose. Many of these addresses are used to identify either a group of nodes or a protocol. Some examples include:

224.0.0.0
 Base Address (Reserved)

224.0.0.1
 All Systems on this Subnet

224.0.0.2
 All Routers on this Subnet

224.0.0.3
 Unassigned

224.0.0.4
 Distance Vector Multicast Routers

224.0.0.5
 OSPFIGP OSPFIGP All Routers

224.0.0.6
 OSPFIGP OSPFIGP Designated Routers

224.0.0.9
 RIP2 Routers

224.0.0.10
 EIGRP Routers

224.0.0.13
 All PIM Routers

224.0.0.22
 IGMP

A full list can be found at the IANA site (*https://www.iana.org/assignments/multicast-addresses/multicast-addresses.txt*).

The IPv6 packet at the bottom of Figure 8-5 has a Layer 3 address of FF02::1:2. The beginning of FF identifies this as an IPv6 multicast. We can see that the frame address begins with 33:33 and ends with 01:00:02, which is taken from the last portion of the Layer 3 address.

Like IPv4, IPv6 has several reserved multicast addresses:

FF01:0:0:0:0:0:0:1
 All Nodes Address

FF01:0:0:0:0:0:0:2
 All Routers Address

FF01:0:0:0:0:0:0:C
 Variable scope allocation

FF01:0:0:0:0:0:0:FB
 mDNSv6

FF02:0:0:0:0:0:0:1
 All Nodes Address

FF02:0:0:0:0:0:0:2
 All Routers Address

FF02:0:0:0:0:0:0:3
 Unassigned

FF02:0:0:0:0:0:0:4
 DVMRP Routers

FF02:0:0:0:0:0:0:5
 OSPF

FF02:0:0:0:0:0:0:6
 OSPF DRs

FF02:0:0:0:0:0:0:9
 RIP

FF02:0:0:0:0:0:0:A
 EIGRP

A full list can be found at the IANA site (*http://www.iana.org/assignments/ipv6-multicast-addresses/ipv6-multicast-addresses.xhtml*).

As you can see, the reserved IPv4 and IPv6 multicast addresses have similar purposes.

Structure

As stated previously, a multicast topology requires that several components and protocols operate together. In the following sections, we will explore the structure and operation of both IGMP and PIM.

Structure: Internet Group Management Protocol

Officially, IGMPv3 is the current version, though there are some cases where intero-perability with a previous version is desired. Version 3 is described in RFC 3376, which obsoletes RFC 2236. However, we will take some of the language from an even earlier document: RFC 1112 Host Extensions for Multicasting. This is because several of the multicast concepts originated in RFC 1112. RFC 1112 also describes IGMPv1. Some important rules from RFC 1112 are:

- Membership of a host group is dynamic; hosts may join or leave groups.
- There is no restriction on the location or number of members in a host group.
- A host may be a member of more than one group at a time.
- A host need not be a member of a group to send datagrams to the group.
- A host group may be permanent or transient.
- A permanent group has a well-known, administratively assigned IP address.

As mentioned earlier, routers will eventually get involved in the forwarding of multi-cast datagrams but only if the time-to-live (TTL) field is greater than 1. A TTL of 1 is the default for multicasting. As we build our examples later in this chapter, this becomes a critical piece of information.

Importantly, RFCs 1112, 2236 (version 2), and 3376 (version 3) only discuss what we might call local area network multicast. Inter-network multicast (dealing with the routing and addressing) is covered by another set of RFCs that are concerned with Protocol Independent Multicast.

RFC 1112 does include some host conformance levels that indicate the level of sup-port for multicast. These are not immediately apparent in the packet structure. These levels of support are:

- 0—no support
- 1—support for sending but not receiving (hosts cannot join groups)
- 2—full support

IGMP version 3

As we read through some of the RFC content, each version sought to make improve-ments or add to the protocol capabilities. From RFC 3376:

> This document specifies Version 3 of IGMP. Version 1, specified in [RFC-1112], was the first widely-deployed version and the first version to become an Internet Standard. Version 2, specified in [RFC-2236], added support for "low leave latency", that is, a reduction in the time it takes for a multicast router to learn that there are no longer

any members of a particular group present on an attached network. Version 3 adds support for "source filtering", that is, the ability for a system to report interest in receiving packets *only* from specific source addresses, as required to support Source-Specific Multicast [SSM], or from *all but* specific source addresses, sent to a particular multicast address. Version 3 is designed to be interoperable with Versions 1 and 2.

The whole point of IGMP is to allow Internet hosts to signal their group request for membership. With this signaling, the node is placed into a multicast group. By default, all hosts are part of the ALL HOSTS group, which uses IP address 224.0.0.1. A particular node or router can be part of several multicast groups. To support this, IGMP has functions for joining and leaving a group. With version 3 of the protocol, nodes have greater control over the multicast streams—which streams a node wants and which streams a node wishes to exclude.

Generally speaking, IGMP is a simple protocol that defines a small number of messages. These messages include MEMBERSHIP QUERY, MEMBERSHIP REPORT (Versions 1, 2, and 3), and a version 2 LEAVE GROUP. While version 3 has been around since 2002, version 2 is still widely used and so this chapter will provide examples for both versions. The base format of an IGMPv3 query message is shown in Figure 8-6. A QUERY message is used to learn which groups have members on a particular network. Hosts that have membership in a particular group respond to queries. In the case of the specific query such as the one shown in Figure 8-8, the QUERY is asking about the membership in only the group or IP address specified.

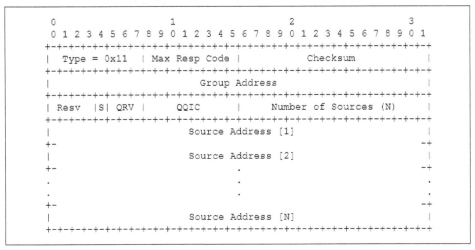

Figure 8-6. RFC general format for an IGMPv3 query

Each query message includes the following fields:

Type
    8 bits. The following messages are defined in RFC 3376:

Type Number (hex)	Message Name
0x11	Membership Query
0x22	Version 3 Membership Report
0x12	Version 1 Membership Report [RFC-1112 (*https://tools.ietf.org/html/rfc1112*)]
0x16	Version 2 Membership Report [RFC-2236 (*https://tools.ietf.org/html/rfc2236*)]
0x17	Version 2 Leave Group [RFC-2236 (*https://tools.ietf.org/html/rfc2236*)]

Queries are used to solicit group membership information. Membership reports are used to announce that a host is part of a multicast group. Membership reports are generated upon joining a group and after timer expiration. Routers record this information so that they can understand end hosts that desire to participate in a particular multicast stream.

Maximum Response Code or Time
8 bits. In membership queries, this field is used to specify the maximum amount of time for a corresponding report. The time increment is 1/10 of a second. All other messages set this value to zero. It is primarily used to keep the routers up to date regarding group membership and the required forwarding of multicast streams.

Checksum
16-bits, the one's complement of the one's complement sum of the 8-octet IGMP message. When computing the checksum, the checksum field is zeroed.

Group Address
32 bits, this is the IP address used for the group. In a HOST MEMBERSHIP QUERY, this field is set to 0s and in a HOST MEMBERSHIP REPORT this value is filled in.

Reserved
Set to 0 for transmissions and ignored at the receiver.

S-flag
1 bit, suppresses router side processing; when set it tells the router to suppress the corresponding normal timer updates

Querier's Robustness Variable (QRV)
Querier is the sender of the query. This 3-bit field has a maximum value of 7. The recommended value is 2 and it is used to help tune for the expected packet loss on a network. Higher values correspond to more lossy networks.

Querier's Query Interval Code (QQIC)
8 bits, this depicts the time between messages from the sender of the query. The QQIC is actually derived from the Querier's Query Interval (QQI).

Number of Sources (N)

16 bits, specifies how many source addresses are present in the Query. This number is zero in a General Query or a Group-Specific Query, and non-zero in a Group-and-Source-Specific Query.

Source address

32-bit address that is the multicast stream origin, the number of addresses here should match the number of sources field.

Additional Data

Included in the checksum calculation but ignored otherwise.

Figure 8-7 depicts an actual IGMPv3 GENERAL MEMBERSHIP QUERY. If we were to expand the IP header for this IGMP packet, the IP protocol ID field value would be 2.

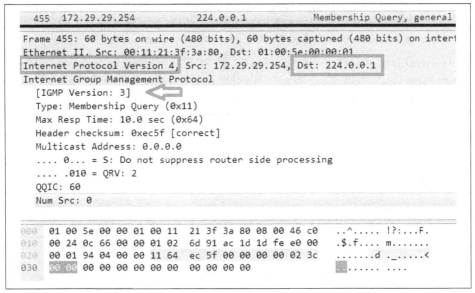

Figure 8-7. Packet showing IGMPv3 membership query

The last field (Num Src) of the packet is highlighted to show the "additional data" field.

Figure 8-8 depicts a SPECIFIC MEMBERSHIP QUERY. This query addresses membership in the multicast group used for the chapter stream example that we will see later.

```
Ethernet II, Src: 00:11:21:3f:3a:80, Dst: 01:00:5e:63:63:63
Internet Protocol Version 4, Src: 172.29.29.254, Dst: 239.99.99.99
Internet Group Management Protocol
   [IGMP Version: 3]
   Type: Membership Query (0x11)
   Max Resp Time: 1.0 sec (0x0a)
   Header checksum: 0x99f2 [correct]
   Multicast Address: 239.99.99.99
   .... 0... = S: Do not suppress router side processing
   .... .010 = QRV: 2
   QQIC: 60
   Num Src: 0
```

Figure 8-8. Packet showing IGMPv3-specific membership query

The difference between these two queries is that the Layer 3 addressing for the specific query is aimed at a particular group address: 239.99.99.99. This is seen in both the IP header and the IGMP packet. Remember that the goal of the QUERY is to discover group members (general or specific groups) on the network.

The general format for the MEMBERSHIP REPORT is shown in Figure 8-9. Membership reports contain the groups to which a host belongs. Figure 8-9 also indicates that each record contains the information on the right side of the image.

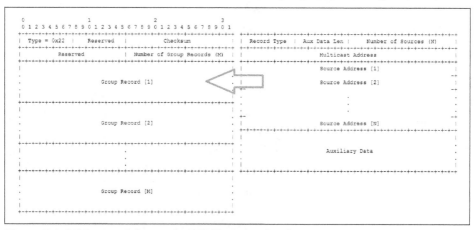

Figure 8-9. RFC general format for IGMPv3 membership report

The following fields have been added for the MEMBERSHIP REPORT message type:

Number of group records
   16 bits, contains the number of records.

Group record

Each one of the group records contains the information seen on the righthand side of Figure 8-9.

Record type

There are several types of record. Record type indicates the reception state of an interface that would participate in the multicast traffic. These are typically for the filtering of a multicast address:

- 1—MODE_IS_INCLUDE
- 2—MODE_IS_EXCLUDE
- 3—CHANGE_TO_INCLUDE_MODE
- 4—CHANGE_TO_EXCLUDE_MODE
- 5—ALLOW_NEW_SOURCES
- 6—BLOCK_OLD_SOURCES

RFC 3376 has the following brief explanation regarding INCLUDE and EXCLUDE modes:

In INCLUDE mode, reception of packets sent to the specified multicast address is requested *only* from those IP source addresses listed in the source-list parameter. In EXCLUDE mode, reception of packets sent to the given multicast address is requested from all IP source addresses *except* those listed in the source-list parameter.

The next couple of fields would be added for these options.

Auxiliary Data Length

Length of the extra data at the end of the record, which may be 0; IGMP does not define this data.

Number of Sources

The total number of IP addresses listed as a source.

Source Addresses

32-bit IP addresses listed as the multicast stream origin.

Figure 8-10 displays an IGMPv3 MEMBERSHIP REPORT.

```
Ethernet II, Src: ec:b1:d7:43:89:74, Dst: 01:00:5e:00:00:16
Internet Protocol Version 4, Src: 172.29.29.1, Dst: 224.0.0.22
Internet Group Management Protocol
   [IGMP Version: 3]
   Type: Membership Report (0x22)
   Reserved: 00
   Header checksum: 0x8837 [correct]
   Reserved: 0000
   Num Group Records: 1
 ⊿ Group Record : 239.99.99.99  Change To Include Mode
     Record Type: Change To Include Mode (3)
     Aux Data Len: 0
     Num Src: 0
     Multicast Address: 239.99.99.99   ⇦
```

Figure 8-10. Packet showing IGMPv3 membership report

In this packet the record fields have been expanded showing the record type (3) and
the multicast address for the stream group.

IGMP versions 1 and 2

For comparison and for compatibility, the packet formats for versions 1 and 2 are
included in this section. Fields descriptions are included to show the differences
between versions.

Version 1. Figure 8-11 depicts the general format for version 1.

```
 0                   1                   2                   3
 0 1 2 3 4 5 6 7 8 9 0 1 2 3 4 5 6 7 8 9 0 1 2 3 4 5 6 7 8 9 0 1
+-+-+-+-+-+-+-+-+-+-+-+-+-+-+-+-+-+-+-+-+-+-+-+-+-+-+-+-+-+-+-+-+
|Version| Type  |    Unused     |            Checksum           |
+-+-+-+-+-+-+-+-+-+-+-+-+-+-+-+-+-+-+-+-+-+-+-+-+-+-+-+-+-+-+-+-+
|                         Group Address                         |
+-+-+-+-+-+-+-+-+-+-+-+-+-+-+-+-+-+-+-+-+-+-+-+-+-+-+-+-+-+-+-+-+
```

Figure 8-11. RFC 1122 general format

The following fields are part of this general format.

Version
   4 bits, indicates the version of IGMP.

Type
   4 bits, message type for this packet. A value of 1 indicates a HOST MEMBER-
   SHIP QUERY and a value of 2 indicates a HOST MEMBERSHIP REPORT.

An example of an IGMP version 1 HOST MEMBERSHIP REPORT can be seen in
Figure 8-12.

```
Internet Group Management Protocol
  [IGMP Version: 1]
  Type: Membership Report (0x12)
  Header checksum: 0x0c9c [correct]
  Multicast Address: 225.0.0.99 (225.0.0.99)
```

Figure 8-12. Packet showing IGMPv1 membership report

The value of 0x12 is used because the version and type fields are 4 bits.

Version 2. RFC 2236 is an update that describes the interaction between hosts and routers. If needed, IGMPv1 and IGMPv2 can interoperate. There are several changes to the header:

- No version number; instead, the IP protocol ID is specified as 2
- Max response time is added
- Router alert included in the IP header

The general format is shown in Figure 8-13.

```
0                   1                   2                   3
0 1 2 3 4 5 6 7 8 9 0 1 2 3 4 5 6 7 8 9 0 1 2 3 4 5 6 7 8 9 0 1
+-+-+-+-+-+-+-+-+-+-+-+-+-+-+-+-+-+-+-+-+-+-+-+-+-+-+-+-+-+-+-+-+
|      Type     | Max Resp Time |           Checksum            |
+-+-+-+-+-+-+-+-+-+-+-+-+-+-+-+-+-+-+-+-+-+-+-+-+-+-+-+-+-+-+-+-+
|                         Group Address                         |
+-+-+-+-+-+-+-+-+-+-+-+-+-+-+-+-+-+-+-+-+-+-+-+-+-+-+-+-+-+-+-+-+
```

Figure 8-13. RFC 2236 general format

Examples of IGMPv2 membership queries are shown in Figure 8-14.

```
Ethernet II, Src: 00:05:5e:28:11:80, Dst: 01:00:5e:00:00:01    Ethernet II, Src: 00:05:5e:28:11:80, Dst: 01:00:5e:7f:00:01
Internet Protocol Version 4, Src: 172.31.31.254, Dst: 224.0.0.1  Internet Protocol Version 4, Src: 172.31.31.254, Dst: 239.255.0.1
Internet Group Management Protocol                             Internet Group Management Protocol
  [IGMP Version: 2]                                              [IGMP Version: 2]
  Type: Membership Query (0x11)                                 Type: Membership Query (0x11)
  Max Resp Time: 10.0 sec (0x64)                                Max Resp Time: 1.0 sec (0x0a)
  Header checksum: 0xee9b [correct]                             Header checksum: 0xfef4 [correct]
  Multicast Address: 0.0.0.0                                    Multicast Address: 239.255.0.1
```

Figure 8-14. Packets showing general and specific IGMPv2 membership queries

The address used in the left packet is to the general "All Hosts" address of 224.0.0.1 as this is not a specific query. In addition to the addressing used we can see the values of 10 and 1 seconds for the Max Response Time. These correspond to the hexadecimal values of 64 and 0a, respectively. Recall that the time increment is 1/10 of a second. Calculating the value for the general query we have ($(6\times16^1) + (4\times16^0)$) × .1 = 10.

Examples of a MEMBERSHIP REPORT and LEAVE messages are shown in Figure 8-15.

```
Ethernet II, Src: 3c:97:0e:1b:81:33, Dst: 01:00:5e:00:00:fb      Ethernet II, Src: 00:1b:21:7c:7f:ec, Dst: 01:00:5e:00:00:02
Internet Protocol Version 4, Src: 172.31.31.15, Dst: 224.0.0.251 Internet Protocol Version 4, Src: 172.31.31.1, Dst: 224.0.0.2
Internet Group Management Protocol                               Internet Group Management Protocol
  [IGMP Version: 2]                                                 [IGMP Version: 2]
  Type: Membership Report (0x16)                                    Type: Leave Group (0x17)
  Max Resp Time: 0.0 sec (0x00)                                     Max Resp Time: 0.0 sec (0x00)
  Header checksum: 0x0904 [correct]                                 Header checksum: 0x9638 [correct]
  Multicast Address: 224.0.0.251                                    Multicast Address: 239.99.99.99
```

Figure 8-15. Packets showing both the IGMPv2 membership report and leave group messages

The LEAVE message appears when the stream is no longer needed. This message signals to the local router that the host no longer desires to receive this particular stream, though other hosts may. The destination address of 224.0.0.2 is to All Routers.

IP Router Alert

IGMP messages are sent with the IP router alert option set in the IP header. The router alert option is defined in RFC 2113. The RFC discusses the problem of getting routers more involved with a particular type of traffic without incurring much additional overhead. The problem is that the routers are limited by the next hop knowledge possessed by the routers. To quote from RFC 2113:

> The goal, then, is to provide a mechanism whereby routers can intercept packets not addressed to them directly, without incurring any significant performance penalty. This document defines a new IP option type, Router Alert, for this purpose. The Router Alert option has the semantic "routers should examine this packet more closely".

Protocol Independent Multicast and IGMP messages get routers more involved without significantly impacting the standard operation of the routers. An example of an IP packet with the Router Alert option set is shown in Figure 8-16.

The type, length, and value (router shall examine packet) seen in the router alert option fields are the same for all messages and specified by the RFC.

```
Ethernet II, Src: 3c:97:0e:1b:81:33, Dst: 01:00:5e:7f:ff:fa
Internet Protocol Version 4, Src: 172.31.31.15, Dst: 239.255.255.250
   0100 .... = Version: 4
   .... 0110 = Header Length: 24 bytes
 ▷ Differentiated Services Field: 0x00 (DSCP: CS0, ECN: Not-ECT)
   Total Length: 32
   Identification: 0x143c (5180)
 ▷ Flags: 0x00
   Fragment offset: 0
   Time to live: 1
   Protocol: IGMP (2)
 ▷ Header checksum: 0x5573 [correct]
   Source: 172.31.31.15
   Destination: 239.255.255.250
   [Source GeoIP: Unknown]
   [Destination GeoIP: Unknown]
 ◢ Options: (4 bytes), Router Alert
    ◢ Router Alert (4 bytes): Router shall examine packet (0)
       ◢ Type: 148
          1... .... = Copy on fragmentation: Yes
          .00. .... = Class: Control (0)
          ...1 0100 = Number: Router Alert (20)
       Length: 4
       Router Alert: Router shall examine packet (0)
Internet Group Management Protocol
```

Figure 8-16. Packet showing IGMP with the router alert option

IGMP Snooping

So, how do we deal with the bandwidth consumption problem presented by all of this multicast traffic? Remember that multicast traffic is forwarded everywhere throughout the Layer 2 topology. Another question is why nodes bother sending a MEMBERSHIP REPORT when all you have to do is grab the multicast frames streaming all over the network? IGMP snooping is a technique used by switches to learn the locations of multicast sources and destinations by examining IGMP messages. By observing the join and membership messages, the network can direct the multicast traffic to interested nodes. Other parts of the network will not receive the traffic because the switch will block the multicast traffic on those ports. This technique conserves bandwidth. Should a node in another part of the network issue a join request, the multicast traffic will also be sent down the associated port. The opposite is true if a node leaves the multicast group. Because membership in multicast groups is dynamic, IGMP snooping responds by dynamically removing ports. Static membership for ports can also be created. This might be used if the administrator knew of desired and more permanent membership demands. Routers can engage in the same sort of throttling as they communicate directly with hosts via IGMP and other routers via

PIM. In this way, excessive multicast traffic is prevented from interrupting Layer 3 traffic.

Structure: Protocol Independent Multicast (PIM)

Configuring routers to forward multicast traffic requires some extra steps and some additional processes. The last stop on our protocol structure tour is Protocol Independent Multicast (PIM). Like IGMP, PIM is encapsulated in IP packets but the protocol ID used is 103. The destination address for PIM messaging is 224.0.0.13. As stated earlier in this chapter, PIM is used to complete the Layer 3 requirements for multicasting between routers. This section will examine this protocol and we will go through a layer 3 topology example later in the chapter.

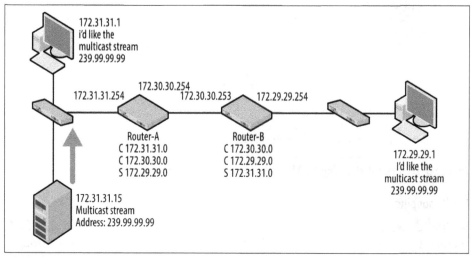

Figure 8-17. The multicast routing problem

As we can see, the routers possess unicast routing tables and do not have any idea how to get the multicast stream from the 172.31.31.0 network to the 172.29.29.0 network. This is where PIM comes in. PIM is a multicast routing protocol that uses the underlying unicast (or multicast) routing information base to connect multicast recipients and sources across the routed topology. PIM has several modes of operation: sparse, sparse-dense, and dense. Both sparse and dense modes are described in their own RFCs:

- RFC 3973 PIM Dense Mode (PIM-DM)
- RFC 7761 PIM Sparse Mode (PIM-SM)

RFC 7761 describes one method to deploy PIM. To quote:

It builds unidirectional shared trees rooted at a Rendezvous Point (RP) per group, and it optionally creates shortest-path trees per source.

An important idea, at least for sparse-mode, is the Rendezvous Point (RP). The RP serves as the root of the tree. The tree is non-source specific and so can be established anywhere in the routed topology. Data from the sender/source is sent to the RP. In addition, those wishing to join the multicast group send their join requests to the RP. In this way the multicast stream is connected. Dense-mode does not utilize a Rendezvous Point, making it less complex to configure at the expense of extra traffic being sent into the Layer 3 topology.

In either mode, designated routers act on behalf of the group hosts to ensure that the multicast traffic is forwarded on. This also means that in addition to the unicast routing tables seen in the topology diagram, each router possesses a multicast routing table. An example of a multicast routing table entry can be seen in Figure 8-18.

```
Router-A#
Router-A#sh ip mroute
IP Multicast Routing Table
Flags: D - Dense, S - Sparse, B - Bidir Group, s - SSM Group, C - Connected,
       L - Local, P - Pruned, R - RP-bit set, F - Register flag,
       T - SPT-bit set, J - Join SPT, M - MSDP created entry,
       X - Proxy Join Timer Running, A - Candidate for MSDP Advertisement,
       U - URD, I - Received Source Specific Host Report
Outgoing interface flags: H - Hardware switched
Timers: Uptime/Expires
Interface state: Interface, Next-Hop or VCD, State/Mode

(*, 239.255.255.250), 00:00:28/00:02:32, RP 0.0.0.0, flags: DC
  Incoming interface: Null, RPF nbr 0.0.0.0
  Outgoing interface list:
    FastEthernet0/0, Forward/Dense, 00:00:28/00:00:00
```

Figure 8-18. Router IPv4 multicast routing table

Routers exchange PIM messages and while there are many types, these messages share a common format, shown in Figure 8-19.

```
 0                   1                   2                   3
 0 1 2 3 4 5 6 7 8 9 0 1 2 3 4 5 6 7 8 9 0 1 2 3 4 5 6 7 8 9 0 1
+-+-+-+-+-+-+-+-+-+-+-+-+-+-+-+-+-+-+-+-+-+-+-+-+-+-+-+-+-+-+-+-+
|PIM Ver| Type |   Reserved    |            Checksum            |
+-+-+-+-+-+-+-+-+-+-+-+-+-+-+-+-+-+-+-+-+-+-+-+-+-+-+-+-+-+-+-+-+
```

Figure 8-19. RFC PIM common header

The fields listed are explained here:

Version
> The current version of the protocol is 2.

Type
> The following messages are defined for PIM:

Message Type	Destination
0 = Hello	Multicast to ALL-PIM-ROUTERS
1 = Register	Unicast to RP
2 = Register-Stop	Unicast to source of Register packet
3 = Join/Prune	Multicast to ALL-PIM-ROUTERS
4 = Bootstrap	Multicast to ALL-PIM-ROUTERS
5 = Assert	Multicast to ALL-PIM-ROUTERS
6 = Graft (used in PIM-DM only)	Unicast to RPF'(S)
7 = Graft-Ack (used in PIM-DM only)	Unicast to source of Graft packet
8 = Candidate-RP-Advertisement	Unicast to Domain's BSR

Reserved

Set to 0.

Checksum

16-bits, the one's complement of the one's complement sum of the 8-octet IGMP message. When computing the checksum, the checksum field is zeroed.

For a base configuration, the common messages include the HELLO and the JOIN/PRUNE. HELLO messages are periodically sent out all interfaces configured for multicast, which allows routers to learn of multicast neighbors. HELLO messages are also used in sparse mode to elect routers that will act as the multicast designated routers. The general format and an example of a HELLO message from the topology can be seen in Figure 8-20.

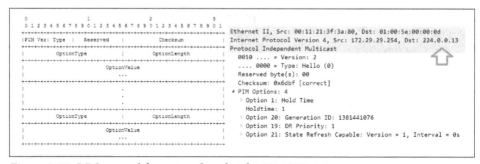

Figure 8-20. RFC general format and packet for PIM HELLO

PIM HELLO messages can contain several options. There is a wide variety and an official list is maintained by IANA outside of the RFC and a complete list is located on the IANA site (*http://www.iana.org/assignments/pim-parameters/pim-parameters.xhtml*).

The following table presents a few examples:

Value	Purpose	Reference
1	Hold time	RFC 7761
2	LAN Prune Delay	RFC 3973
19	DR priority	RFC 7761
21	State refresh	RFC 3973
22	Bidirectional capable	RFC 5015

For our example, the only significant field is the hold time. The hold time value is the length of time before the next expected HELLO message. The RFC suggests a length of 30 seconds. HELLO messages can also be triggered by events such as bootup of connections. This interval is 5 seconds. In this example, we also see a Generation ID. The Generation ID is a random value that refers to the interface used for the HELLO message. Because we are using DENSE mode for our PIM deployment, we are not concerned about DR priority.

JOIN/PRUNE messages are used when hosts wish to be part of a multicast group or have lost interest in the source. The general format and an example can be seen in Figure 8-21.

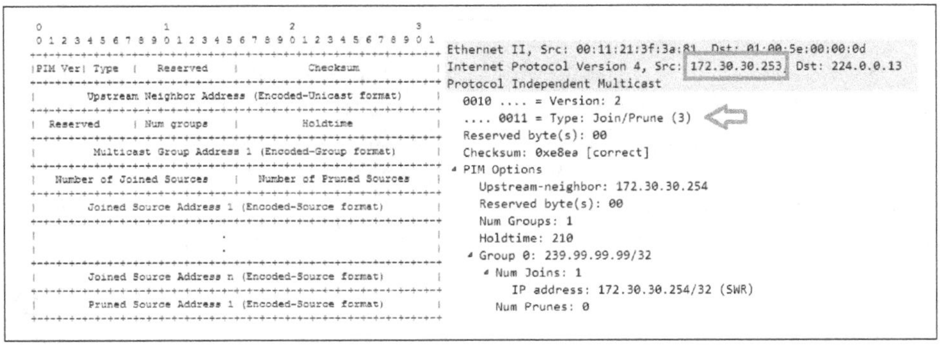

Figure 8-21. RFC general format and packet for PIM JOIN/PRUNE

JOIN/PRUNE messages are both type 3 messages. The purpose is indicated in the Num Joins and Num Prunes fields. As the names suggest, in one case the stream is desired (JOIN) and in the other it is not (PRUNE). These messages directly impact the routers forwarding of multicast streams. Routers send these messages to their upstream neighbor. It is important to note that upstream and downstream are relative to the direction of the multicast stream.

In this example, we can see the standard IGMP header followed by options that are tailored for this JOIN/PRUNE message. The source IP for this message was 172.30.30.253 and it was sent to the PIM destination address of 224.0.0.13 but it was a notification for the upstream neighbor 172.30.30.254.

The upstream neighbor is closer to the root of the multicast tree. This field is actually 8 bytes long instead of the typical 4 bytes necessary for an IP address. The extra bytes are for the address family; encoding type; the Reserved, S (Sparse), W (Wildcard), and R (Rendezvous Point) bits; mask length; and finally, the source address. The address family is IANA assigned and the encoding matches the address family. This address family is IPv4 (value=1) and the native encoding is 0. In this example (172.30.30.254/32 (SWR)), only the mask length is specified with the other bits being set to 1. The hexadecimal values seen in a capture would be:

```
01 00 07 20 ac 1e 1e fe
```

The hold time is the length of time that the PRUNE state must be kept alive failing a receipt of a JOIN or GRAFT message. GRAFTing (type 6 message) is the process of rejoining a pruned stream. JOIN/PRUNE messages can be used to indicate more than one group at a time. Thus the Num Groups field can be greater than one and the Num Joins (per group) field can also be greater than one.

A note on timers

Both IGMP and PIM have a collection of timers. The messaging between systems is there in order to help determine where multicast streams should flow. Nodes join groups and routers join these same groups. Some systems can be configured such that network devices can leave without notification and timers exist so that devices do not have to constantly signal their group membership interest. At the same time, conservation of resources dictates that group membership should not persist indefinitely without occasional notification from group members. As a result, the timers associated with these protocols have the task of keeping track of and aging out membership and advertised information. Many of these timers (advertisement/solicitation rates, aging time, etc.) are configurable parameters.

A note on state

Both PIM dense-mode and PIM sparse-mode dramatically change the way that routers handle the forwarding of traffic because there is an addition to their forwarding information base. Like other routing protocols, such as Open Shortest Path First (OSPF), this is due to the router's knowledge of its "State" or what the router understands about its network connections. For multicast, the state is contained within the Tree Information Base (TIB). The TIB has a slightly different structure in the two modes because of the different approach taken, most notably the Rendezvous Point (RP).

Generally speaking, the router keeps track of multicast stream sources, networks that contain hosts requesting the multicast stream, and any RPs in the topology. Routers do not need to keep track of individual hosts. Each active interface is part of the state and has timers associated with the traffic that might be forwarded. Both modes of operation specify a "General Purpose State" in which the routers are aware of HELLO message timers and network conditions. The state is modified by the IGMP/PIM messages seen or the expiration of timers.

Operation

Let's work through a couple of examples. To start, we simply have a small local area network without routing or external connectivity, as shown in Figure 8-22.

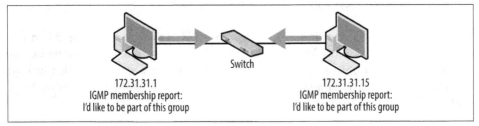

Figure 8-22. Initial multicast topology

If we assume that initially there are no multicast sources, there isn't much to see. But the network nodes do not know this. When a node joins the network it performs a multicast announcement just in case. The specific behavior is somewhat dependent on the operating system and configuration. For the most part, this consists of a small number of MEMBERSHIP REPORTS. The output from a Windows 10 host is shown in Figure 8-23.

```
172.31.31.1        224.0.0.22        IGMPv3    Membership Report / Join group 224.0.0.251 for any sources
172.31.31.1        224.0.0.22        IGMPv3    Membership Report / Join group 224.0.0.252 for any sources
```

Figure 8-23. Windows 10 default multicast messages

These correspond to addresses reserved for multicast DNS (RFC 6762) and link-local multicast name resolution (RFC 4795). Because this node did not receive an answer (no messages from other nodes and a multicast router is not present), this traffic does not get repeated very often.

In our second example, we will add a multicast source to this basic topology (Figure 8-24). Recall that initially the IP TTL values for IGMP messages are all set to 1, meaning that everything happens locally. The only modification to our initial topology is that one host (172.31.31.15) will be providing a multicast stream. The other host (172.31.31.1) will signal its desire to be a member of that multicast group.

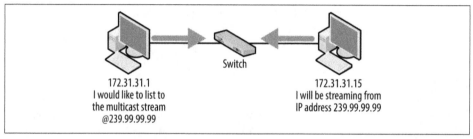

Figure 8-24. Multicast topology with nodes signaling interest

To set this up, we will be using VLC (*http://www.videolan.org*) to provide the multi-cast stream. We will also use VLC to connect to the stream. Remember that we do not have a router and so this is pretty straightforward. The only real trick is that instead of connecting to a unicast address, we will connect to a multicast destination IP. A portion of the stream configuration is shown in Figure 8-25.

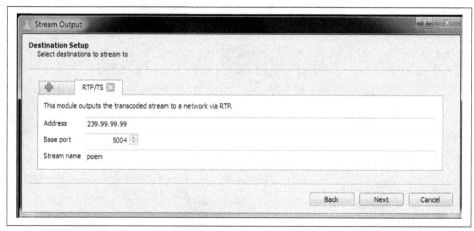

Figure 8-25. VLC multicast configuration

The server is configured to generate a Real-Time Transport Protocol (RTP) stream via the multicast IP address of 239.99.99.99 and using port 5004. RTP is used for a variety of real time data transmissions including Voice over IP. The multicast address is selected by the systems or network administration at the time of configuration. Recall that the multicast address space runs from 224.0.0.0 to 239.255.255.255, though many of these are reserved. The list of reserved address can be found at *http://www.iana.org/* and far exceeds those included in this chapter. Administrators are well advised to take a look at addresses. This list provided the basis for the address used for our example.

Once the stream begins, this traffic will commence from the server, even without any clients present.

```
61    172.31.31.15    239.99.99.99    5004    MPEG TS    PT=MPEG-II tr
62    172.31.31.15    239.99.99.99    5004    MPEG TS    [MP2T fragmen
63    172.31.31.15    239.99.99.99    5004    MPEG TS    Audio Layer 3
64    172.31.31.15    239.99.99.99    5004    MPEG TS    [MP2T fragmen
                                                 ...
Frame 61: 1370 bytes on wire (10960 bits), 1370 bytes captured (10960 bits) o
Ethernet II, Src: 3c:97:0e:1b:81:33, Dst: 01:00:5e:63:63:63
Internet Protocol Version 4, Src: 172.31.31.15, Dst: 239.99.99.99
User Datagram Protocol, Src Port: 52118 (52118), Dst Port: 5004 (5004)
Real-Time Transport Protocol
```

Figure 8-26. Multicast RTP stream

On the network, packets are coming from the host 172.31.31.15 but to a destination of 239.99.99.99 and port 5004. Clients joining the group will simply listen to this collection of packets instead of ignoring them. Because they are multicast frames, they are transmitted throughout the network. Nodes wishing to join send a MEMBERSHIP REPORT for the stream source.

```
1897   172.31.31.1    224.0.0.2              IGMPv2    Leave Group 239.99.99.99
                                                 ...
Frame 1897: 64 bytes on wire (512 bits), 64 bytes captured (512 bits) on interface 0
Ethernet II, Src: 00:1b:21:7c:7f:ec, Dst: 01:00:5e:00:00:02
Internet Protocol Version 4, Src: 172.31.31.1, Dst: 224.0.0.2
Internet Group Management Protocol
   [IGMP Version: 2]
   Type: Leave Group (0x17)
   Max Resp Time: 0.0 sec (0x00)
   Header checksum: 0x9638 [correct]
   Multicast Address: 239.99.99.99
```

Figure 8-27. IGMP leave group message

When the client is done listening to the stream, it disconnects with a LEAVE GROUP message. This example depicts version 2 packets but version 3 behaves in the same way.

Adding a Router

As we have seen, there is not much to the Layer 2 IGMP and multicast operation. It is now time to take a first step toward Layer 3 multicast operation by involving the router. During the first stages of the connection, group membership must be established. Multicast routers send out MEMBERSHIP QUERY messages to the local network. Hosts respond with MEMBERSHIP REPORT messages in order to indicate the groups to which they belong.

Once a router is added to the topology things change because there is the potential need to forward multicast into the unicast-based routed domain. Once multicast is enable on the router with the following commands:

```
ip multicast-routing
int f0/0
    ip igmp version 3
    ip pim dense-mode
```

The router becomes active in the topology and tries to determine the multicast needs on the live interfaces.

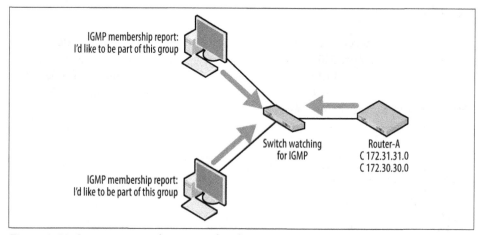

Figure 8-28. Step 1 – router discovery of nodes interested in the stream

From the router, QUERY messages are sent to the all hosts using an address of 224.0.0.1 and a TTL of 1. Recall that by default network nodes are members of this group. The host-based REPORT messages generated in response are sent to the IP address of the host group also using a TTL of 1 and the appropriate multicast MAC address. Per RFC 1112, hosts try not to flood the network with all of these multicast responses by using random values in timers associated with the IGMP message.

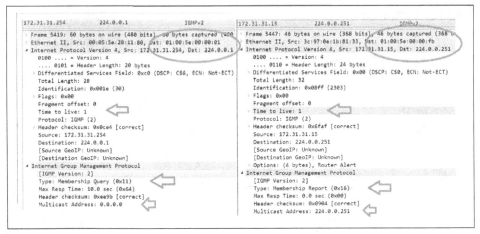

Figure 8-29. Packets generated at this point in the connection

In these first two packets we can see the change to the IP addresses and the corresponding MAC addresses. While both MAC addresses begin with 01:00:5E, the latter half is changed to reflect the layer addresses of 224.0.0.1 and 244.0.0.251. What follows is a list of the packets exchanged between the router and the 172.31.31.15 host. From this exchange it is clear that the host is attempting to join the groups indicated by the addresses of 224.0.0.251, 224.0.0.252, and 239.255.255.250.

```
172.31.31.254     224.0.0.1          IGMPv2   Membership Query, general
172.31.31.15      224.0.0.251        IGMPv2   Membership Report group 224.0.0.251
172.31.31.15      224.0.0.252        IGMPv2   Membership Report group 224.0.0.252
172.31.31.15      239.255.255.250    IGMPv2   Membership Report group 239.255.255.250
```

Figure 8-30. Packet list from this point of the connection

These groups correspond to addresses reserved for multicast DNS (RFC 6762), link-local multicast name resolution (RFC 4795), and what is called the organizational-level scope (RFC 5771), respectively. This last address sounds complex but the idea is that addresses in the 239.0.0.0–239.255.255.255 range are to be used in a single local domain.

At this point, there are no active groups or multicast sources on this particular topology. Thus, the multicast traffic (which can be expensive in terms of bandwidth) will die down. However, routers will continue to query the network periodically for group membership. Should a node or router wish to join a group, this desire is signaled immediately without waiting for the membership query.

A Layer 3 Example

In our fully routed example, shown in Figure 8-31, we will now have to solve the problem of getting to another unicast network.

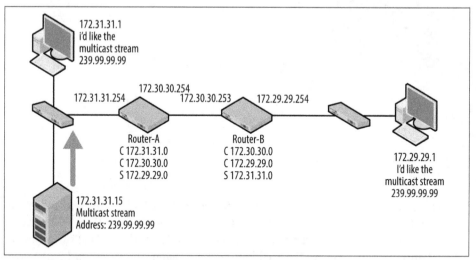

172.31.31.1
i'd like the
multicast stream
239.99.99.99

172.30.30.254
172.31.31.254   172.30.30.253   172.29.29.254

Router-A   Router-B
C 172.31.31.0   C 172.30.30.0
C 172.30.30.0   C 172.29.29.0
S 172.29.29.0   S 172.31.31.0

172.29.29.1
I'd like the
multicast stream
239.99.99.99

172.31.31.15
Multicast stream
Address: 239.99.99.99

Figure 8-31. Solving the layer 3 multicast routing problem

In this case, we will be using PIM-dense mode. Both of the routers have multicast routing enabled and the interfaces active. The significant portions of the configurations for both routers are shown in Figure 8-32.

```
hostname Router-A                                   hostname Router-B
!                                                   !
ip multicast-routing                                ip multicast-routing
!                                                   !
interface FastEthernet0/0                           interface FastEthernet0/0
 ip address 172.31.31.254 255.255.255.0              ip address 172.29.29.254 255.255.255.0
 ip pim dense-mode                                   ip pim dense-mode
 duplex auto                                         ip igmp version 3
 speed auto                                          duplex auto
!                                                    speed auto
!                                                   !
interface FastEthernet0/1                           interface FastEthernet0/1
 ip address 172.30.30.254 255.255.255.0              ip address 172.30.30.253 255.255.255.0
 ip pim dense-mode                                   ip pim dense-mode
 ip igmp version 3                                   ip igmp version 3
!                                                   !
ip route 172.29.29.0 255.255.255.0 172.30.30.253   ip route 172.31.31.0 255.255.255.0 172.30.30.254
```

Figure 8-32. Router configurations used for this chapter

Note that with these configurations, we first solve unicast routing and then multicast routing.

Dense-mode makes the router configuration reasonably straightforward and as the setup is completed, we can examine the network for the correct transmissions and requests. Starting with the host that will receive the multicast stream (172.29.29.1) we can see that it attempts to join the correct multicast group.

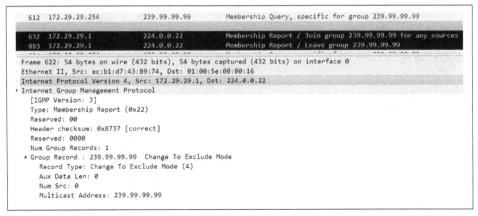

```
  612  172.29.29.254        239.99.99.99       Membership Query, specific for group 239.99.99.99

  632  172.29.29.1          224.0.0.22         Membership Report / Join group 239.99.99.99 for any sources
  883  172.29.29.1          224.0.0.22         Membership Report / Leave group 239.99.99.99

 Frame 622: 54 bytes on wire (432 bits), 54 bytes captured (432 bits) on interface 0
 Ethernet II, Src: ec:b1:d7:43:89:74, Dst: 01:00:5e:00:00:16
 Internet Protocol Version 4, Src: 172.29.29.1, Dst: 224.0.0.22
 Internet Group Management Protocol
    [IGMP Version: 3]
    Type: Membership Report (0x22)
    Reserved: 00
    Header checksum: 0x8737 [correct]
    Reserved: 0000
    Num Group Records: 1
    Group Record : 239.99.99.99  Change To Exclude Mode
       Record Type: Change To Exclude Mode (4)
       Aux Data Len: 0
       Num Src: 0
       Multicast Address: 239.99.99.99
```

Figure 8-33. Packets from 172.29.29.1 during connection attempt

This packet list depicts the QUERY from the router regarding groups membership for 239.99.99.99, the host MEMBERSHIP REPORT for the same group, and the subsequent LEAVE message when the host severed the connection. The EXCLUDE mode indicates that the host would be willing to accept any source.

Figure 8-34 depicts the traffic between the routers in which we can see the PIM message exchange.

```
  550  172.30.30.254        224.0.0.13         Hello
  603  172.30.30.253        224.0.0.13         Hello
  795  172.30.30.253        224.0.0.13         Join/Prune
```

Figure 8-34. Packet list for PIM messages sent between the routers.

At the source we can see that the RTP stream is flowing (Figure 8-35).

```
 172.31.31.15         239.99.99.99      5004   57018 → 5004   Len=1328
 172.31.31.15         239.99.99.99      5004   57018 → 5004   Len=1328
 172.31.31.15         239.99.99.99      5004   57018 → 5004   Len=1328
 172.31.31.15         239.99.99.99      5004   57018 → 5004   Len=1328
 172.31.31.15         239.99.99.99      5004   57018 → 5004   Len=1328
```

Figure 8-35. RTP packets from the source

Everything looks great except that the recipient cannot receive the multicast stream. Looking in-between the two routers we also notice that the RTP stream is not being forwarded by Router-A. A little more investigation and we can find the source of the problem. The RTP stream has an IP time-to-live set to 1, which means that the routers will stop forwarding the traffic at the first hop.

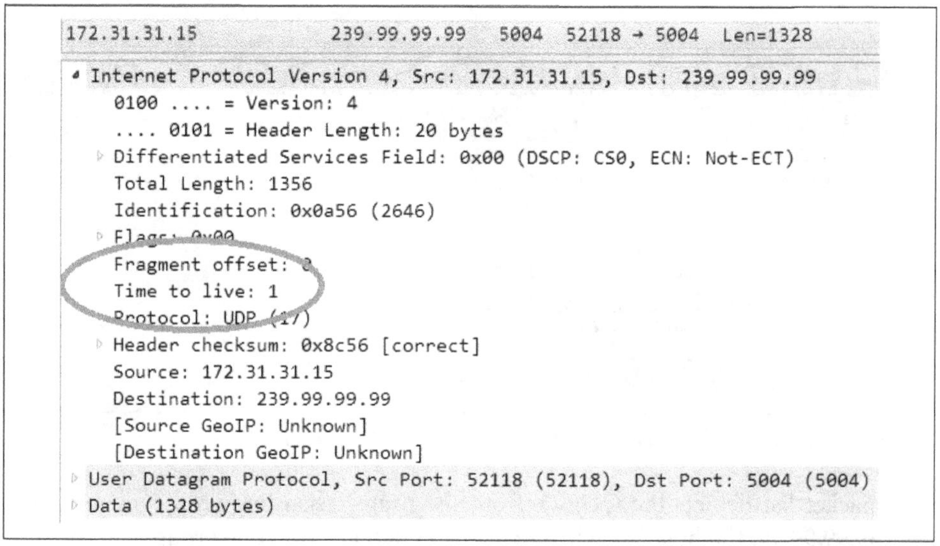

```
172.31.31.15              239.99.99.99   5004  52118 → 5004  Len=1328

Internet Protocol Version 4, Src: 172.31.31.15, Dst: 239.99.99.99
    0100 .... = Version: 4
    .... 0101 = Header Length: 20 bytes
  Differentiated Services Field: 0x00 (DSCP: CS0, ECN: Not-ECT)
    Total Length: 1356
    Identification: 0x0a56 (2646)
  Flags: 0x00
    Fragment offset: 0
    Time to live: 1
    Protocol: UDP (17)
  Header checksum: 0x8c56 [correct]
    Source: 172.31.31.15
    Destination: 239.99.99.99
    [Source GeoIP: Unknown]
    [Destination GeoIP: Unknown]
User Datagram Protocol, Src Port: 52118 (52118), Dst Port: 5004 (5004)
Data (1328 bytes)
```

Figure 8-36. RTP packets with low TTL value

So, even though the routers and host were cooperating for this configuration, the stream source was not and the destination could not receive the stream. To complete this build, it was necessary to increase the time-to-live (TTL) at the source in the VLC configuration.

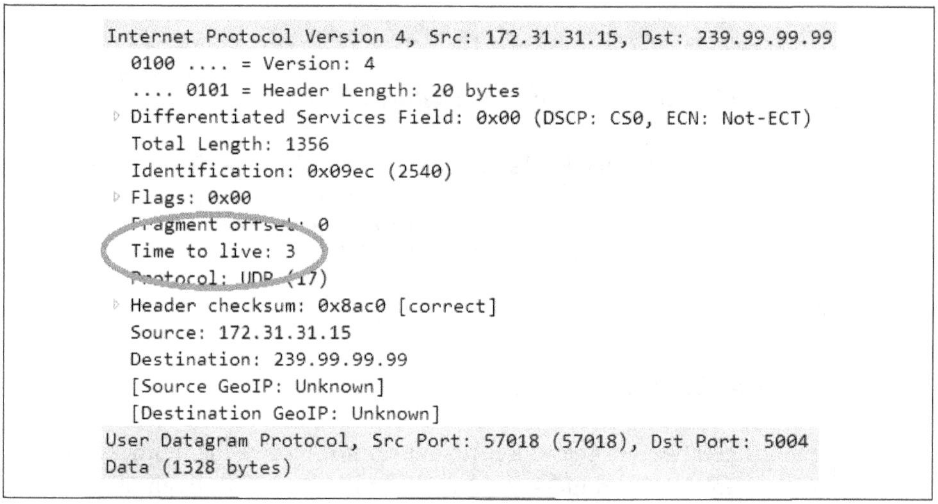

```
Internet Protocol Version 4, Src: 172.31.31.15, Dst: 239.99.99.99
    0100 .... = Version: 4
    .... 0101 = Header Length: 20 bytes
  Differentiated Services Field: 0x00 (DSCP: CS0, ECN: Not-ECT)
    Total Length: 1356
    Identification: 0x09ec (2540)
  Flags: 0x00
    Fragment offset: 0
    Time to live: 3
    Protocol: UDP (17)
  Header checksum: 0x8ac0 [correct]
    Source: 172.31.31.15
    Destination: 239.99.99.99
    [Source GeoIP: Unknown]
    [Destination GeoIP: Unknown]
User Datagram Protocol, Src Port: 57018 (57018), Dst Port: 5004
Data (1328 bytes)
```

Figure 8-37. RTP packets with the proper TTL value

Once the TTL update is done, the multicast stream can reach all of the destinations. As a last check, we can take another look at the router multicast routing tables with the show ip mroute command, as shown in Figure 8-38.

```
Router-A#sh ip mroute
IP Multicast Routing Table
Flags: D - Dense, S - Sparse, B - Bidir Group, s - SSM Group, C - Connected,
       L - Local, P - Pruned, R - RP-bit set, F - Register flag,
       T - SPT-bit set, J - Join SPT, M - MSDP created entry,
       X - Proxy Join Timer Running, A - Candidate for MSDP Advertisement,
       U - URD, I - Received Source Specific Host Report
Outgoing interface flags: H - Hardware switched
Timers: Uptime/Expires
Interface state: Interface, Next-Hop or VCD, State/Mode

(*, 239.255.255.250), 01:59:45/00:02:27, RP 0.0.0.0, flags: DC
  Incoming interface: Null, RPF nbr 0.0.0.0
  Outgoing interface list:
    FastEthernet0/0, Forward/Dense, 00:01:32/00:00:00
    FastEthernet0/1, Forward/Dense, 00:04:43/00:00:00

(*, 239.99.99.99), 01:59:43/00:02:59, RP 0.0.0.0, flags: DC
  Incoming interface: Null, RPF nbr 0.0.0.0
  Outgoing interface list:
    FastEthernet0/1, Forward/Dense, 00:02:32/00:00:00

(172.31.31.15, 239.99.99.99), 00:01:47/00:02:59, flags: CT
  Incoming interface: FastEthernet0/0, RPF nbr 0.0.0.0
  Outgoing interface list:
    FastEthernet0/1, Forward/Dense, 00:01:51/00:00:00

(*, 224.0.1.40), 01:59:53/00:00:00, RP 0.0.0.0, flags: DCL
  Incoming interface: Null, RPF nbr 0.0.0.0
  Outgoing interface list:
    FastEthernet0/1, Forward/Dense, 01:59:53/00:00:00
```

Figure 8-38. Updated router IPv4 multicast routing table

At this point we can see that the multicast source is identified as 172.31.31.15 and that the router is processing the destination 239.99.99.99. The receiver now picks up the multicast stream.

Security Warning

Most protocols have some weaknesses in either their structure (fields, etc.) or their basic operation. IGMP and PIM are no different. Both are clear text and have fields that are reserved or filled with zeros. Once configured, the sum of the operation is automatic. Messages can be forged and some devices can be victimized by denial-of-service attacks. By forging messages, routers can be tricked into believing that group members exist where they should not.

PIM messages can also be forged and RFC 3973 states that routers should not accept messages without having first received a valid HELLO message. It is also possible that architectures using the PIM-SPARSE mode may be more vulnerable as they have the Rendezvous Point, which represents a single point of failure.

Because both protocols are encapsulated in IP, the RFCs have guidelines for operation with an IPSec Authenticated Header. In addition, RFC 4609 provides some guidelines for security with PIM sparse mode.

IPv6

IPv6 makes ample use of multicast, though it is primarily for router discovery and learning about other hosts on the network. This process is called NEIGHBOR DISCOVERY and includes several ICMPv6 message types. The IGMP functionality of group membership is served by the IPv6 Multicast Listener Discovery (MLD) which is described in RFC 4604. MLD version 2 performs the functions of IGMPv3.

Summary

Multicast traffic can be both challenging to run successfully and once running can consume valuable network resources at an alarming rate. Multicast is a challenge because traditional IP networks operate based on the principle of reaching unicast destinations. By default, routers have no knowledge of multicast destinations. Routers must be told how and to where this traffic should be forwarded. Multicast can be damaging because in many ways it is treated like Layer 2 broadcast frames in that multicast is sent everywhere within the Layer 2 domain. This "forwarding everywhere" approach can consume network resources and clog network pathways. At Layer 3, multicast traffic can cause the same problems.

Addressing both the challenge of reaching multicast destinations and the cost of multicast traffic are the Internet Group Management Protocol (IGMP) and Protocol Independent Multicast (PIM). Together these protocols provide mechanisms for hosts to signal their interest in joining multicast groups and to receive multicast traffic. In addition to Layer 2, these protocols can also facilitate transmissions over a Layer 3 routed infrastructure. This chapter explained the structure and operation of both IGMP and PIM. Several examples were included that covered Layer 2 and Layer 3 operations. These explanations are supported by packet capture and configuration examples for the various network segments.

Reading

RFC 1112: Host Extensions for Multicasting
RFC 2236: Internet Group Management Protocol, Version 2
RFC 3376: Internet Group Management Protocol, Version 3
RFC 2113: IP Router Alert Option
RFC 4604: Using Internet Group Management Protocol Version 3 (IGMPv3) and Multicast Listener Discovery Protocol Version 2 (MLDv2) for Source-Specific Multicast
RFC 3973: Protocol Independent Multicast—Dense Mode (PIM-DM): Protocol Specification (Revised)

RFC 4609: Protocol Independent Multicast—Sparse Mode (PIM-SM) Multicast Routing Security Issues and Enhancements

Review Questions

1. What are the current working versions of IGMP and PIM?
2. What IPv4 address is used for All Hosts?
3. What IPv4 address is used for PIM messages?
4. A streaming server uses a multicast address for the source IP.
   a. TRUE
   b. FALSE
5. Network hosts signal their interest in a multicast group via an IGMP query.
   a. TRUE
   b. FALSE
6. Routers can act as both multicast routers and clients.
   a. TRUE
   b. FALSE
7. Hosts can be a member of more than one multicast group.
   a. TRUE
   b. FALSE
8. What is a Rendezvous Point?
9. PIM dense mode does not require a Rendezvous Point.
   a. TRUE
   b. FALSE
10. A router that forwards both unicast and multicast traffic can do so with entries from a single routing table.
    a. TRUE
    b. FALSE

Review Answers

1. Versions 3 and 2, respectively
2. 224.0.0.1

3. 224.0.0.13

4. FALSE—A streaming server sends to a multicast address.

5. FALSE—Network hosts signal their interest in a multicast group via an IGMP MEMBERSHIP REPORTS.

6. TRUE

7. TRUE

8. A Rendezvous Point is the root of a multicast tree. Senders forward multicast traffic to it and receivers get the multicast traffic from it.

9. TRUE

10. FALSE—Multicast routers have both a unicast and multicast routing table.

Lab Activities

Activity 1—The Internet Assigned Numbers Authority

Materials: A computer with an Internet connection

Visit the IANA websites described in this chapter. See if you can find the following:

- IPv4 reserved multicast addresses
- IPv6 reserved multicast addresses
- PIM Hello options

Activity 2—Your Multicast

Materials: A computers with a network connection, Wireshark

1. Start Wireshark and capture on your active network connection.
2. Filter for the IGMP messages.
3. Why are these messages there? What is their purpose? Can you find them on the lists from the previous activity?

Troubleshooting: If you cannot capture IGMP on your host, see if you can capture from another on the same network. Multicast traffic should pass through most Layer 2 network devices.

Activity 3—Streaming Media

Materials: VLC and two networked computers

1. Download and install VLC on both computers. One of these will be the server. VLC can be found at the VideoLAN site (*http://www.videolan.org/vlc/index.html*).
2. Using the guides at VideoLAN (*https://wiki.videolan.org/Documentation:Streaming_HowTo_New/*), configure one end as a streaming server.
3. Connect to this server from the other VLC node.
4. What traffic results? Can you control this traffic?

Activity 4—Mbone

Materials: A computer with an Internet connection

1. Investigate the current state of MBone. Some reasonable places to start looking:

   - *http://www.ics.uci.edu/~rsilvafi/243d/Ass6/MBONE.htm*
   - *http://www-mice.cs.ucl.ac.uk/multimedia/projects/mice/mbone_review.html*
   - *http://www.cs.ucsb.edu/~almeroth/classes/S99.290I/art1.html*

2. What is the status of the multicast backbone project? What ISPs support multicast? Are there hopes of reinventing the architecture?

Activity 5—A Small Routed Topology

Materials: router, network nodes, and VLC

1. Build the topology shown in Figure 8-39.

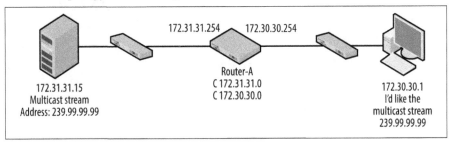

Figure 8-39. Activity 5 topology

2. Configure the routers for multicast routing, ip pim, and igmp as shown in this chapter.

3. See if you can configure the source and clients to successfully transmit a multicast stream.

About the Author

Bruce Hartpence is a faculty member in the Network, Security, and Systems Administration (NSSA) Department in the Golisano College of Computing and Information Science (GCCIS) at Rochester Institute of Technology (RIT) in Rochester, New York. He splits his time between teaching, projects, and writing.

Learn from experts.
Find the answers you need.

Sign up for a **10-day free trial** to get **unlimited access** to all of the content on Safari, including Learning Paths, interactive tutorials, and curated playlists that draw from thousands of ebooks and training videos on a wide range of topics, including data, design, DevOps, management, business—and much more.

Start your free trial at:

oreilly.com/safari

(No credit card required)

Printed in the USA
CPSIA information can be obtained
at www.ICGtesting.com
JSHW052332141123
51994JS00004B/7

9 781449 306557